STORIES FROM TRAILBLAZING WOMEN LAWYERS

Stories from Trailblazing Women Lawyers

Lives in the Law

Jill Norgren

NEW YORK UNIVERSITY PRESS

New York

NEW YORK UNIVERSITY PRESS
New York
www.nyupress.org
© 2018 by New York University
All rights reserved

Library of Congress Cataloging-in-Publication Data
Names: Norgren, Jill, author.
Title: Stories from trailblazing women lawyers : lives in the law / Jill Norgren.
Description: New York : New York University Press, 2018. | Includes bibliographical references and index.
Identifiers: LCCN 2017054992 | ISBN 9781479865963 (cl : alk. paper)
Subjects: LCSH: Women lawyers—United States.
Classification: LCC KF299.W6 N65 2018 | DDC 340.092/520973—dc23
LC record available at https://lccn.loc.gov/2017054992

Dedicated to the women of the legal profession

And, especially, Brooksley and Linda for their commitment to

gathering the history of American women lawyers

CONTENTS

It was 1967. The Vietnam War was raging. The African American civil rights movement was full-blown, but many women of all races were only just beginning to consider the discrimination that they experienced in family life, school, sports, and work. I was in my mid-twenties, a married political science graduate student at the University of Michigan. For a while, Ann Arbor felt like it would be my Waterloo. While canvassing for the candidates of my political party, I learned that ladies did not mess in the messy business of politics. Charles, my ever-polite next door neighbor who worked on the line at General Motors, told me this as he asked, "Why is a cute little girl like you running around asking people to vote? You should be at home." I was dismayed, but I laughed.

That same year, at a party at the home of my husband's academic adviser, I was told by the host that ladies did not wear pants suits (mine was apple green and softly tailored). Across the length of his crowded living room, the otherwise politically liberal Dr. O. bellowed, "Oh, here are Mister and Mister Norgren." I was dismayed but held my tongue.

And then, in quick succession, I discovered that my professional ambitions had to include a male protector if I were to be awarded foundation research funds to conduct fieldwork in eastern Kentucky coal country, and was told that I would receive only honorable mention for a national grant fellowship because my husband already earned the munificent amount of six thousand dollars a year. This was not life as I wanted it to be, or knew it ought to be.

Like the women in this book, I have had to work my way over and around personal and professional hurdles to have a fair shot at equal treatment and opportunity as a wife, professor, and writer. I am not a lawyer, but I have lived through, and understand, American society as experienced by these legal Trailblazers. The United States of the 1950s and 1960s presented women with few opportunities for professional aspiration outside of nursing, teaching, and library work. Virtually no lawmakers were women, the Pill was new, and control of one's body was an evolving experience. Like it or not, and to be fair many did like it, women were expected to be homemakers.

A colleague once told me that I should become a lawyer. I did not take his advice, but, in my own way, I have come to inhabit the world of lawyers. As a writer I have dug deep into the history of American women lawyers in order to explore how, in the nineteenth and twentieth centuries, they used ambition, intelligence, changing social mores, and legislation to battle their way into the male-dominated profession of law.

Stories from Trailblazing Women Lawyers is the third book that I have written about women lawyers in the United States. It draws upon an extraordinary set of oral histories made available to me by the American Bar Association's (ABA) Commission on Women in the Profession along with the Senior Lawyers Division.

In 2005, at the urging and direction of Brooksley Born and Linda Ferren, the Commission on Women initiated a unique, national oral history project. The mission set out by Born and Ferren, organizers of the Women Trailblazers Project (WTP), was a simple but daunting one: one hundred outstanding senior women lawyers would be asked to recount their personal and professional histories in interviews conducted by younger female colleagues. The women to be interviewed were selected on the basis of their accomplishments, contributions that illuminate the role of women in the profession beginning in the post–World War II period. Many were recipients of the prestigious Margaret Brent Women Lawyers of Achievement Award given by the American Bar Association's Commission on Women in the Profession. Personal and professional considerations led some women to decline the opportunity to participate. Several women have given interviews that will not be available to the public for a number of years.

The typed transcripts of these interviews run from one hundred to five hundred pages. Most number about two hundred pages. The interviews were conducted in offices and homes. They often required several sessions, in some instances stretching over a period of months. The interviewers knew their subjects, permitting a comfortable rapport. These volunteer interviewers received an identical list of broad, open-ended questions to be asked of their subjects. The interviews began with a discussion of childhood and then followed the subject's life through higher education and law school. Interviewers posed questions concerning the lure of a legal career and then asked about job interviews and first legal positions. Considerable time was spent on the development of each woman's career, including discussions that focused upon ambition, barriers, mentors, and outcomes. Interviewees were encouraged to chronicle important cases or policy developments in which they participated. Some of the Trailblazers used the conclusion of the interview to reflect on women's changing place in the field of law.

The interviews were recorded and the tapes subsequently used to create written transcripts. Each subject received a copy of this preliminary transcript, which she could edit before the final version was typed and filed.

The women who were interviewed have had careers at private law firms; government agencies; state and federal courts, including the Supreme Court of the United States; Congress; law schools; and public interest legal organizations. The project organizers sought to ensure diversity "with race, ethnicity, geography, and professional backgrounds being key considerations." Economic background was not a consideration. A reading of all of the interviews, however, reveals that many of these women came from recent immigrant families or families where the lack of money or poor parental health, including alcoholism, shaped their lives. Many Trailblazers worked their way through college and law school; quite a few received scholarship support or help from members of their extended families.

The selection of senior attorneys and retired women lawyers as the focus of the project permitted the women who gave their oral histories to reflect on the many stages of their careers. The oldest interviewee was born in 1916, the youngest in 1951, with the majority born in the 1930s and 1940s.

Some of the women who gave oral histories were videotaped, permitting me to learn more about them by watching body language and listening to the way in which they answered questions. I have also brought in the stories of certain women who did not participate in the project, using their articles and memoirs, media reporting, and archived Internet interviews to report on their careers. The project's oral histories, along with my additional research, do not constitute a scientific sample of trailblazing women lawyers. Yet from the one hundred histories available to me, patterns emerged that I am now certain would be repeated over and over were this narrative to cover the lives of five hundred or a thousand such women.

The importance of these oral histories became apparent to me as soon as I began to read them. I had been given the opportunity to write these women into history in their words, comparing their experiences and creating an original history of certain women in the profession. The women who agreed to participate are leading representatives of the many fields of law. They are women attorneys who, in courtrooms, board rooms, and classrooms, have rattled the world with insistent and successful demands to shape society through the use of law. Theirs is a dramatic story of how professional women dared to challenge established rules, thereby breaking law's glass ceiling. Their histories also permit us to consider whether having a far larger number of women lawyers makes a difference. The oral histories reveal women lawyers who broke the dominant mold of male legal practice, while others did not. They describe women who practiced law-as-usual during the day while attending meetings to challenge existing gender law at night. They reveal how women lawyers changed institutions and institutional practices.

This book interweaves social and legal history with individual experience to describe a society that was, particularly in the 1960s and 1970s, in flux. I made the decision to present the challenges and accomplishments of these women using a linear chronology of life and career. It struck me as logical to follow the natural progression of events and experiences that had resulted in a notable career. Flashbacks are fashionable in novels, less useful in biography. The selection of representative yet diverse experiences from each life and career stage permitted me to juggle dozens of lives on my story board and still create one story, one narrative of ambitious women who set out to become lawyers at a time when patriarchy prevailed. Thus, the oral histories meld into a larger chronicle in which individual personalities both stand out and blend into a collective memoir and a history of outstanding women in the modern profession of law. In the words of anthropologist Jennifer Cole, it explores the "unruly terrain where person and history meet."

Reviewing the book *Notorious RBG* in 2015, journalist Jennifer Senior wrote that the "cold universe of belittlement" experienced by Ruth Bader Ginsburg and women of her generation was "unimaginable to this female book critic, who will hand in her review to a female editor, who in turn reports to another female editor." *Stories from Trailblazing Women Lawyers* captures the stories of several generations of women lawyers who, with their insistence on equal treatment, helped to create an America where Senior and her generation of women must read these stories in order to understand on whose shoulders they stand and what, exactly, the Trailblazers had to endure in order for that to happen.

* * *

Several years ago Brooksley Born and Linda Ferren approached me. They offered to give me complete access to the one hundred oral histories conducted under the aegis of the American Bar Association's Women Trailblazers in the Law Project. They asked if I would write a book based upon these histories. *Stories from Trailblazing Women Lawyers* grew out of that offer and so, first and foremost, I wish to thank Brooksley and Linda for that offer, and for their faith that a non-lawyer could shape a narrative from these important and fascinating interviews. Further thanks are owed to the American Bar Association's Senior Lawyers Division as well as its Commission on Women for their sponsorship of this unique national initiative. The busy women who told their stories gave untold hours of time. Everyone interested in the history of women in the profession of law owes them a debt of gratitude. Equally, the women lawyers who participated in the project as interviewers are to be thanked for their time and a job done well. During interviews they occasionally offered comments or extra encouragement. Otherwise, they were paragons of impartiality and quiet, leaving the stage to the women being interviewed. Thanks also to the anonymous individuals who transcribed the interviews. And thanks to the organizations that have archived the full interviews: the Library of Congress and the Schlesinger Library. In addition, they are on the website of the Senior Lawyers Division of the ABA and the Robert Crown Law Library at Stanford Law School.

My agent, Cecelia Cancellaro, encouraged me in the writing of this book. Heartfelt thanks are owed to her, and to Philippa Strum, who read and offered comments on an early draft. Flip's friendship and encouragement have been responsible for much of what I have accomplished in my writing career. Sheila Cole, Wendy Chmielewski, Deborah Klimburg-Salter, Barbara Babcock, Janet Pickering, Serena Nanda, Tim and Alice Stroup, and the members of New York's Women Writing Women's Lives seminar have also wrapped me in the warmth of friendship and the gift of patience during the writing of a book that would not be hurried. Elena Rohner aided me as a resourceful research assistant.

Anonymous readers read my proposal and final manuscript, improving structure and content. I thank them. I am grateful to New York University Press for publishing this book. Clara Platter, my editor, Amy Klopfenstein, and copy editor Emily Wright helped in numerous ways and have my thanks.

Gratitude is also owed to the three generations of my family for their interest in this project, especially my husband, Ralph, who is always there for me, and who knows how to fight for a comma better than anyone I know.

Introduction

Against the Odds

Who were the first women lawyers in the United States, and when did they start to practice law? Beginning in the 1860s, a small number of intrepid rebels dared to imagine that they might enter the profession. Their names included Barkaloo, Bradwell, Couzins, Foltz, Lockwood, and Ray. They were responding to the liberal spirit of post–Civil War America as well as buried ambitions. In their fight to become lawyers, some of these women drew upon the statement in the 1848 Seneca Falls Declaration of Sentiments chastising men for monopolizing "nearly all the profitable employments." Their struggle to open the profession of law to members of the female sex was largely one of individual effort and perseverance, encouraged by the early women's movement and both aided and hindered by the decisions of nineteenth-century legislatures and courts.

The desire of these women to be part of what most men and women saw as the gritty world of law discouraged the faint of heart. Lawyer and Columbia University trustee George Templeton Strong refused to imagine a world in which there might be lawyers named Belva or Myra. In 1869 he wrote in his diary, "No woman shall degrade herself by practicing law. . . . if I can save her."[1] Strong, and other opponents of women lawyers, hid personal social views behind moral pieties. The impact of their actions should not be underestimated. In the legal field, men like Strong controlled legal apprenticeships, law school admissions, and county and state bar association licensing.

In spite of these gatekeepers, a handful of stubborn women aspirants found male lawyers, often husbands or brothers, who were sufficiently progressive to open their offices to female apprentices (at a time when most individuals trained for the law in this apprenticeship system). Others attended the small number of law school programs—Washington

University, the University of Iowa, Union College (later Northwestern), the University of Michigan, Boston University, and Hastings College of the Law—that came—some grudgingly—to accept women in the 1870s or 1880s.

Belva Lockwood, a forty-year-old widow living in Washington, D.C., was among the first women in the United States to join the legal profession. With struggle, she won admission to the D.C. bar in 1873 but then found federal court practice closed to her. Beginning in 1874, Lockwood repeatedly walked up Capitol Hill from her downtown home to lobby for rights-granting legislation that would open all of the federal courts to her and other qualified women lawyers. After a bruising five-year contest in which, she said, no amount of lobbying on her part was "too daring," Congress passed an antidiscrimination bill entitled "An act to relieve certain legal disabilities of women."[2] On March 3, 1879, the justices of the Supreme Court had no choice but to have Lockwood sworn in to its bar as its first woman member, granting her the privilege to practice before the Court. In 1880 Lockwood made her first argument before the high court.

Membership in the profession, of course, did nothing to guarantee employment. The United States Supreme Court had admitted Lockwood to its bar, but in the nineteenth century neither the federal nor state governments hired women lawyers. The growing fields of railroad and corporate law were closed to them, as were most local law firms. In 1886 Illinois attorney Catharine Waugh (later McCulloch) graduated from law school. Encouraged by friends to settle in Chicago and to "capture my share of the large fees floating about," Waugh "sallied forth" with letters of recommendations and a list of contacts.[3] After interviewing she dragged herself home, later writing that she "collapsed with chagrin and failure" after Mr. J. told her that "he disapproved of women stepping out of their true sphere, the home." Pompous Judge J. spoke to her "with his eyes still clinging to his newspaper," while "[b]ristly, bullet headed little Mr. B. exclaimed vehemently, "I don't approve of women at the bar, they cant [sic] stand the racket." He advised her to go home and take in sewing. Waugh retreated to Rockford, Illinois, her home town, rented a modest office, and boarded with her parents until her marriage in 1890 to Frank McCulloch, with whom she established a law partnership. The two practiced together while raising a family.

One-woman firms or joint practices with brothers or husbands became the norm, but each of the early pioneers put a particular stamp on her career. Beginning in 1868, Chicago matron Myra Bradwell drew upon her legal education to build a national publishing empire. Ada Bittenbender, a temperance activist, built a reputation in Lincoln, Nebraska, as a nearly unbeatable trial attorney and in 1888 became a paid cause lawyer in Washington, D.C., for the National Woman's Temperance Union. Connecticut's Mary Hall did not believe that women should argue in court, but Bittenbender, California lawyer Clara Foltz, and Catharine Waugh McCulloch preferred the courtroom to the quiet of back-office work.

The employment discrimination these women faced limited their career opportunities and their earnings. Still, in the face of prejudice, Catharine Waugh McCulloch "collapsed with chagrin and failure" only once. Like her sister-colleagues across the country, McCulloch networked whenever she could, and created her own opportunities and challenges. In 1888 she accepted nomination as the Prohibition Party candidate for state's attorney in Illinois. In Illinois women could run for elective office even though they could not vote. She lost but ran ahead of the ticket. In 1907 McCulloch ran for justice of the peace in Evanston, Illinois, winning election from the all-male voting pool. She was reelected in 1909.

Belva Lockwood matched McCulloch's interest in elective politics. She campaigned for the U.S presidency coast to coast in 1884 and 1888 on the Equal Rights Party ticket, using lecture fees to finance her electioneering. In Massachusetts, attorney Lelia Robinson wrote well-received law books for the lay public. In her first, *Law Made Easy* (1886), she laid out "those elementary principles of law which everyone must have in order to conduct the daily affairs of life intelligently."[4] Robinson also believed in bringing about change in society through political activism. She joined the Second Nationalist Club of Boston and spoke about running for elective office in 1892 before her untimely death in the summer of 1891.

Excluded from men's social clubs where so much business was conducted, as well as the more prestigious law schools, Robinson and her colleague Mary Green on the east coast and Clara Foltz, in California, established professional clubs and law classes through which women might network and educate one another. Robinson and Green founded the Boston Portia Club, named for the young heroine in Shakespeare's *Merchant of Venice* who, disguised as a man, plays the role of a lawyer. They invited women lawyers and law students to join the club and to meet monthly at a local hotel for dinner and discussion.

Working with the technologies of their day, women lawyers also used newspapers and chain letters (a forerunner of blogging) to exchange information and opinions as well as to pass along the names of clients to women colleagues in other parts of the country. Myra Bradwell used the pages of her newspaper, the *Chicago Legal News,* to report on suffrage and antidiscrimination employment politics. She wrote feature stories about women lawyers. When Lavinia Goodell contested her exclusion from the Wisconsin Supreme Court bar, Bradwell published the legal briefs that Goodell had filed.[5]

Magazines also figured in this mix. In 1889, while writing her second book, *The Law of Husband and Wife, Comp. for Popular Use*, Lelia Robinson undertook to survey all of the women lawyers in the United States. Through the survey she hoped to acquaint female and male attorneys with the full extent of women's accomplishments in law. Her article, published in *The Green Bag: A Useless but Entertaining Magazine for Lawyers*, presented seventy-eight sketches of American women who had, by this time, trained for the profession of law. This group was part of the 208 women who identified themselves as attorneys in the 1890 U.S. Census.

Women at the University of Michigan law school similarly saw the value of networking. Two years before Robinson's survey, they initiated a correspondence club of women attorneys. In their chain letters, members of what they called "the Equity Club" copied out personal news. In their writing they also wrestled with myriad professional issues, including the propriety of wearing their hats in court, acceptance of pro bono clients, and whether to think of themselves as women lawyers, or simply lawyers. In one of her letters, Catharine Waugh McCulloch wrote about running for elective office and her belief that having the male voters in her county hear a woman speak in public helped on the "woman question."[6] Lelia Robinson sent a long letter about her extraordinary year as a lawyer in the Washington Territory. In her only letter to the Equity Club, Belva Lockwood argued that members should lobby to give the national government, rather than local and state governments, control over domestic law.

The Equity Club women also interrogated themselves as to whether the "female constitution" permitted them to compete as attorneys. The correspondents did not see themselves as prisoners of the female condition. Yet they understood that doing the work of housewife and lawyer could cause a woman's health to suffer. Many practiced regimens for healthy living that included calisthenics, good diet, dress reform, and even, in Lockwood's case, the regular use of an adult tricycle. The young Catharine Waugh spared no words in giving her advice: "My creed includes no corset, broad, low heeled shoes, reform under garments, dresses in one piece hanging from the shoulders, no tea, little coffee or pork, few pies and cakes, much sleep, a little hoeing in the flower beds and a day in bed when occasion demands instead of sitting and suffering."[7]

By the early 1890s a sense of professional community had emerged among these women. In 1893 the United States hosted a world's fair in Chicago. Women lawyers seized upon the exposition as a place to draw attention to their numbers and to meet in person. Organized by Chicago lawyer Ellen Martin, they held the first American congress of female attorneys. During the program, older participants reminisced about the early struggle against discrimination. Kansas Populist Mary Ellen Lease, sometimes called "Yellin' Mary," followed with a quiet lawyer's talk analyzing political movements. Belva Lockwood used her time to present the case for a permanent international court of arbitration. Her friend Clara Foltz presented a paper, esoteric in nature, titled "Evolution of the Law." During the meeting Martin lobbied, successfully, for the group to establish a National League of Women Lawyers, which was meant to be an organization of influence and networking but "not to be in any sense a bar."[8]

Established women lawyers also sought to expand the community of female attorneys by establishing formal law classes and institutions. Although by 1900 the number of women lawyers approached one thousand, women were still discouraged from taking up law as a career. Yet, as early as 1873, Belva Lockwood had corresponded with

President Ulysses Grant and members of Congress about her plan for a sexually integrated national university "worthy of the Capital" that would include a law program.[9] Clara Foltz, restless and ambitious and persistently seeking opportunities for herself and other women, established her own Portia Club, holding law classes for California women that included tutorial trips to local criminal courts. In the late 1880s a number of wealthy New York City women started the Women's Law Class, motivated by their realization that charity work in the city's tenements required knowledge of local law. Some years after the class began, the chancellor of New York University (NYU) agreed to take over the program and to set up a separate women's law class at his law school.[10] In 1890 NYU began accepting women students in its regular law school. And in Washington, D.C., twenty years after Lockwood had failed to interest the government in a showcase public university, her friend, D.C. lawyer Ellen Spencer Mussey, revived the idea of a woman's law school. In ten years, with the help of Lockwood's protégée, Emma Gillett, the two women built the Washington College of Law into a nationally known program.[11]

The New Century

This first generation of women lawyers, along with women whom legal historian Felice Batlan describes as lay practitioners involved in cause lawyering, were a bridge to the next generation of women attorneys.[12] The new generation also had difficulty finding good jobs, but they were smart and determined, and made opportunities for themselves. Rosalie Loew (later Whitney) graduated from one of the first classes at NYU to accept women. For a short time she practiced with her father and then accepted a position as the first woman lawyer at the New York Legal Aid Society. In the Midwest, Florence Kelley took a law degree from Northwestern University to facilitate her work as an Illinois state factory inspector. Beginning in 1899, she used this training as the head of the newly created National Consumers League. Like temperance attorney Ada Bittenbender a decade earlier, Kelley combined the roles of reform advocate and cause lawyer. In her work for the Consumers League she created a model that influenced twentieth-century civil rights and civil liberties organizations.[13]

Solo and family practice remained the norm, but the careers shaped by Kelley and Loew suggest that small changes were occurring in what might be considered female-appropriate legal work. Life in fast-growing urban areas was changing. Factory conditions, health, safety, and wage issues commanded attention, as did immigration and child protection. Women were visible in Progressive Era policymaking and were commanding respect. In 1899 the nation's first juvenile court opened in Chicago. By 1920 nearly every state had a juvenile court system. Increasingly, both the voting public and political officials thought that women might be uniquely suited to work in these courts.

Between January 1919 and August 1920 two federal constitutional amendments were ratified: the Eighteenth, prohibiting the "manufacture, sale, or transportation of intoxicating liquors," and the Nineteenth, stating that "the right of citizens of the United States to vote shall not be denied or abridged by the United States or by any State on account of sex." These long-sought amendments also created opportunities for a new generation of women lawyers.

One of the first women lawyers brought into national government service was New Yorker Mary Quackenbos. In 1906, she conducted risky private investigations into peonage in the South, where she collected dozens of affidavits from turpentine camp workers held against their will. Notice from this work led the NYU law graduate to be hired as a special assistant United States district attorney for the Southern District of New York. This marked her as the first woman hired for a senior position in the Department of Justice.[14]

In 1920 Annette Abbott Adams was brought into the U.S. Justice Department as an assistant attorney general. During her year in Washington, Adams argued five Supreme Court cases, winning four. Mabel Walker Willebrandt followed Adams as assistant attorney general and, from 1921 to 1929, was also responsible for enforcement of the National Prohibition (Volstead) Act. She made aggressive use of tax laws in the fight against illegal liquor, earning the moniker "Prohibition Portia." She was equally involved in the reform of the federal prison system. Her friend, Judge John Sirica, later said, "If Mabel had worn trousers, she could have been President."[15] But in her Women's Trailblazers Project oral interview, Judge Shirley Hufstedler suggests that putting Willebrandt in the "equivalent of a cabinet position . . . [occurred] because it was the days of prohibition, and they wanted to give this job, which had all kinds of hairy probabilities of being a disaster, to a female, so if she flunked the course there was only a woman who was to blame, that's the way it really was."[16]

Willebrandt urged professional women to fight sex discrimination but to do so "not by mannishness, that only confesses weakness. . . . It is preposterous because it is parody."[17] In 1928 she actively campaigned for Herbert Hoover, expecting, in return, to be named attorney general. He passed over her. She resigned her government position and returned to a private practice specializing in radio and aviation law with offices in D.C. and Los Angeles. In 1938 Willebrandt became the American Bar Association's first female committee chairperson, head of its committee on aeronautical law.[18]

The openings used by Adams and Willebrandt may have occurred, as Hufstedler argues, for cynical reasons, but suffrage politics was also in play. New women voters were being wooed by both political parties, and many male politicians believed that women wanted aggressive enforcement of Volstead Act violations and would be proud to see a woman lead the campaign.

After Adams and Willebrandt, more women were recruited for Washington agencies, including the Children's Bureau and the Women's Bureau. From 1928 to 1947, Helen R. Carloss nearly equaled Willebrandt's record of aggressive prosecution while serving at the Internal Revenue Service, arguing before the Supreme Court sixteen times and filing numerous briefs in Volstead Act and tax-related cases. Bessie Margolin and Beatrice Rosenberg also had extraordinary careers and were repeat players before the Supreme Court. Margolin, an expert on the Fair Labor Standards Act and, later, the Equal Pay Act and the Age Discrimination in Employment Act, argued twenty-seven cases before the Court as assistant and associate solicitor at the Department of Labor. From 1943 to 1972, as an attorney in the Justice Department's criminal division with an expertise in search and seizure law, Rosenberg argued more than thirty cases before the high court.

Recruitment of women lawyers to work in legal aid societies and local courts, particularly those dealing with domestic or family issues, also reflected a change in public opinion about careers appropriate for women.

In 1918 NYU law school graduate Anna Moscowitz Kross joined New York City's Corporation Counsel assigned to the Family Court. Jane Bolin, the first African American woman to graduate from Yale Law School (1931), joined New York City's law department as assistant corporation counsel in 1937 after six years of private practice with her father and, later, her husband.

Bolin was hired by corporation counsel Paul Windels, a close political advisor to Mayor Fiorello LaGuardia. The selection of Bolin, a Republican, followed on the heels of her campaign for a seat in the New York State Assembly. Although she was unsuccessful, in a year when Franklin Roosevelt and the Democrats crushed Republican candidates, both Windels and LaGuardia had noticed the smart, politically savvy lawyer, interested in her, in part, as a way to address problems in Harlem following the riot of 1935.

Once Bolin was hired, Windels assigned her as trial counsel in the Court of Domestic Relations of New York County. Bolin's biographer has written that with her appointment, New York blacks gained "an advocate working on the inside of the city's judicial system who fully appreciated the seriousness of their plight."[19] The African American press celebrated Bolin as "a Sepia Portia," and the white press treated her with respect.[20] In 1939, two years after Domestic Relations Court justice Rosalie Whitney recommended Bolin to LaGuardia for a judgeship, the mayor made the appointment. Bolin became the nation's first African American woman judge. LaGuardia won credit for appointing a woman of color. It is likely, given the nature of race politics in the city in the late 1930s, that Bolin's race influenced the mayor's decision more than her gender did. She remained on the bench until 1978, influencing reforms particularly in the areas of probation and the juvenile placement facilities used by her court.

Nineteenth-century women lawyers made significant use of their training in the causes of their day, which included suffrage, temperance, criminal justice reform, opposition to monopolies, and international peace. Nothing changed in the new century. Women attorneys continued their fierce commitment to reform and the protection of rights.

Harriet Pilpel is representative of an outstanding group of cause lawyers who, early in the twentieth century, dedicated themselves to the protection of civil rights and liberties. After graduating second in her 1936 Columbia Law School class, Pilpel was hired by the law firm of Greenbaum, Wolf & Ernst. Partner Morris Ernst, one of the founders of the American Civil Liberties Union (ACLU), took Pilpel on as his protégée and helped her to shape a career that included work for the firm as well as pro bono cases.

Pilpel quickly developed legal expertise in sex education and reproductive rights litigation, in part through her work with birth control advocate Margaret Sanger. She successfully represented the famous Kinsey Institute in a lawsuit against the U.S. Customs Service that claimed that the institute's sex-related literature was "grossly obscene." She also argued numerous cases for Planned Parenthood and authored the Planned Parenthood amicus brief ("friend of the court") in *Roe v. Wade*. Pilpel was the rare woman of her generation to shape a career in civil liberties, and to do so working out of a private (nonfamily) law firm.

This distinguished Pilpel from another early champion of social justice, her contemporary Dorothy Kenyon. A New Yorker and 1917 graduate of NYU law school, Kenyon had a more fluid career than Pilpel, working on behalf of many social justice organizations. She and Democratic activist Dorothy Straus established a law firm in the decade of the 1930s that they used to help labor, women's, and consumer causes. In 1946 President Harry S. Truman appointed Kenyon as the U.S. representative to the United Nations Commission on the Status of Women. She served in this position until 1950, speaking on the importance of education for girls and citizen rights for married women.

Throughout the 1950s and 1960s, as a member and often officer of organizations such as the ACLU, the American Association of University Women, and Consumers Cooperative Services, Kenyon took the lead in advocating progressive legislation pertaining to labor, civil rights, and social problems. She also sought to influence judicial decisions. Kenyon co-authored the Florida Civil Liberties Union amicus brief in the 1961 case of *Hoyt v. Florida*, an unsuccessful attempt to have the U.S. Supreme Court declare that Gwendolyn Hoyt's trial before an all-male jury violated her rights under the Fourteenth Amendment. Hoyt argued that the all-male jury was the product of an unconstitutional Florida statute providing that no woman should be called for jury service unless she volunteered for it.

Late in 1965, Kenyon teamed up with lawyer and ACLU national board member Pauli Murray. The two women had been asked to write a portion of the ACLU's brief in *White v. Crook,* described by Murray as "a double-barreled challenge of the constitutionality of all-white, all-male juries."[21] Murray and Kenyon authored the section that dealt with exclusion from jury service on the basis of sex. Murray's groundbreaking article "Jane Crow and the Law: Sex Discrimination and Title VII," co-authored by Mary Eastwood, supported their argument, and was included as an appendix. In 1966 a federal court ruled unanimously in favor of the plaintiffs with respect to the issues of sexual and racial bias.[22] When Ruth Bader Ginsburg wrote her ground-breaking 1971 brief for *Reed v. Reed,* challenging Idaho's mandatory preference for fathers over mothers as the administrator of a child's estate, she put Kenyon's and Murray's names on the cover, in order to honor their trailblazing work on behalf of women's rights.

Constance Baker Motley joined the NAACP Legal Defense and Education Fund (LDF) in 1945 as a law student and stayed on as counsel until 1964. Nongovernmental organizations (NGOs), like family law firms and certain government agencies, proved, in small ways, to be places where women lawyers, at midcentury, might find space to build a career. Motley graduated from Columbia Law School in 1946. Twenty women matriculated with her, including Bella Abzug, later a member of Congress, and Beatrice Shainswit, who became a judge on the New York Supreme Court.[23]

By the end of law school Motley, an African American, had immersed herself in civil rights law, assisting Thurgood Marshall as his clerk at LDF. She worked on cases that laid the groundwork for the iconic school desegregation appeal, *Brown v. Board of Education.* In the early 1960s she argued ten civil rights cases before the Supreme Court, winning nine.[24] Jack Greenberg, director-counsel of LDF, said of her work, "[She] was a dogged opponent of Southern segregationists, who found her tougher than Grant at Vicksburg."[25]

Motley shifted the focus of her career to politics and government service after Marshall passed her over for the job of LDF director-counsel. In 1964 she capitalized on her respected public reputation, media name recognition, and effective networking to win election as a state senator from Manhattan's Upper West Side. Barely a year later she became

Manhattan borough president. And then, on January 26, 1966, Motley was called to the White House, where she presumed staff intended to interview her as a possible nominee for the federal bench. Instead, Lyndon Johnson, the president who loved to surprise people, called her into his office and said that he was ready then and there to call in the media and to name her as his nominee to the U.S. District Court for the Southern District of New York. Clearly pleased with himself, the president told Motley, "You take this position on the district court and just work your way up."[26] Johnson was waiting for the opportunity to bring Thurgood Marshall onto the U.S. Supreme Court (which he did in 1968) and suggested that Motley, too, might one day see herself in high court robes. At the age of forty-five Constance Baker Motley became the first African American woman named to the federal bench. Her friend and political supporter Bella Abzug shot off congratulations: "Being a first is always both an honor and a burden."[27]

Women in the South and Southwest

Southern and southwestern women had not been part of the first generation of women lawyers, but that changed after World War I when new female public figures emerged: Helen Carloss, Lucy Somerville Howorth, Olga Herrmann, Burnita Shelton Matthews, Betty Runnells, and Dade County Juvenile Court judge Edith Atkinson (elected 1924–33), among others.

Carloss and Howorth were Mississippi lawyers who made midlife careers in Washington, D.C. Howorth had applied to Columbia's law school before it opened its doors to women. Rather than apply to nearby New York University, she attended the University of Mississippi, where, in 1922, she graduated at the top of her class. Influenced by her politically active family, Howorth joined a host of local civil and social welfare organizations, worked as her mother's campaign manager, and herself won appointment to the Mississippi Board of Examiners, and as a U.S. District Court magistrate hearing civil and criminal cases. In 1931 Howorth, a Democrat, was elected to a seat in the Mississippi House of Representatives. In 1932 she supported Franklin D. Roosevelt for president and was rewarded with an appointment to the Board of Appeals of the U.S. Veterans Administration. She remained a government attorney until 1954.[28]

Olga Herrmann Lapin never practiced law in the nation's capital, but in 1930 she established a solo practitioner law firm near the east Texas oil fields. Born in Georgia and raised in Texas, in 1927 Olga Herrmann became the first woman graduate of the Houston School of Law, lured to the study of law while serving as secretary to a former Texas appeals court judge.

In 1930, newly married to Jack Lapin, Olga heard about the discovery of oil near a Texas farming town called Kilgore. Jack knew oil fields. Olga sized up the town and noticed that there were no lawyers. She seized on this opportunity, rented office space in Kilgore, purchased *Vernon's Annotated Texas Statutes* and form books, installed a telephone, and printed business cards.

As Kilgore became an oil boom town, Olga Lapin prospered. Her son Mart, later her law partner, reports that she had no lack of clients, "particularly those who may have been defrauded as to their mineral rights."[29] Through her representation of landowners and oil operators, Olga became fluent in the language and complexities of the "oil patch." She was conversant with the oil field slang. This made prospective clients comfortable hiring her to bring lawsuits involving the oil fields.

She was well received by the legal community, with the exception of one county judge who refused to have her practice in his courtroom. Still, as a litigator Lapin had persistent concerns. She feared that jury members would consider a woman inferior to her male opponents. To protect the interests of her clients, Lapin associated herself with a local male trial lawyer, sharing her fees. She practiced law in Kilgore for fifty years. Like many of the women of her generation, unable to find jobs with established law firms, Olga Lapin created her own.

Making Room for a Few Women Judges

Since they first entered the legal profession in the nineteenth century, women, like their male colleagues, aspired to judicial positions. Belva Lockwood and several other Washington, D.C., women lawyers spoke plainly about wishing to serve on the U.S. Supreme Court. Catharine McCulloch's election as justice of the peace early in 1907 established a benchmark as she showed that women could win local judicial office. In the 1920s and 1930s, while female jurists were still unusual, women like Edith Atkinson, Rosalie Whitney, and Jane Bolin were appointed or elected as county and state jurists.

The record on the federal side, however, was deplorable. Women lawyers were shut out of the federal judiciary until 1934, when the U.S. Senate confirmed President Franklin D. Roosevelt's nomination of Ohio judge Florence Allen for the Sixth Circuit Appeals Court. She became the first woman to serve on the federal bench after Genevieve R. Cline who, in 1928, had been named by President Calvin Coolidge to serve on the U.S. Customs Court.

Allen had been elected to the Cuyahoga County, Ohio, Court of Common Pleas in 1920, inspired to run, she said, by Catharine McCulloch's earlier election as a justice of the peace, and aided by newly enfranchised women voters. She supported the Democratic Party, women's causes, and law and order. In 1922 Allen moved her career forward by winning election to the Ohio Supreme Court. Six years later she was reelected. Allen was the only Democrat on an otherwise Republican court. She gained national attention as a smart, tough, effective jurist. Women's organizations, believing the appointment of women to federal judgeships was long overdue, began pitching Allen's candidacy, helping her to win the Sixth Circuit appointment.[30]

Allen's name had also been mentioned as early as 1930 for a place on the U.S. Supreme Court. In 1939, when Justice Louis D. Brandeis announced his retirement, her supporters argued that it was time to nominate a woman to the high court and pressed President Roosevelt to do so. Wise to the longstanding power of men's clubs and bar associations, women had formed the National Association of Women Lawyers (NAWL), an organization committed to lobbying for the appointment of women to influential government positions. Members contacted Roosevelt, urging him to nominate Allen to replace Brandeis. Rumors swirled, but the White House did not put Allen on its list of possible candidates. Some observers blamed the men of the high court; others blamed the president. Attorney Lucy Howorth claimed that Allen "would have been appointed to the Supreme Court . . . but someone around the President asked the views of the [members of] the Supreme Court and the word came back that the presence of a woman would make the judges 'uncomfortable,'" unable to put their feet up while discussing cases.[31]

This first missed opportunity did not keep Allen's supporters from repeatedly sending her name to the Roosevelt White House. Subsequently, President Truman was also urged to nominate Allen. Truman, however, shied away from nominating a woman to any judicial position. From 1945 to 1952, he sent the Senate the names of four individuals for Supreme Court positions, twenty-six for the courts of appeal, and 101 for the district courts.[32] Only in 1949 did he respond to pressure from women leaders and the NAWL by nominating Burnita Shelton Matthews for a district court judgeship. When confirmed, the Mississippi-born D.C. resident became the first woman to serve as a U.S. district court judge.

Dwight Eisenhower did not even match Truman's record while John F. Kennedy had nominated only one woman before his assassination in 1963. That woman, Judge Sarah Tilghman Hughes, became part of the iconic tableau of tragedy photographed aboard Air Force One on November 22, 1963, when she administered the oath of office to Lyndon B. Johnson following President Kennedy's death.

A Texas lawyer, politician, and Dallas district court judge, Hughes won a place on the U.S. district court for the Northern District of Texas because of her myriad accomplishments and through her long-time alliance with fellow Texans Johnson and speaker of the House Sam Rayburn. She had long championed women's rights, including the right of Texas women to serve on juries. In June 1970, Hughes was a member of the three-judge panel whose unanimous opinion declared Texas abortion laws unconstitutional, a decision later upheld by the U.S. Supreme Court in *Roe v. Wade*.[33] Two years later Hughes authored her court's opinion in *Taylor v. Sterrett*, an important decision in support of prisoner plaintiffs contesting poor jail conditions.

Thus, until Jimmy Carter's election in 1976, U.S. presidents demonstrated no particular inclination to nominate women to the federal bench. Male federal judges were also reluctant to hire women law graduates as law clerks. Justice William O. Douglas was an early exception.

He sought out graduates from law schools in the Ninth Circuit and in 1944 tapped University of Washington graduate Lucile Lomen to clerk for him. She later had a three-decade-long career with General Electric. Years after clerking for Douglas, Lomen made an observation critical to understanding the price of discrimination. She wrote that a concrete benefit of clerking was the "number of doors that have been open to me as a woman in the profession because of that year."[34] Twenty-two years elapsed before a second woman was taken on as a Supreme Court clerk. In 1966 Margaret J. Corcoran, a Harvard Law School graduate, began a clerkship for Justice Hugo Black. Two years later Martha F. Alschuler joined the chambers of Justice Abe Fortas.

Conclusion

The profession of law was not closed to women in the early decades of the twentieth century. It is absolutely the case, however, that prejudice and discrimination, including law school admission quotas and firm "we do not hire women" policies, made it difficult for all but the best and the boldest to seize a career in law. This remained true until the late 1960s.

A small number of the Trailblazers who provided oral histories for this book began their legal careers in the 1940s and 1950s. They experienced the quick-moving changes of their profession as established attorneys. Most of the women interviewed, however, joined the profession in the mid-1960s and 1970s, a period of extraordinary social and legal change, one with a new vocabulary for the discussion of social justice and civil rights thanks to writers, activists, and legislators. In 1953 French existentialist Simone de Beauvoir's influential *Le Deuxième Sexe* (*The Second Sex*) became available in an English translation. Betty Friedan published *The Feminine Mystique* a decade later. Her book was credited by many observers with sparking a new phase in the U.S. women's rights movement that, after winning universal female suffrage in 1920, had been engaged with issues of jury service, an equal rights amendment to the federal Constitution, fair employment, and family planning, among other issues.[35] Helen Gurley Brown's 1962 bombshell book *Sex and the Single Girl* was also important, selling several million copies immediately following its publication. Brown offered unmarried women advice about money, careers, independence, and sex in a how-to that the *New York Times* called a "spirited manifesto" that celebrated the single woman and "torpedoes the myth that every girl must be married."

Brown's message about independence and sexuality played to a public newly introduced, in the early sixties, to the birth control pill. Moreover, both Friedan's and Brown's ideas mixed effectively with private and public institutional actions that began to acknowledge, and act against, sex discrimination. In 1963 Congress enacted equal pay legislation and, in the following year, passed the landmark Civil Rights Act of 1964, which outlawed many forms of discrimination, including employment discrimination toward women. As a logical sequel, Congress then debated financial support for child care for working parents. Both the House and the Senate passed the 1971 Comprehensive Child Development Act. President Richard Nixon, however, vetoed the bill in the name of protecting Americans from the deleterious effect of what he labeled a "communal" approach to child-rearing.

The child care bill attracted considerable attention. In contrast, Title IX of the 1972 Education Amendments (P.L. 92–318; 86 Stat. 235) drew little public notice and was not even mentioned by President Nixon when he signed the act. Title IX barred educational institutions receiving federal funds from discriminating against students or employees because of their sex. Representative Edith Green, a long-time advocate for equal education, drafted the legislation with women's rights activist Bernice Sandler and moved it through the House with Representative Patsy Mink while Indiana senator Birch Bayh cosponsored Title IX in the Senate. To avoid unwanted attention, the congresswomen buried the ground-breaking legislation in an omnibus education bill and urged women activists not to lobby. The *New York Times*, however, caught on. Understanding the significance of Title IX, the newspaper's editors argued against passage, calling the legislation "educationally unsound."[36] In this instance, however, women had the last word. Following enactment of the bill and announcement of the necessary federal regulations, school quotas for women fell and school-based female sports exploded. Years later Sandler said that Title IX "has been the most important step for gender equality since the 19th Amendment gave us the right to vote."[37]

For women applying to law school, long used to gender quotas and other forms of discrimination, the unfolding impact of the women's movement, Title IX, and the empty seats created by the Vietnam War draft created a game changer. Applications were now judged on merit. By the year 2000 half of law school seats would be filled by women. And surely, as this happened, some of the newly accepted students walked law school halls singing the contemporary feminist anthem, Helen Reddy's 1972 hit, "I Am Woman."

1

Cataloguing Childhood Influences

Catcher in the Rye, the iconic coming-of-age novel, opens with the alienated Holden Caulfield telling us, "[T]he first thing you'll probably want to know is where I was born and what my lousy childhood was like. . . . and all that David Copperfield kind of crap."

Well, yes. Beginnings are the foundation of a biography. So, we do want to know what people were important to the Trailblazers early in life. Who supported, or discouraged their aspirations. Who or what put them on the path to law school. The women say that the stories, and the answers, involve parents but also grandparents, aunts and uncles, siblings, teachers, friends, and neighbors. Birth order, gender, hometown culture, race, and religion accounted for aspirations and ambition but also deterrents. No one template shaped the childhoods of Trailblazers or determined how gender would influence school achievement. Each woman's experience was unique, but some patterns do emerge, beginning with those that occurred in childhood and adolescence.

Sara-Ann (Sally) Determan, a retired partner at Hogan and Hartson, says that she never thought about being anything but a lawyer, like her father. In first grade she drew a stick figure walking into an office. Not yet able to spell the name of her future profession, Determan called her picture "Sally Layer." She wanted to be a lawyer, in part to please her father. By the age of twelve she was sneaking into his briefcase and reading transcripts. She recalls thinking, after making her way through a rape trial report, "Woo hoo hoo, this is the life."

In Texas, Irma Herrera's Mexican American family saw the makings of a lawyer in her before she did. She was an inquisitive and argumentative child who loved to read, and relatives told the young Herrera that she was *"abogada sin libros"* (a lawyer with no training; literally, a lawyer with no books). At the age of five, in 1923, Shirley Adelson Siegel sat next to strangers on a Pennsylvania Railroad car and talked for the entire two-hour trip. Arriving home, her family said that Shirley was such a chatterbox she should become a lawyer. Soon afterwards, her kindergarten teacher asked class members what they wanted to be as grownups. Shirley did not miss her chance. Although she had no idea what a lawyer was (except that they got to talk), she replied "lawyer." Florence Roisman thinks the idea of becoming a lawyer was "implanted" into her brain because, when she was a baby, her father, a lawyer, wheeled her around in a pram while neighbors called her the "little lawyer-kin" and assumed she, too, would become an attorney.

In Los Angeles Miriam Wolff shaped her vision of the future with more concrete information. She benefited from having a neighbor who worked in the local DA's office handling high-profile criminal cases. From sixth grade on, Wolff would visit court to listen to him. Her father, a doctor, encouraged these outings and also introduced his daughter to family friends who were judges. Although the year was 1927 and Wolff was eleven, friends and family knew that she intended to be a lawyer.

Fathers and Mothers

Fathers figure strongly in this story. Not surprisingly, a dozen were lawyers. This was not unimportant, but their transcendent power lay in the ability to make or diminish their daughters' sense of worth, and their interest in challenging society's gender expectations. More than half of these Trailblazer daughters were the first born. Psychotherapists call being oldest "kind of loaded to be domineering," with first-born children tending to be very strong, opinionated, determined, and highly responsible.[1] Other Trailblazers had no brothers. One daughter spoke frankly of her father, who wanted, but did not have, a son. As a result he treated her as his son. Joanne Garvey's dad had two daughters; Garvey was playing catch "with a glove" at the age of three. Sally Determan said, "I think I was the son my father was destined not to have. . . . [M]y mother never said I couldn't be anything that I wanted to be, but my father was so ego-involved in the fact that I had chosen so early to be a lawyer like him, and of course that was the reason I chose as early as I did." Both of Tamar Frankel's parents supported her "almost without reservation." Frankel believed that her father saw her as his first born, and "to some extent I was a boy in that sense." Jodi Bernstein, however, had a brother and said her dad made a "fetish" of treating them equally.

Esther Lardent was an only child. Her parents were Holocaust survivors; she was their "hope." Her parents encouraged Lardent to become a doctor or lawyer and discouraged her from learning to cook or to sew. Her father would show Esther pictures of Golda Meir and say, "You see, see what she can do, you see." Lardent was certain that if her parents had a son he would have been the focus, "but instead it devolved to me."

Roberta Ramo said of her father, "[H]aving three daughters it never occurred [to him] that we couldn't do anything we wanted to do." He held Ramo and her sisters to this expectation by having "extremely high standards." She tells the story of her dad, later in life, being asked if he didn't wish he had a son. To anyone who dared to say that to him, her father would reply that they were right: he was sorry he and his wife had not had a fourth child because he thought three daughters weren't quite enough and a fourth girl "would really be the icing on the cake."

Mothers, while sometimes reluctant or even hostile in the face of a daughter's professional ambitions, were, more often, nurturing heroines. Low-salary moms and homemaker moms counseled these daughters not to count on the support of a husband, and to have sufficient education to earn their own way.

Some mothers tried to dispel stereotypes for both girls and boys. During her early childhood in San Mateo, California, Mary Cranston's mother found the only female pediatrician practicing in the Bay Area after nuns told her second-grade twin daughters that women could not be doctors. While Cranston was training to become an attorney, her twin, Susan, became the first female board-certified vascular surgeon in the United States. Nancy Duff Campbell took her young son to a woman pediatrician. He was quite surprised to learn in elementary school that men could be doctors. Barbara Robinson's two-year-old son knew that his mom was a lawyer. Told by his grandmother that he was so good at defending his baby brother he ought to grow up to be a lawyer, the child replied, "Oh Gamma, I can't be a lawyer, only girls are lawyers."

As a child Shirley Hufstedler spent much more time with her mother than with her father. Her life decisions as an adult were influenced "by mom conversations," a story not uncommon among these women. Hufstedler's mother left school when she married and expressed to her daughter dissatisfaction with her subsequent role as a woman. Hufstedler reports that her mom had strong views about those expectations and constraints: "She didn't call it discrimination, but that's what she was talking about."

By the time Karen Mathis was born in 1950, twenty-five years after Hufstedler, her mother had named society's expectations "discrimination," and engineered a solution for Karen, her eldest daughter. As a child Karen's mom, a graduate of Kathryn Gibbs Secretarial School, began to call her K.J. Asked how she had decided on this nickname for her daughter, her mother said, "Because no one will know if you are a man or a woman and they won't discriminate against you."

Many daughters were prepared by mothers to have the professional life forbidden to mothers, grandmothers, and aunts. Other daughters spoke specifically about honoring their mothers by not permitting fathers, husbands, or society to curtail their ambitions. One element of these Trailblazers' drive toward becoming professionals was their desire to be surrogates for their older female kin.

In families of all backgrounds—religious, racial, and economic—it was commonly reported that fathers did not want their wives to be employed, even where they had trained for a career and worked before getting married or having children. In the decades of the '40s, '50s, and '60s, societal pressure pushed women into domestic lives. Husbands argued that a working wife would bring disgrace on the household and questions of why the "man of the house" could not support his family. Carolyn Dineen King's mother, who had practiced law for several years before her marriage, was in this position. King's father, illogically, believed women should have every educational opportunity but insisted that his wife not work because it would be a "poor reflection on him." As King grew up, her mother spoke highly of women becoming involved in law, telling her daughter and other young women, "There's a whole world out there of things that you can do in addition to teaching." Cornelia Kennedy's mother taught by example, returning to law school once her children went to school.

Zona Hostetler's father left his family of four children in 1945 when she was nine. Her mother also taught by example. She commuted sixty miles a day from rural Virginia to Richmond, the state's capital, to work at secretarial jobs and then as an office manager for a personal injury law firm. Smart and ambitious, Hostetler's mom figured out that she and the other secretaries could do a lot of the work the lawyers were doing.

Zona refers to her mother as a "pioneer" in the creation of the paralegal profession in Virginia, a woman who gave talks throughout the United States about how she and the firm were breaking new ground. Hostetler experienced this example of female professionalism first-hand as a summer employee at the law firm.

Patricia King's single working mom, learning of King's interest in a legal career, said simply, "[G]o for it." While corralling her seven children, Wendy Williams's mother found time to clip items from the newspaper about how girls could do anything, and she would leave them on her eldest child, Wendy's, pillow.

In contrast, several daughters reported no words of encouragement but eventually took flight as professional women because of their silent observation of their home situation. Gail Harmon's mother was "very capable but high-strung, [a] frustrated person." Harmon perceived that she had enough of her mother's characteristics that she would need a life outside of the house to give her life balance. Joan Klein's family offered her no encouragement to study or get good grades. She, too, looked and listened and concluded that "[m]y dream was to have a life unlike my mother's." Klein liked neither the way her mother was treated nor the way her mom lived: "She had no independence about anything. [Father] called her 'woman.'"

Ada Shen-Jaffe says that it was to her advantage that her parents, as recent immigrants from China, "were somewhat oblivious to and therefore less susceptible to the American cultural 'norms' of the *Mad Men* era." Her father encouraged Shen-Jaffe to sign up for debate class where, for the first time, Ada heard someone being ridiculed for having been bested "by a girl." At the same time Ada's mom discouraged her from signing up for a typing class so that she would not be able to rely on that skill to earn a living. (She questions now—with humor—how her mom could have foreseen "that in the PC/MAC era typing would become an indispensable life skill.")

Family, Friends, and School

Mothers and fathers were not alone in offering encouragement or, in some instances, arguing for lesser ambitions. An African proverb suggests, as Hillary Clinton famously noted some years ago, that "it takes a village to raise a child." Other family members, friends, and teachers augmented or, sometimes, trumped the influence of parents. Older siblings were role models, some exerting a powerful influence and provoking an intense desire to imitate. Roberta Ramo and her two sisters joined their parents in dinner discussions. She said a friend observed that trying to talk at the Ramo dinner table was like "trying to get in the on ramp at the LA freeway on a bad day." Everyone learned how to be heard, excellent training for the law.

As the eldest, some of the Trailblazers were put in charge of younger siblings. In other instances siblings cast protective arms. While she was a junior political science major in college, one of Maryann Saccomando Freedman's older brothers came to her saying that he did not see job ads for people in political science: "You'd better start thinking about how you are going to make a living." Telling this story, Freedman paused to underscore her belief that not everyone thought girls went to school to find husbands. "This girl never went to school to find a husband; this girl went to school in order to be able to earn a living that was substantially better than my parents' living."

Some brothers and Trailblazers protected one another and, in one instance, literally flew into the skies together. Congresswoman Patricia Schroeder grew up moving about the United States in a family "without any gender stereotyping." Her father, a pilot and businessman, believed in giving his children the tools needed to be independent. He taught Pat and her younger brother to fly while they were young, and by age fifteen they were at the controls. Schroeder said that her parents "always felt that the most important thing we could learn was how to bankroll ourselves"—so she and her brother followed that advice. They developed entrepreneurial ventures. While still living with their parents, they arranged to buy cars at the end of the season in Detroit, then fly to Detroit and drive them home to Des Moines, where the siblings would sell them.

Constance Harvey speaks powerfully of the pain and toll of being born into, and growing up in, violent, segregated Mississippi—her village. She was in the second group of African Americans to integrate the University of Mississippi law school and was almost killed along with a group of poll watchers in 1968 in Marshall County. Meals with her parents and siblings provided "our own school about life," including the tumultuous politics of her childhood years. But she also turned to the company of elderly relatives "to listen to how things use to be." Her favorite grandparent always had advice for her. When she complained about segregation and racism her grandfather would say, "Times were worse than they are now." Harvey was grounded in the fact that there had been two different racial worlds and "you did not venture into the white world if you were black." The history that she learned from family, "the unfairness and the pain associated with that," infuriated her. This upbringing, in her view, "had quite a bit to do with what I wanted to do in life."

Maryann Freedman's educational ambitions were supported by her brother, but female relatives in their Italian immigrant community worked hard to undercut her aspirations. They thought, Freedman said, she was being "'high falutin'" for going on in school. In her presence they asked, "Who does she think she is?" One of these women relatives said, "There is nothing that makes me happier than scrubbing my floors and making them gleam and that should be enough for Maryann too."

Yet opinions were divided, and laced with humor. During the discussion of clean floors versus Maryann's dreams of higher education, another relative responded, "Nobody wants to eat off your floor and if Maryann wants to go to college, she should go to college, and if Maryann wants to go to law school, she should go to law school, because no one wants to eat off her floor either."

In other villages messages were unequivocally supportive. In Patricia King's family, only one uncle had attended college. When King's college scholarship money ran out, he mortgaged his property in order to finance her sophomore year of study. Betty Murphy's father died when she was young; an uncle paid for her undergraduate years at Ohio State.

As champions of talent and the drive for betterment, some teachers were important mentors, urging these young women on, often giving them the first information they obtained about good high schools and colleges outside the local area. Freedman's teachers in Buffalo, New York, recognized her outstanding drive and intelligence, encouraged her, and made certain she signed up for courses that would prepare her for the all-important (and prestigious) New York State Regents tests, while friends were placed in secretarial courses. Esther Lardent's high school newspaper adviser urged her to try for a top college.

But not every teacher bestowed encouragement. Some teachers could, and did, respond to their students' class, race, and ethnicity as well as gender with cutting, dispiriting words. Antoinette Dupont views social prejudice as the root of a much-repeated opinion voiced by a New London, Connecticut, Latin teacher who told Dupont's aunt that her niece "should not go to college and that most people with Italian immigrant parents were better suited to work at Woolworth's." Latina and African American girls heard from teachers that aspiring to be lawyers or physicians was an unreasonable goal. Mexican American Trailblazer Antonia Hernandez, raised in a civic-minded East Los Angeles family, never believed that being a girl excluded intellectual interests. In 1965 Hernandez wrote an essay about her dreams and ambitions for her high school English teacher. The teacher returned her paper with a drawing of a sad face, accompanied by the comment "that it was wonderful to dream, but [she] had to be practical [as she] was not college material."

Irma Herrera, a self-described Chicana, went to segregated parochial schools in Texas. The nuns demanded that only English be spoken. Very early in school they gave the message "that it was not okay to be who we were." The Spanish nuns, Herrera felt, "viewed themselves as superior because they were light-skinned women."

Elsewhere, middle-class high school girls were told that college offered them only two options: a teaching degree or an Mrs. Degree. Most Trailblazers attended local high schools. A few attended all-girls' schools where parents, or daughters, sought the absence of distractions they associated with coeducational institutions. Others enrolled in public girls' schools that were known for their high academic standards, ones that required high test scores for admission. Immigrant Ilana Rovner, born in Riga, Latvia, in 1938, was sent to Philadelphia High School for Girls. She loved the "incredible" mix of races, ethnicities, and religions, and the educational preparation. Rovner was a complete fan of single-sex education and elected to go to Bryn Mawr. At college she was told that women could "accomplish anything." The all-women's school filled her "with a sense of hope and possibility."

Barbara Robinson also attended Bryn Mawr, where she expanded her already well-honed leadership skills. As president of the Undergraduate Association, she called for more respectful relations with the maids and porters, asking that they be called by their last names. She says that the college administration went "ballistic." Still, like Rovner, she found an atmosphere respectful of the students, one that included an expectation that each young woman would go on to a serious career. She believed that Bryn Mawr, by making women the main focus, immunized them from feeling like second-class citizens. Yet, while spending time at the nearby all-male Haverford College, Robinson noticed that the intellectual life there was "livelier."

Robinson had long heard that women's colleges were valuable because they did not perpetuate the underestimation of women. Supporters argued that women achieve in an environment where their accomplishments receive more notice. Yet Robinson felt that most Americans would think of a gender-segregated place as diminishing young women's opportunities. Judith Areen, admitting some inconsistency given an undergraduate career spent at coed Cornell, thinks otherwise. She sees reasons why "all-girl schools are maybe very good things at certain points for women to develop confidence."

In 1958, at all-women's Smith College, Stephanie Seymour's dorm mates talked a great deal about "those boys' schools where they couldn't get in." The revived women's movement had not yet geared up, but the women at Smith understood that they lived in a world with gender boundaries, even if they avoided them while at Smith. Still, Seymour liked Smith and appreciated knowing that there were plenty of women in the world who were just as smart as men despite not having equal opportunities. This knowledge, she said, "really motivated her."

There was, and is, of course, another school of thought. Norma Shapiro rejected the opportunity to attend Bryn Mawr on scholarship. She felt that if she was going to be in a man's world, she had to go to college with men. She chose the University of Michigan, taking summer business courses at the then very male world of the University of Pennsylvania's Wharton School.

Other women, like Shapiro, used coeducational schools to hone leadership skills and find the lively intellectual life Robinson spoke of. Janet Reno, the first woman to serve as U.S. attorney general, described herself as six feet one inch tall and "gawky" by the time she entered her coed high school in 1952. She found a place for herself there, however, in part by learning extemporaneous speaking. In her senior year Reno won the state championship. She had also voiced an interest in science, but after she became state champion, the speech teacher told her, "[Y]ou can sit in a lab for the rest of your life or you can come out and do something worthwhile."

Childhood, of course, is about the formation of identity. Reading, in school and at home, offered a window on the wider world through frames featuring fictional characters—*Little Women*—as well as biographical ones. Pop culture female heroines—Nancy Drew, Cherry Ames, and Sue Barton—figured in many Trailblazers' imaginations. Occasionally, the Hardy boys made an appearance along with TV's Perry Mason and, in the case of Rya Zobel, born in Germany, all of the Karl May adventure and science fiction books. Dreams both shaped and expressed maturing identities. Janet Reno's childhood dream was to become state attorney and to "stand up next to [Senator] Claude Pepper who would say to her, 'Now Janet, you're doing a good job.'" Jodie Bernstein, fascinated by politics from a very early age, and an activist by personality, "had this adolescent vision of running for the Senate." Around the age of eleven Betty Ellerin realized there were career options for a woman that did not include becoming a teacher. She, too, had a "real dream" that she was going to be a United States senator. Or maybe a member of the House of Representatives.

Religion

In a variety of ways, religion shaped the kind of person these young women became and the values, secular and religious, that they brought to their adult lives and careers. Most Trailblazers followed family religious traditions at least until college. Marcia Greenberger went to Jewish religious school and had her bat mitzvah ceremony in 1959 although girls were not permitted to read from the Torah. But Judith Resnik first engaged with something that "could be recognized as feminism" when she argued against participating in bat mitzvah education because she thought that the religious training for a bat mitzvah girl was "a second class program."

Maryann Freedman visited different houses of worship. Members of her extended family were observant Catholics, including two aunts who were nuns, but her father was an anticleric. To help her shape a religious identity, he sent her to the various churches and synagogues of their community to get "full exposure to the world." Ada Shen-Jaffe's father was a secular humanist. While she was a teenager he would take Ada and her two siblings to different religious services each weekend—various Christian churches, Jewish synagogues, a Shinto temple—and then quiz them about the experience at dinner.

Race and Ethnicity

African American and Mexican American Trailblazers formed identities in circumstances that were often quite different from those of their Caucasian counterparts. Segregation, racism, and discrimination marked their lives, personalities, and ambitions. Constance Harvey is eloquent in describing the mental stamina she developed to work against the racism of 1950s and 1960s Mississippi. As an adult Harvey believes she has become better at accepting things she cannot change. But when she was young, "[I]f I couldn't change it, I would die trying. I just had serious problems with anybody being mistreated for something that they had no control over."

Perseverance became the mark of Harvey's personality and character. Her upbringing influenced her early desire to be a missionary doctor, but civil rights activist Medgar Evers called Harvey to civil rights work (only two weeks before he was assassinated). She attended Tougaloo, "a radical college," where she became president of the student body, and worked for social justice activist Fannie Lou Hamer when she ran for Congress. Harvey lived through the murders of Evers, Malcolm X, Dr. King, and Bobby Kennedy, tragedies that "shook" her life and "hurt her heart." She marched in demonstrations but was "conflicted because she wanted to be nonviolent but was angry and would have fought back if someone spit on her."

Urban Los Angeles differed on many dimensions from the rural character of Harvey's life in Mississippi. In forming an identity, however, Mexican American Antonia Hernandez also found succor, explanations, and direction from her close, politically active family. In sprawling LA she was cocooned by a very large family—"family is everything," she said—and her Latina community. She came to the United States from Mexico in 1955, a time when there was little immigration from that country. There were kids who looked like her in school, but they did not speak Spanish as she did and made fun of her, using "negative terms." Hernandez developed a "comfortable sense of self" from the example of the strong women of her extended family, and a very strong work ethic. Every summer the seven children in Antonia's family worked alongside their parents in the Central Valley farm fields. Entrepreneurial, she also sold crochet goods and tamales starting from an early age: "I'm very good. I can sell you just about anything." And for Hernandez this early life of commercial activity gave her "life skills, social skills, negotiating skills, and also street-smart skills."

LaDoris Cordell grew up in suburban Philadelphia in an African American community. As a child she encountered only white people at school. She believed that being "the only black kid [at school] taught her survival skills, how to adjust," something that prepared her for college, law school, and work. She made friends with white kids, but an unspoken rule prohibited having play dates at each other's houses. Part of her motivation for doing very well in school was to prove to the white teachers "that she was worth something."

A comfortable sense of self in the matter of gender developed naturally and with the support of family for some Trailblazers. Hernandez says that she "never saw being a woman and a girl mutually exclusive with pursuing my intellectual pursuits or my political activity." Judith Resnik had "the good fortune" to have a mother who was admired for her brightness. Her parents thought "that being a smart woman was absolutely fine." At her high school "there was nothing wrong with being a smart female," and Resnik was one of two people out of a class of six hundred who were both first in their class.

The Impact of Local Culture

Other Trailblazers experienced their communities differently and were stifled by social conventions that did not celebrate smart girls. With shame, Sally Determan relates that she did not graduate first in her high school class. She "deliberately put wrong answers on tests because it was socially uncomfortable to be singled out." Hers is a familiar story: "Being a fat brain and coming from the richer part of the community . . . that was social death. About ninth grade, I started to make sure I never had any perfect papers. . . . I didn't get over that until I went to college."

Maryann Freedman, born in 1934, not only had relatives who thought her ambitions made her "high falutin"; she also dealt with the inescapable knowledge that "boys in my generation didn't like smart girls and I was smart, got good grades. They didn't like ambitious girls and I was ambitious. They didn't like girls whose careers in life were going to exceed theirs and to a large extent, mine has." Florence Roisman, the "little lawyer-kin," was discouraged by her mother from trying out for a special high school because boys did not like smart girls. Roisman came to think that she would do better socially if people didn't think she was very smart, "a message that her mother reinforced." Lynn Schafran's southern mother wrapped her advice in a cliché, telling her daughter that "you catch more flies with honey than vinegar"—and said that on a date she should not show how smart she was.

Some Trailblazers recount that they escaped these pressures by attending all-girls' high schools. In South Carolina at Lourdes Academy, Elizabeth Lacy "never had that social issue of 'Gee, I don't want to look too smart for the guys.'" She graduated class valedictorian. Marcia Greenberger went to Philadelphia High School for Girls because her intellectual parents thought academic rigor was more important than a coed school. Greenberger said, "There was certainly no sense in my family of going to a girls' school because it was going to be empowering. . . . But it was very empowering."

Empowerment also came through global politics. In her interview Sally Determan, raised in small-town Pennsylvania, discussed the impact of an event far beyond family and community, namely, the Soviets' 1957 launching of *Sputnik*, the first artificial earth satellite. She said that the subsequent space race "freed up a lot of small town bright kids because the society as a whole started focusing on its bright kids in ways that they didn't in the pre-*Sputnik* era."

College: The End of Childhood

The selection of an undergraduate college similarly followed diverse circumstances, advice, and aspirations. Trailblazers went to college because they were ambitious. Most were happy to fulfill the expectations of their parents that they would join the great wave of Americans going to college following World War II. Immigrant children and those from poor families aspired to rise above their home circumstances. Surprisingly, perhaps, a healthy handful of Trailblazers started college intending to take a pre-med or science curriculum, but none spoke of selecting a college because of its strong science offerings. Most changed their minds quite quickly, but Loretta Argrett, later head of the Justice Department's Tax Division, majored in chemistry at Howard University and worked as a scientist for a number of years before changing careers. Joan Hall chose Nebraska Wesleyan because of her Methodist religion.

Chance encounters led to the expansion of knowledge and choice. Determan, for example, was set to attend Penn State University. While waitressing, however, she met a young woman who was headed for Mount Holyoke College. This well-read, sophisticated coworker talked up the benefits of an all-women's college, leading Determan to abandon her plans for Penn State and begin school at Connecticut College. Patricia King grew up in all-black neighborhoods in Norfolk, Virginia, and attended segregated schools. John Perry, a high school physics teacher, recognized her abilities and encouraged her to consider college. He told King that she needed to take the SAT, and paid her application fee. He gave her advice about non–African American schools and scholarship funds. King attended Wheaton College, where she had her first experiences with white people.

Peggy Quince also grew up African American in the segregated world of Norfolk. Unlike King, she did not feel ready to go to a white school after having known virtually no whites and, instead, took a scholarship to Howard University. Loretta Argrett also came north from the Mississippi Delta in order to attend Howard. She relates going to downtown D.C. in the mid-1950s to shop and knowing that "Garfinkel's didn't particularly want blacks to come in its swanky store. That wasn't all that difficult for me because I come from an environment where those sort of barriers were prevalent." Argrett's comment makes an interesting contrast to one made by the author Toni Morrison. She, too, had opted to attend historically black Howard, expecting, as Morrison told a *New York Magazine* interviewer in 2012, "some sort of Utopia for African-American intellectuals." Instead, she found herself "in a segregated city, on a campus segregated de facto by skin tone instead of race. The cruelties of racism were starker than in Ohio (where she was raised); even worse was the realization that its victims could be almost as cruel to their own kind." Thinking, perhaps, of women like Argrett and Quince, Morrison concluded, "I had friends who lived in the South, and they absorbed it, and it doesn't stand out as foreign to them."[2] But it did to Morrison.

Family finances guided many college decisions. Trailblazers came from both middle- and working-class families. Mormon Christine Durham selected Wellesley College (where she beat out TV journalist Diane Sawyer as their dorm's song leader) over Brigham Young University when she won "a very generous scholarship." New Yorker Betty Ellerin went to Indiana University for a few months "to get away," but came back to New York University, which also gave her a scholarship and the opportunity to complete a BA and law degree in six years. She supplemented her scholarship with pay from waitressing.

Bernice Donald, one of ten children, and the first in her family to go to college, received no counseling about schools or scholarships. She attended the University of Memphis as a commuting student because she could not afford dorm fees. Judith Lichtman also commuted from home her first two years at Hofstra College. Florence Roisman and Wendy Williams were among a number of Trailblazers who attended state or local universities because of their low tuition.

School reputations and culture along with family alumni influenced yet other decisions. Ruth Abrams, raised in the suburbs of Boston, enrolled at Radcliffe in 1949 because her Harvard Law–educated father "liked it best." Nearly two decades later Ada Shen-Jaffe went where her father told her, Jackson College at Tufts University. Ada was sent to the Boston area because her parents had heard there were "a lot of smart, eligible Chinese boys there for her to meet." Shen-Jaffe thrived at Jackson, forming an all-female rock band called "The Rhythm Method" (which had male groupies) and winning election as president of her class.

Growing up in Kansas City, Gail Harmon called herself "a rebel, an outsider." She did not want to go to Vassar, where the women of her family went and where, a sister-in-law told her, she "would meet Kansas City people [at socials], marry one and come back." Instead, Harmon went to Radcliffe, where she believed there would be greater freedom. She found a sense of freedom but she also felt alone, in part, because she "did not know how to banter with the guys."

Nancy Duff Campbell, brought up middle-class in Indianapolis, was the child of parents who did not use gender to present options. They were "very egalitarian with respect to [their three children] who were permitted to 'make mistakes.'" At the airport when "Duffy" went off to New York's Barnard College, her physician father counseled her, "[T]here's a lot of traffic so be careful crossing the streets. . . . [and] don't have any unwanted pregnancies." Elizabeth Lacy traveled from Wisconsin to South Bend, Indiana, in order to attend St. Mary's College. Although the University of Wisconsin was Lacy's state school, her parents would not think of having their daughter apply—"they considered it a 'sin hole.'"

Ada Shen-Jaffe's parents raised "the marriage question" in frank terms. As young women many of these Trailblazers were exploring the geometry of independence, and marriage was, quite logically, part of the future that they chewed over. Ultimately, more than 90 percent of the Trailblazers married, a status supported by most parents.[3] Not surprisingly, given the culture of the 1950s and early 1960s, many were pushed and cajoled by parents and teachers to think about finding a husband. Joan Klein was not unique in being cautioned that college should be used to obtain a "teaching degree or Mrs. Degree." Marna Tucker's mother wanted her to marry but the family called her degree in education "insurance," in case she did not marry.

Some parents brought to these arguments the belief that too much education spoiled their daughters for the marriage market. Judith Lichtman was given this caution upon announcing her interest in obtaining a PhD in political theory. Patricia Schroeder was raised to be an independent child and teenager. Her mother taught first grade and was "a great role model because she worked." She was supportive of her daughter's ambitions. Yet even this working mom raised the marriage question when Schroeder enrolled at law school. Schroeder said of her mother that "she was never quite as sure as my dad that I should go to law school. When I went to Harvard Law School she just lost it. She was, '[L]ook at you, I want to be a grandmother; who will marry a woman lawyer from Harvard?' But most of the time she tried to suck it up."

Conclusion

The variety of childhood experiences that shaped the identities and decisions of these women is striking. Yet, the people, institutions, and rites of passage are familiar. Family, friends, and neighbors, along with schools and houses of worship, intertwined with innate personalities, and helped to shape ambition and empowerment. In these oral histories some Trailblazers make it quite clear that empowering themselves occurred in opposition to family or local culture.

Working through the mix of these norms and concerns, Trailblazers ultimately made their own decisions about enrolling in law school and about marrying, or remaining single. Most did marry, rejecting the 1950s adage at Bryn Mawr College that only those who do not pursue careers marry or, in the tougher language of the dorms, "Only our failures wed." Once married, however, these women created their own timetables. Some delayed having children until their careers were well underway. Jodi Bernstein and Patricia Wald played it differently. Once they started families, these two Trailblazers put off full-time work and serious career building until their children were all in school. And yet other Trailblazers built careers and raised families at the same time. And a smaller number of Trailblazers, married or single, had no children.

2

The Lure of Law

In 1960 Trailblazer Katherine Huff O'Neil worked for Richard Nixon after his selection as the Republican Party's presidential nominee. O'Neil had graduated Phi Beta Kappa in 1960 from Stanford. She had, she believed, "the perfect education" to go into the Foreign Service, which she would have loved, but she thought that no women could apply. As a single woman she was also disqualified from the kind of Presbyterian missionary work in the developing world that also appealed to her. Looking for a postgraduation job, O'Neil turned to her former Stanford professor, Neil Cotter, who arranged for her to interview at the Republican National Committee (RNC). She was hired as a staff member for the RNC's Young Republican Division. She worked there during Nixon's campaign, hoping for a job inside the White House. Democrat John F. Kennedy's defeat of Nixon in the presidential campaign of 1960 landed Republican Katherine Huff O'Neil at Harvard Law School (HLS) as a member of the class of '64:

> When I left the Republican National Committee, the director was a man from Oregon named Hal Short. He was appalled that a mere secretary could get admitted to the Harvard Law School and was further leaving the Young Republicans, which I had been running on a secretary's salary which would also inconvenience him. We had a very strange exit interview in which he attempted to undercut my confidence by questioning my motives and laying out a very bleak future for me in the field of law and emphasizing how unfortunate it was that I was leaving probably the best job that I would ever have, namely being a secretary at the Republican National Committee.
>
> I decided to go to law school when Nixon lost and I knew that Republican jobs would be few and far between. If Nixon had won I would have probably gotten a job inside the White House and my life would be different.

Mindful of the bleak experiences of my Aunt Mary Belle when she graduated from LSU with a law degree and knowing that prospects were equally grim for contemporary women law grads, before applying to law school I checked out my job prospects. My Uncle Carlos assured me that he would find a place for me in his law firm in Baton Rouge. Judge John Minor Wisdom of the Fifth Circuit, former New Orleans neighbor and father of my pal Kit Wisdom, was encouraging when the prospect of a clerkship was discussed. And Sen. Roman Hruska, Republican of Nebraska, father of my pal Jana . . . was certain that I'd find a job as legislative assistant on The Hill either with him or with another Republican.

O'Neil, later a founding partner of Graf & O'Neil, went to law school after arriving at a fork in the road. Law school was not a long-sought dream; rather, it was an at-the-moment alternative. Women as talented as these Trailblazers often went through childhood and college with no thoughts of becoming an attorney. O'Neil was not alone with her dreams of Foreign Service or missionary work. Tamar Frankel, later a law professor and practitioner, was born into a family of lawyers in Israel. She wanted to be an actress. She belonged to an organization of young people interested in the theater whose head asked her parents' permission for Tamar to study acting at his studio. "They refused. She conceded."

Other Dreams

Frankel also wanted to become a concert pianist. She practiced seven hours a day. That dream did not materialize. So, if you ask whether she chose to be a lawyer, Frankel says, "I think the first choice was *not* to be a lawyer, but to choose another vocation. But then it became, kind of, almost the third choice, and I took it. Once I took it, I committed, and I did the best I could." She says that in the late 1930s in Israel girls were treated very similarly to boys, creating a fair playing field in obtaining a legal education and entering the practice of law.

Elizabeth Cabraser built an extraordinary reputation as a plaintiffs' lawyer specializing in consumer class action cases. As with Frankel, however, her talents were multifold and the lure of the law competed with the possibility of becoming a professional drummer.

[I] certainly never thought at all about being a lawyer growing up. I wanted to be a musician, and if I couldn't be a musician I wanted to be a physicist. . . . There was, of course, the Beatles on *Ed Sullivan*. You know, I immediately fell in love and was going to be a musician. [I fell in love with] John Lennon, of course. But I loved watching Ringo Starr, and decided I would be a drummer. And so that's what I did. So my parents had to put up with me being in garage bands throughout my high school career. [I recorded] a series of obscure garage band recordings. [At college] I would go for a couple of quarters, and then I would quit and go tour with my band [called] The Truth About Radio [or] Rosie and the Riveters. . . . I did backup for session work for various touring bands.

[But] the summer after I graduated Berkeley I had to figure out what to do, and I heard that they were giving—I was living in San Francisco, heard they were giving the LSAT down the street at San Francisco State, so I went down and took the LSAT. And then . . . applied to the University of California Law School at Berkeley . . . figuring, okay, I've done what I can about higher education, now I'll go get a music job or something and forget the whole thing. But I got in, so I went. It was kind of the path of least resistance.

In addition to an interest in the arts, a number of Trailblazers majored in English, or started careers in journalism. Georgetown law professor Wendy Williams was on her way to a UC–Berkeley PhD in English before her "aha moment."

I was an English major. I was pretty good at it and really loved it. But was thinking—you know, it was a time of such activism—I was thinking, I want to do something more for the world . . . I can probably do law school. . . . That was also when the bottom was falling out of the English Ph.D. market, and people, brilliant people with fabulous work, were not getting jobs except in Junior colleges, if at all. . . . So I switched from graduate school to law school at Boalt Hall [UC–Berkeley's law school]. And I was intimidated, really intimidated. And I hated courses like Corporations. I just, you know, had a bad attitude. I wanted to be a civil rights lawyer.

Trial lawyer and National Labor Relations Board chair Betty Murphy also had no thoughts of a legal career during her days as a class-cutting undergraduate at Ohio State. Bachelor's degree in hand, in the early 1950s she began supporting herself as a freelance reporter while living in Paris, Belgrade, Istanbul, and New Delhi. She next joined United Press International (UPI) in Washington, D.C., as a writer. Wanting to cover the U.S. Supreme Court, Murphy signed up for night classes, Constitutional Law and Legislation, thinking, she said with a laugh, that they might give her "the edge" over senior UPI reporters who also wanted to cover the high court. She loved her classes at American University's Washington College of Law and finally matriculated but graduated still not knowing what career suited her, what road to take. A conversation with the dean ended her uncertainty when he laid out the options: "You have to decide whether you want to be a reporter with a legal background, or a lawyer with a reportorial background. . . . [W]hat it really boils down to, you have to decide whether you want to *make* the news or you want to *report* the news." Laughing, she answered, "I want to make the news."

New York State chief judge Judith Kaye, like Murphy, originally envisioned a career in journalism. In the late 1950s at Barnard College she created a combined major of Spanish and Latin American Civilizations, intending to be a reporter in a Latin American country. Kaye had no inkling that she would end up in law:

Never crossed my mind at the time. No, absolutely not, I was going to be a journalist. . . . It wasn't until after graduation when I started looking for a job that I realized what an impossible idea it was. Nobody would hire me at all. . . . I think a large part of it was my gender. You know just back then there obviously were *some* women. I remember at the *Herald Tribune* there was Judith Crist. . . . So there were some women, but very few. And I just wasn't one of them. And I remember just travelling around in great despair unable to find a job. . . . Finally in desperation I took a job with the *Hudson Dispatch* of Union City, New Jersey. . . . I was the social reporter.

But that got grim, very quickly. It was not what I envisioned for myself. . . . I think I encountered Tony Lewis at the time, maybe his writings or just finding out about him. He had attended the Yale Law School. He didn't do a whole graduate program at the Law School, but he did take a year or so at Yale and it enabled him to do this magnificent Supreme Court reporting and you know, he's such a superstar. So I began to think

about law school. My parents were devastated, shocked and horrified. . . .
[They] were not too keen on my becoming a lawyer because nobody
would marry me.

Kaye said she tested the waters during her first year at NYU law
school, uncertain about a career in law and still harboring hopes of becoming an international journalist. Slowly, she made the commitment
to a career in law.

Federal judge Cornelia Kennedy's father was a lawyer who encouraged his daughter to go to law school. Kennedy, seriously considered
for the U.S. Supreme Court position that ultimately went to Sandra Day
O'Connor, was one of several Trailblazers who anticipated becoming a
physician or scientist. Looking back, Kennedy says the fact that her attorney father was always worried about other people's problems seemed
punishing, so she enrolled in college with a pre-med major. Organic
chemistry formulas and memorization made her reconsider. Only after
this falling out with science in 1944 did she enter the University of Michigan's law school.

Tax lawyer Loretta Argrett came to law as a second career. She had
established herself as a successful chemist at the National Institutes of
Health and Walter Reed Hospital. In her midthirties, Argrett began
thinking about whether to remain in the world of science:

> Over time, I realized that, while I really loved research chemistry—it's
> very intellectual, but solitary. . . . I was involved in [community activities]
> because there was an interrelationship with other people, while at the
> same time fulfilling a desire and historic need to do what I could to help
> make this world a better place. . . . I come from a line of people in my
> family who were leaders in their community in the civil rights area. My
> maternal grandfather, Ernest Jones, was a founder of the NAACP chap-
> ter in his county, at a time when it was dangerous to do something like
> that. . . . So, I wanted to help in the struggle, too, but I tend to be a more
> private person. . . . And then as time went on, and my husband went to
> MIT and Harvard to get a graduate degree in urban planning, I saw how
> excited he was about what he was doing. I started thinking about what
> I wanted to do with the rest of my life. It's just by happenstance that I

looked at law. [A friend] said, why don't you go to law school. . . . It was like planting a seed.

The suggestion took time to gestate, but in 1972, with the encouragement of her husband, Argrett, the mother of a nine- and an eleven-year-old, entered Harvard Law School. Argrett was not alone as a mom of older children who made the decision to go to law school. In 1962 Minnesota state judge Rosalie Wahl's resume included a husband, four children, a sixteen-year-old college degree in sociology, and a host of community organizing experiences. Practicality told her the family would benefit from a second income. Reality told Wahl that there was not much she could do with her dated sociology degree. A chance seating at a dinner party put her next to a young woman lawyer with several children, and in short order Wahl, inspired by this woman's example, had enrolled in the local law school. She graduated five years later, by then the mother of five.

Oregon appeals and supreme court judge Betty Roberts applied to law school at the age of thirty-nine after being told that despite her master's degree, she was too old to enter a PhD program. Roberts was one of several Trailblazers who considered entering PhD programs, generally a six- to eight-year commitment. She found law school's shorter three-year program attractive, believing that legal training prepared graduates for any number of opportunities.

Early Dreams of Law

On the other side of the equation, law did capture the hearts and minds of some women at an early age. Here, the decision to pursue an education in law was neither an alternative nor a default mode but rather an ambition held for years before actually crossing the threshold of a law school. There were many Sally Determans.

Marygold Melli, born in 1926 and later a University of Wisconsin faculty member, grew up fascinated by law and lawmaking:

It sounds silly, but I think I developed my interest in being a lawyer from reading newspapers. My father always read the newspaper at a table. . . .

So when I was four years old or so, I would sit on his lap and he would read me the funnies. Eventually, you know, I got to where I looked at other things, so I became a great newspaper reader because of my father. . . . and I observed that the people who had influential positions in the world were often lawyers.

So my interest in being a lawyer didn't stem from going down to the courthouse. I had never been in the courthouse. It stemmed from reading who the famous people were in the world and deciding that that was the way to get ahead, being a lawyer. And also at some point, probably I was in eighth grade, even high school, I can remember reading Oliver Wendell Holmes, who said that the law is the calling of thinkers, and I remember thinking that through and saying, "I think that's what I want to do."

Other great men influenced young girls who became great women. As a history buff Carla Hills, later secretary of Housing and Urban Development, was similarly mentored by works of history and the writings of statesmen like Alexander Hamilton. Growing up she thought that the people who had made a contribution in American history were usually trained in law. For Third Circuit judge Dolores Sloviter, the influential man was Clarence Darrow, the book, his biography of a life in law.

Other Trailblazers came to the law because of their dads. Baltimore attorney and women's bar activist Connie Putzel acknowledged that her father was the catalyst: "My father was Senior Vice-President of a regional conglomerate in the business of finance. My father came home every night and sat at the dinner table complaining about government regulation and how frustrating it was for him. And I got to thinking about what he was saying and one night, for no reason that I can recall, I told him I thought I'd like to go to law school. My father's face lit up and he said, 'Sounds good to me.'" That was 1943.

Some daughter fulfilled fathers' (and mothers') abandoned dreams. Myrna Raeder's workaholic CPA dad had hoped to become an attorney but did not have the financial opportunities "to be able to do that." When Raeder, later a law professor, told him she wanted to be a lawyer, "he was incredibly supportive."

Federal judge Phyllis Kravitch was influenced by her lawyer–civil rights activist father and, for a time, worked cases with him.

Early on I fell in love with ballet and I thought I was going to be a great ballerina. I think it was probably by the time I was a teenager that I decided, started thinking about law school, although back then there were no women lawyers and certainly no women on the bench or anything as we have here today. I remember one incident when I was about 12 [1932]. My father was one of the only lawyers in Savannah, he was a trial lawyer and if the court appointed him to represent an indigent, he would take the case. And he was appointed to represent an indigent African-American man in a highly-publicized and very unpopular case. And as a result, I was the only little girl in my scout troop that was not invited to another child's birthday party, which upset me terribly. And my father's way of dealing with my disappointment was to explain the Constitution and the Sixth Amendment and I remember that he said, "When you are a little older, you'll understand there are more important things in life than birthday parties." I didn't know what he meant at the time but as time went by, I remembered that and became more interested in a legal career.

Joan (Jodi) Bernstein was also born in the 1920s. She was close to an aunt who was a doctor and had another relative who taught history. But Bernstein was not drawn to these careers:

I knew I didn't want to do those and from a very early time. . . . I mentioned being aware of Franklin D. Roosevelt. From a very early time I was interested and intrigued with politics and with democratic institutions and with government generally. I was just intrigued with it. . . . And my father was interested, maybe that was the reason. He was active in politics. As my mother's brothers were, although they were Republican and my father was a Democrat, which really meant that there were interesting differences that I became aware of. . . . And then, of course, when Roosevelt was elected he was all our hero and the only president I ever knew until I was in college. . . . From an early time it seemed to me that if you were going to have any sort of career life, or whatever you ended up doing, in that arena you needed to be a lawyer. And that was what really drove me, so I decided sort of early, I talked about it in junior high and high school.[1]

In selecting a career in law, Kravitch, Raeder, Putzel, Melli, Hills, Sloviter, and Bernstein, born in the 1920s and early '30s, experienced the influence of the ideas and achievements of men—Holmes, Hamilton, Darrow, and Roosevelt—along with family members and neighbors. They did not mention knowing about, or being influenced by, early women lawyers, suffrage, or female activism. Only slowly did this change.

To Fight for Civil Rights

The history of racial injustice in the United States and elsewhere motivated women of several generations to pursue the legal education that would help them advance social justice. Pioneering civil rights lawyer Frankie Muse Freeman was one of the first. Freeman was born in 1916, in Danville, Virginia. Her mother taught school and her father was a railway postal clerk:

> I remember when everything in Danville was racially segregated. The NAACP lawyers were coming but that was no change. What happened was my parents—and the Black community which you'd have called a middle-class community—decided, well, if we can't borrow money from a white bank, we'll get our own. So my father and some other people, they started the bank. The same thing was true with respect to a hospital. Because everything was racially segregated, all of us felt we had to do what we could to change it. When I was saying things need to be changed that was when I was in high school, but I said I'm gonna go to law school. But my decision that actually became a commitment and a passion . . . to be a lawyer when I was in college. We knew the lawyers . . . they'd stay with us, because they didn't stay at any [segregated] hotel.
>
> I think that because our parents and the people around us did not accept racial discrimination, we [she and her seven siblings] did what we could. . . . When I announced that I wanted to be a lawyer . . . there were people who really questioned this. Except that neither one of my parents questioned it. By that time you see, they really knew me. [Laughs]

Freeman worked for the federal government after college, and then attended Howard law school, graduating in 1947 when, as she said, "[C]ivil rights issues were gaining attention." Freeman left law school committed to a career as a civil rights attorney. Thurgood Marshall offered her a job on the east coast working for the NAACP, but she had already made up her mind to join her husband in St. Louis. She became a solo practitioner after neither white- nor African American–owned firms would take her on and almost immediately began helping, pro bono, the local NAACP chapter with cases: "You didn't get paid by the NAACP, but did get a lot of publicity and sometimes that brought in some clients." In 1954, as lead attorney, Freeman argued and won the landmark NAACP desegregation case *Davis v. St. Louis Housing Authority*. She went on to become general counsel of the St. Louis Housing Authority.

Days before his assassination on November 22, 1963, President John F. Kennedy had Freeman come to the White House. He planned to nominate her as the first woman to serve on the recently created (1957) U.S. Commission on Civil Rights. Lyndon Johnson nominated Freeman after Kennedy's death. She was confirmed by the Senate on September 15, 1964, and served for sixteen years—always the only woman—through the administrations of Johnson, Nixon, Ford, and Carter.

More than a generation after Freeman took up the work of a civil rights attorney, at the age of fourteen, future mediator Linda Singer read about the Scottsboro Boys:

> I loved nineteenth century novels. I also read a number of biographies. What made me want to go to law school was, that when I was fourteen I read *The Scottsboro Boys*. I don't even know how it happened to be in my house, but I just picked it up and was mesmerized and got very interested in civil rights when I was just a teenager. . . . I went back and forth [in college] about whether it was a possibility. It's what I really wanted to do, but then I got married and I had a baby and I wasn't sure whether it was something I could do. I wanted to be a leader in the civil rights movement. [Being a lawyer] was the way I could think of doing that. And representing poor people and causes as well.

At Radcliffe, class of '63, Singer read everything she could lay her hands on about Earl Warren and the Supreme Court, and took the only law course that was available to undergraduates, a class given by Paul Freund, Harvard's famous constitutional law professor.

Linda Singer, born in 1941, was an early example of a Trailblazer who brought a new set of experiences and motivation to her choice of law as a career. She and other Trailblazers responded, in making this choice, to the rapid changes of post–World War II America. Social, political, and legal movements, initially formed, and shaped, decades before by, among others, W. E. B. DuBois, Mary Church Terrell, Carrie Chapman Catt, Alice Paul, Crystal Eastman, Ida B. Wells, Roger Baldwin, Margaret Sanger, the NAACP legal teams, and "Rosie the Riveter," began to manifest themselves in new and even more powerful ways. A better-educated, worldlier middle class squared off, prepared to reargue American civic ideals. For nearly one-third of the Trailblazers, events of the racial- and gender-rights movements, including issues of economic justice and equality of opportunity, directed them, in some cases compelled them, to legal careers.

Janet Reno, born in 1938 and later the first woman U.S. attorney general, was schooled to understand the power of the law, and committed to becoming an attorney by the time she was fourteen:

> My mother and father told me what Joseph McCarthy was about and how important it was to see what Mr. Welch [lawyer for the U.S. Army] was doing and to follow it and to understand how he was using the law. How important it was the people speak out and that their rights not be impaired without due process of law. She and my father encouraged us to read history and to appreciate history. We followed the events of *Brown v. Board of Education* and being a lawyer seemed to me to be a person who could reach out and take problems that existed in the community, the wrongs that existed in a community, and use the law to be a problem solver to work out solutions for their problems and to correct these wrongs.

Reno expressed a core, optimistic belief of this new generation, that they could, and would, change the world for the better. Law would be the instrument of their power. In her 2014 memoir, U.S. senator Elizabeth Warren used similar words in describing her decision to go to law school. She said that becoming a lawyer followed from the belief that it was possible to "argue our way to a better world."[2]

Mary Schroeder, later a Ninth Circuit judge, met student leaders of the civil rights movement in 1960 while a Swarthmore College undergraduate. She joined the movement first by organizing a lunch-counter sit-in. She also signed on as a summer intern in the office of Illinois senator Paul Douglas and had the opportunity to study the legislative process. Her experience learning about Congress, along with her racial-rights activism, convinced Schroeder that she should apply to law school. She had no trouble "putting together that she'd need a law degree if she wanted to affect public policy."

Ada Shen-Jaffe had been an activist throughout her time in college. In her senior year she became class president. On May 4, 1970, a month before graduation, members of the Ohio National Guard shot and killed four unarmed students at Kent State University who were protesting the invasion of Cambodia by the United States and the expanded war in Vietnam. Weeks after what some called a massacre, with tension high on most university campuses, Shen-Jaffe delivered her senior class president graduation speech. She announced that seniors had voted to send the class gift to the Harlem Free Breakfast Children's Program run by the Black Panthers. Parents stormed out and hate mail ensued. A year later, during a master's program internship, Shen-Jaffe made her commitment to law. With the assistance of a Columbia Law School professor, she succeeded in helping a number of homeless individuals displaced by a HUD urban renewal project:

> One night, as I drove up towards the community center, I could see dozens of people milling around. The usual turn-out for a meeting was 8–12 people. Something was up. Folks who had, two years earlier, been displaced by HUD (Housing and Urban Development) Urban Renewal efforts with the promise of new and decent housing had just received letters saying that, after all, no new units would be available to them. Some of these people had been living in corrugated metal shacks along abandoned railway tracks for 18 months waiting for the new housing they had been promised. I asked if I could take a copy of the HUD letter, and took it to my faculty advisor, who sent me to a professor at the law school who had worked for HUD. The professor went up the library ladder in her office in her stocking feet, and started tossing down volumes of 45 CFR [Code of Federal Regulations], and dictating a demand letter to be sent by the community group to HUD citing various federal regulatory violations. I typed the letter on my small, green Olivetti portable typewriter, making a carbon copy (pre–IBM correcting Selectric, pre-computer), and sent it off to HUD. Two months later, as I drove up to the community center,

the place was mobbed with happy people. There was cake, and balloons. HUD had sent out new letters saying that an error had occurred and that, after all, there would be new housing available for the displaced people. I thought, "Wow! Really? This is what happens when you cite a bunch of federal regulations to a governmental agency? People's lives change for the better and those who have made empty broken promises are required to make good? I think I need to go to law school."

At the age of twelve Norma Shapiro, later a federal judge, watched a local Philadelphia transit strike that occurred when white employees resisted the hiring of African Americans conductors:

> The thing I remember the most was the transit strike during World War II. The President put soldiers on the street cars so that they would run because the strike was impeding the war effort. And that made a tremendous impression on me and I decided to spend a lot of my grown life trying to ease inter-racial relations. I was very appalled by discrimination and bias. . . . I became interested in becoming a lawyer when I was in 7th grade. . . . My aunt was a teacher at J. Cook Junior High and she brought home a book called *Liberty for All* and it was a story of the Constitution and two children who had 10 dreams; one about each of the Amendments of the Bill of Rights. And it just captured me. I still have the book. And that is when I decided to become a lawyer. [I talked to my parents about this dream.] They thought I was a little crazy. In the beginning they were indifferent. By the time I was in college they encouraged me. . . . I wanted to be the first woman on the Supreme Court, which I told Sandra Day O'Connor the day I got the Sandra Day O'Connor award.

When she was in seventh grade, Nancy Duff Campbell's class was asked to write about what they wanted to be as adults. It was the mid-1950s, immediately after the Supreme Court's decision in *Brown v. Board of Education*, something her family, like Janet Reno's, talked about along with issues of the McCarthy era. Campbell, later a founder of the National Women's Law Center, wrote that she wanted to be a lawyer and to work on civil rights issues.

Across the United States there was a growing interest in public service as the civil rights and economic justice movements intersected with

President John Kennedy's clarion call at his 1961 inaugural address: "Ask not what your country can do for you; ask what you can do for your country." Americans joined the Peace Corps (1961) and, later, VISTA (Volunteers in Service to America, 1965). Campbell, however, was not interested in law school as "a road to public service in the government sense." Rather, Campbell said, she understood the possibilities of using legal knowledge for work "in the protest, activist sense. It was to be a lawyer and use the private system to make change."

Given her family's political activism, it was not surprising that Antonia Hernandez, later long-time general counsel at the Mexican Legal Defense and Educational Fund, started to think about applying to law school while a UCLA undergraduate:

> I was more into the philosophy of history and taking a lot of the courses at UCLA on that. There was a teacher, a professor of Brazilian history, E. Bradford Smith. He was a . . . lovely man, and I had taken many of his Latin American history courses. So when I went to him . . . for advice about the fact that I was thinking about going to law school. . . . he said, "Go." He said you will do a lot more good for your community with a law degree than with a Ph.D. He said, "I will help you if I can." When I got the Alumnus of the Year Award at UCLA, he came. . . . It was he who had said, "Yes, this is the tool. Law is a tool that you can really use." And he told me, "You would be good at it because you love to bicker and argue."

Conclusion

Antonia Hernandez's conversation with her history professor highlights the degree to which, at the height of the post–World War II civil rights movement, many Americans looked at law as a tool of social change. It was a promise and a mission. But the lure of the law was multifold, with women finding different mentors and career directions in different decades. And for some, it was a close call between becoming a lawyer and becoming a drummer, pianist, or journalist.

Ruth Burg, born in the mid-1920s, for example, was one of the few women to mention the Holocaust as an influence in her choice of careers. Although initially committed to life as a doctor, Burg, always interested in human rights "because of the Holocaust and things of that type," decided that law "seemed to be a good vehicle in which to get involved in all of that."

Reflecting back on their interest in law as teenagers or college students, these Trailblazers did not speak about selecting a legal career in order to become wealthy. Certainly even at that age many wished to be free of the worries experienced by their single mothers or working-class fathers. They wanted the independent life of a career woman. As they got older these women came to understand the appeal of the two-income cushion of a married couple. But as we will see, even those who took positions with private law firms when they graduated law school did not see money as the lure of the work. They were all newcomers in a profession that did not want them. The idea of flying high financially occupied their thoughts far less than just earning *something.* The money-related issues important to most of these women initially concerned independence and reasonable financial security. The lure of law was about myriad other things, which is not to say that many Trailblazers failed to do well financially.

But this is getting ahead of their story. Whatever their motivations and ambitions, very few Trailblazers appreciated what they would encounter as law students.

3

Law School

"You're Taking a Man's Place"

Gaining admission to law school in the mid-twentieth century demanded that women have outstanding college grades. Acceptance to a law program also required that a woman beat the odds in a process that favored male applicants by imposing formal and informal quotas for the admission of women. Neither law firms nor most government institutions hired female attorneys. The thinking at law schools, therefore, was quite simple: Why train women as lawyers if nobody will hire them? Why use a precious place for a woman applicant that could be given to a man?

Between the end of World War II and the late 1960s, very little changed, with the acceptance of women at U.S. law schools increasing at a glacial rate. Shirley Adelson Siegel entered Yale's class of '41 as the sole woman student. Harvard Law School did not even open its law school to women until 1950. By 1961 the number of women admitted at Harvard had worked its way up to twenty in a class that also included 540 men. On the west coast at Boalt Hall, the public law school of the University of California, women fared only slightly better. When Wendy Williams entered Boalt in 1967, women made up 10 percent of her class. This creep-crawl undoubtedly would have continued indefinitely without the demands of the new women's movement in the late 1960s, the declining number of male law school applicants during the Vietnam War as men were drafted, and the passage, in 1964 and 1972, of two key pieces of federal antidiscrimination legislation.

* * *

Massachusetts Supreme Judicial Court justice Ruth Abrams, Radcliffe '53 and Harvard Law School (HLS) '56, was a local, raised in suburban Newton. She was one of the first women to win admission to Harvard.

Abrams's dad practiced law and his daughter, often sent on business errands, knew her way around law books and courthouses. Her father was open in his desire that his daughter go to law school: "He thought there was a great future for women in the law." Like a number of Trailblazers, she applied to Harvard because it was well regarded and had the shortest application of any law school. Most of the women admitted immediately after HLS became "coed" in 1950 came from Radcliffe. Abrams says this was because Harvard trusted the Radcliffe grading system.

Judge Abrams's acceptance pleased her father, but her mother's family raised the traditional cry that becoming a lawyer would hurt her chances of getting married and having children. As she prepared to enter HLS in September 1953, Abrams herself had doubts "as to whether I could lead a traditional life after law school—and I didn't." Abrams's 2009 chronicle of her three years at HLS spells out many of the experiences and reactions of women who followed her in various law schools throughout the 1950s, '60s, and early '70s:

> HLS was overwhelming, absolutely overwhelming. Picture a big class with mostly men. I did make one friend the very first day—a lawyer in NY now, Bob Gelfman.
>
> They did not have anything that helped orient you or tell you what law school would be like. There is one session that women still gripe about. The dean had a dinner for women only. Did he do it to be helpful? I do not know. It was a horrible dinner. All the dean said was that we would be lucky to get any job in law, even as a secretary. I don't think Harvard was ready to admit women even after it did so.
>
> The dinner was around November of 1953. If you go to any reunion at Harvard with women, it's coming up on sixty years of women at HLS, and they have the session "What do you want to talk about?"—everyone wants to talk about how terrible that dinner was.
>
> So how did it feel at first? It was fearful . . . absolutely fearful. The thought of getting called on, the fear of not understanding and being part of a small minority in such a big group. Women were not necessarily called on frequently but they had what they called "ladies day" and on that day the faculty called on women. It was announced in advance. "Next week is ladies day." It would be different days in different classes. In some classes it was once a month, in others once or twice a year.

When we were called on the faculty was equal opportunists with critical remarks, men and women. I am not sure that the men did not have some of the same problems. Sink or swim attitudes. They didn't complain and we didn't either. We had to tough it out. There was no women's lib at that time.

Some of the women would talk about ladies day. "Oh God it's ladies day, maybe I will get called on—what should I wear? Big problems—what should I wear!"

Some male classmates treated us well; some I am still friendly with. You had a variety of attitudes. Many professors thought that women were taking the place of a man who had to support his family. Of course, many women have to support themselves—that apparently scared a whole lot of people. It is much more realistic now, and even if you have children it's only 18 years out of a life. Life is expected to be very long. But then people did not expect women to work.

Study groups were 5–8 people. They were named after Harvard Law professors, Casner, Club, Seavey and Leach. They were set up formally because they had what they called the "Ames" competition, when you had to write a brief and make an oral argument—one team versus another team. I was the only woman in my study group but I could write and they would tell me to do the brief. They were happy to have me and I am still friendly with most of them.

I only felt less overwhelmed and more confident after I got into the second year because in the first year they told us one out of every three were going to flunk out. It is a very nervous year and no exams until the end of the year. So you are on edge the whole year. It was really a very hard education. On the other hand, they say that is the way the practice of law is. My first year grades were good but not as good as they were at Radcliffe.

As I selected courses I was not thinking about what kind of law I might want to practice. I just wanted to get done. I knew I could always work with my father and that is what I did for my first year after law school. I wrote briefs and some trial memos. After that I went over to the DA's office, did the appeals cases and became an Assistant DA.

Judge Abrams did not name the dean who hosted the women's dinner. We know, however, that it was Erwin Nathaniel Griswold who became a legend to Harvard's women students. Griswold joined the HLS faculty in 1934. Before being tapped in 1967 by President Lyndon Johnson to become U.S. solicitor general, he spent twenty-one years as head of the law school.

Erwin Griswold and his wife hosted the infamous women's dinner that Harvard-trained Trailblazers talked about for years, some, as Abrams suggests, well after their retirement. In 1950 Griswold had overseen the opening of the law school to women, decades after competing elite schools such as Yale, NYU, Stanford, and the University of Chicago had done so. He was not enthusiastic but had come to believe that a prominent, national school had to make the change.

Understanding the Griswold dinners highlights the insight of the classic Japanese film *Rashomon*. Accounts reflect the particular perspective and focus of the participant. Interpretations of the dinner Judge Abrams called "terrible" abound. Federal district judge Zita Weinshienk, class of '58, told her interviewer, "Griswold invited all the women to his house and his wonderful wife who was in a wheelchair made us feel very warm and welcome, but the dean proceeded to tell us how we were there against his better judgment because all of us were just going to go and have babies and not practice law. So that was the message given to me early on, and that made me more determined than ever to do well at law school."

Judge Antoinette Dupont graduated from the second class at Harvard that accepted women, went to the dean's house, and heard the same mantra. Fifty years later, in her 2006 interview, she offered a rejoinder: "We were always told when I was there that we were taking places that men could take and would never practice law anyway. The amazing thing is, every single woman in my class that graduated practiced law. . . . Unlike the male members of the class that went into business and all kinds of other endeavors and never practiced law. So it strikes me as kind of funny that they told us this . . . the professors, the Dean."

Others had a more understanding response. Supreme Court Justice Ruth Bader Ginsburg, in a 2010 interview for the Academy of Achievement, had this to say about the Griswold dinner:

The dean in those days had a dinner early in the term for all the women in the first-year class, and I think he kept it up until the number of women exceeded 20. In any case, after dinner he brought us into his living room, and each of us sat next to a distinguished professor, invited to be our escort, and he asked [us] to tell him what we were doing in the law school occupying a seat that could be held by a man. Now he did not mean that question to wound. Harvard had only recently begun to accept women, didn't accept women until 1950, 1951, and I came there in 1956, only five years after they started to admit women. There were still some doubting Thomases on the faculty, and the dean wanted the women's answers about what they were doing in law school to arm him with responses to those members of the faculty who still resisted admitting women. So he wanted women's stories so he could report those to his faculty colleagues.[1]

Colorado Supreme Court chief justice Mary Mullarkey shares Ginsburg's opinion of the evening. In a fiftieth Harvard Law class reunion speech, Mullarkey said, "Personally, I thought the dinner was a kind gesture meant to ensure that women felt welcome, although it did have the unintended negative consequence of emphasizing how few women there were in our class. Still, I felt then, and continue to feel, grateful to the Griswolds."[2]

Justice Ginsburg does point to other pressures that existed during her law school years:

For the most part, my professors treated the women in the class fairly. There was no such thing as "Ladies' Day" in any of my classes. "Ladies' Day" was notorious in law schools. It was the day when only women were called on, and the rest of the year they were ignored. I did not have that experience, but I did have this experience: The nine of us [women students] were divided into four sections, so that meant most of us were in a room with just one other woman. If we were called on, we worried that if we failed, if we didn't give the right answer, we would be failing not just for ourselves, but for all women.[3]

The fear of failing other women and, thus, limiting the opportunities of all female lawyers was reported frequently, regardless of the law school, as a source of intense pressure.

Ladies' Day, also, was much discussed. In her book *Pinstripes and Pearls,* author Judith Richards Hope, HLS class of '64, gives a vivid description of what some women faced. She recalls Ladies' Day in Professor W. Barton "Pappy" Leach's law of property section (Leach being one of the two members of the faculty who voted against admitting women to HLS):

> On Halloween 1961, like trained seals doing tricks for an eager audience, the five women in Leach's section, dressed in high heels, skirts, blazers, and pearls, were ready. They left their seats in the front row of the large, fan-shaped classroom seating, mounted the steps to the dais, sat down on five folding chairs that had been arranged in a line facing the rest of the class, crossed their ankles, and waited calmly for the first question they already knew was coming.
>
> Leach left the dais and went to the middle of the classroom, where he stood to interrogate them, surrounded by 140 or so male students, who hooted and laughed and sometimes stomped their feet, thinking it was marvelous fun. Actually, most of the women thought it was fun, too. It seemed totally normal for Harvard Law School then. Nancy [my classmate] remembers, "It was sort of like Picnic at the Zoo Day—and we were the animals in the cages."[4]

Hope believes that Leach's actions as well as his motivations were confusing to the women of her class, and probably to him. She writes that "he seemed to be trying to be entertaining, patronizing, and perhaps even kind, all at the same time. Looking back, it was odd that neither the women in Leach's section nor the rest of the women in our class took offense at the ladies' days: we thought they were just another aspect of the hazing that everyone, male and female, was subjected to that first year."[5]

Judge Mullarkey, appreciative of the Griswolds, had no comparably kind thoughts about Ladies' Day, or Hope's interpretation of it. In an article drawing upon her "Celebration 50" reunion speech, Mullarkey railed at an institution and faculty who considered Ladies' Day an acceptable aspect of a legal education.[6] Mullarkey recalled that she and Pamela Burgy Minzner, a law school friend (later a judge on the New Mexico Supreme Court) sat "paralyzed with fear of being called on" near the front of A. James Casner's classroom (by prearranged seating chart).[7]

They need not have worried. In his two-semester property class, Casner did not call on any woman student until Ladies' Day in the spring term. One Friday, Casner announced that the following Monday would be their time to answer questions he put to them. The topic would be marital gifts. The women prepared all weekend. As the only woman seated in the front row, Mullarkey was called on first. Professor Casner said, "Miss Mullarkey, if you were engaged—and I notice you're not—he paused for laughter—would you have to return the ring if you broke the engagement?" This, Judge Mullarkey noted, was the *sole question* asked of her in a full year of property class meetings. Her friend Pam was asked a question about premarital property settlements. "When it was over," she writes, "we were angry and felt humiliated by the trivial nature of the questions and Casner's very obvious condescension."[8]

Judge Mullarkey also rejects Judith Hope's interpretation of Ladies' Day as "a good-natured form of hazing."[9] Rather, she argues, it was a "very public silencing of women," carried out by Casner (and Leach), who held a named chair at the school and "acted with at least the tacit approval of the administration." And, indeed, within a year of Mullarkey's time at HLS, Casner became the acting dean. She acknowledged that other professors, particularly the younger ones, coped with women students with varying degrees of grace. Still, it made her wonder "to see so many brilliant legal minds completely undone at the mere prospect of calling on a female student." The women did not protest at the time, but Mullarkey later wrote to the *Harvard Law Record*, the student newspaper, saying that she "doubted the practice would have been tolerated if it had been directed at any other identifiable group. Ladies' Day was a mean-spirited game that marginalized women and reinforced the view that women in the law were not to be taken seriously."

Katherine O'Neil matriculated at Harvard Law in 1961. She had finessed the male world of the Republican National Committee, but staff work in Washington, D.C., did little to prepare her for the culture of HLS. Law school was, she said, unpleasant from the beginning. She remembered no women professors and no mentors. The male faculty varied in their treatment of the women students. Many professors were "truly malicious," hoping to humiliate women by calling on them only when a rape case was the topic of discussion:[10] "Some professors were bullies because the thinking was that they were preparing students for Manhattan law firms—others were just mean-spirited men abusing power, and yet others were professors I liked." O'Neil thought of the students as part of the "silent generation." She thought they were all "scared to death."

> We inherited our parents' Depression mentality [the 1930s period of severe economic hardship] and the economic belief that any prosperity was momentary and could vanish at any second. And then there were memories of WWII, food shortages, cousins going off to war, and then the Cold War, Red scares, and McCarthy. *There were reasons why we kept our heads down. . . .* [A] characteristic of the Silent Generation was to be conditioned to take whatever was handed out.

O'Neil could not see how conforming to Harvard Law School's standards made sense. At the same time she discovered that there was a parallel track for the eastern private school boys who were drinking scotch with the professors, and learning about what would be discussed the next day.

> We paid the same tuition, but certainly we didn't get the same advantages. . . . These "elites" banded together and made sure they got the class sections that had the best teachers who would guarantee them to get the jobs they wanted in NYC. I didn't even know there was a preferred section—I thought we were assigned randomly to professors.
>
> An aspect of competition at Harvard was to crush your fellow students in argument in/out of class, to take any advantage when you saw it. Harvard is proud of that. I was disgusted by it, and to think that generations of American leaders have come out of Harvard Law School with that mentality is unsettling.

Whether women should be lawyers was a question raised by numerous individuals. This included Dean Griswold's wife, Harriet, who held strong views about women's proper role and responsibilities. In her Trailblazer interview, O'Neil describes a 1964 luncheon at which the philosopher and ethicist Sissela Bok, wife of faculty member Derek Bok (who succeeded Griswold as dean) gave a talk. Bok argued that women could have a life separate from their husbands. She told the women that it was not imperative to sacrifice their identity for their husbands' careers.

After Bok sat down, Harriet Griswold spoke, according to O'Neil, "jumping up to the lectern and contradicting everything Mrs. Bok had said." Harriet Griswold insisted that if a woman "cared about [her] husband's success, [she] needed to focus 100 percent on serving his interests and his career."[11]

For Trailblazers the law school experience was, before all else, marked by where you were, when you were there, and who your friends or study group partners were. Florence Wagman Roisman, HLS class of '63, described herself as a public school kid who was "staggered" by the elitism of the people she met at Harvard. Yet, she loved being at law school, telling her interviewer, "[T]o quote Robert Bork out of context, I thought it was an intellectual feast. . . . Being a first year student at Harvard Law School was mind expanding. . . . I enjoyed the intellectual challenge and the fact that what we were grappling with were the things that kept society together and made it work."

However, Roisman, later managing attorney at the D.C. Neighborhood Legal Services Program, emphasized that amidst this feast, she did not have a female faculty role model, and that there was no institutional support system.

Litigator Jamie Gorelick reported having the "erroneous" impression that if she stayed on at Harvard and went to law school, she would "in some respects continue her undergraduate experience." This did not happen

> because the law school, at least at the time, was much more like a trade school than it was an academic venture. You didn't really talk very much about "why." You talked about what the law was, what the competing interests were and what the principles were, but it was not a doctrinal conversation. [Yet she] was blessed with really good teachers. . . . Alan Dershowitz. . . . having been a [Judge] Bazelon clerk. . . . was interested in civil commitment and the relationship between the concept of guilt and the right to imprison someone. I observed that in the study of criminal law, I could both learn a skill that was very important to our legal system and also be engaged in the great debates of our time. That interest stayed with me. I came to the law school very interested in civil liberties and civil rights, but I don't know that I would have maintained that interest . . . had I not had professors and friends among the faculty who were interested in the same issues.

So in this mix O'Neil found HLS decidedly unpleasant, while Janet Reno considered it an "exciting part of her life." Many women mulled over being told, as a high compliment, that they "thought like a man." None of the Trailblazers, however, has forgiven fellow students or faculty for their extraordinarily crude, puerile sexual jokes. And not a few women, decades later, still spoke with exasperation about institutions that did not create adequate study lounges or bathrooms for their women students. They had been admitted, but their comfort was of no concern.

Elsewhere

A number of Trailblazers transferred from one law school to another. Their multiple experiences offer the opportunity to view different school subcultures through the same pair of eyes. Katherine O'Neil left Harvard after her first year but returned to law school in 1974, enrolling at Lewis and Clark in Portland, Oregon.

> [Lewis & Clark] was a beautiful campus. We had an eclectic faculty coming entirely from a practice setting. They were all interesting people who were interested in the students and focused on their success. The faculty wanted to share their knowledge of and love for the law, rather than playing mind games and reinforcing their own self-perceived superiority. Many of my classmates were attracted to the law school because of its Environmental Law programs.... In sharp contrast to Harvard Law School, the students at L & C were supportive and helpful of each other.... Parking was a problem because there just weren't enough spots—so the Czar of Parking was the most powerful man on campus. He could give you a parking tag to park elsewhere, which was about as good as a lottery ticket. He could also forgive you part or all of a parking ticket provided you appeared and begged. Some of my best advocacy ever was done to the Czar of Parking.

Christine Durham, a brand-new mom, transferred twice, starting at Boston College in 1969, spending time at the newly established Arizona State University law school, and then completing her degree, in 1971, at Duke. Civil rights activist Father Robert Drinan recruited Durham to Boston College. He took care to welcome her as a student who was a mother, presumably having no concern about the compatibility of parenting and being a lawyer. Yet Dunham did not make light of the fact that being a parent affected her law school experience: "I was just so different from everyone else." There were other women in her classes but not other mothers. She was not invited to join a study group at Boston College or Arizona, perhaps because she did not have time to socialize. Not making close friendships denied her ties with life-long professional associates and acquaintances that help build careers.

But by the time Durham transferred to Duke she had learned how to put herself forward. Through a friend she inherited a course on law and medicine that she taught after graduation. And at Duke Durham put her longstanding beliefs about women's role in the world into action. She graduated as a passionate feminist.

In 1970 Duke's law school was not unusual in permitting certain law firms to come on campus to conduct job interviews only with male students. Other firms also came and interviewed women, but their representatives bluntly asked female interviewees about their contraceptive practices and plans for having children. Durham and her friends started talking about these practices "and got mad."

They made the tactical decision to form a group, appreciating that individuals speaking with the administration would not be as effective as a caucus. In 1970 they formed one of the first women law students' organizations in the country. Members told the law school that they did not think it should be offering interview facilities to firms that discriminated against some of its students. The administration supported the women on this and other issues. For example, there were no women faculty at the law school and no courses on women and the law. The administration gave the newly formed Women's Law Caucus funds that the students used to organize a course on sex discrimination and the law, and to invite women speakers to the Duke campus. Barbara Babcock, then a young public defender in Washington, D.C., came and spoke about her professional experiences. Ruth Bader Ginsburg, a young law professor, also visited Duke, bringing some of the materials she would later publish as a co-author of *Text, Cases, and Materials on Sex-based Discrimination*.

Durham gives an eloquent explanation of the moment and its impact on her:

It was a "heady" time in terms of feminism and law; we were just starting to explore what it meant to have women becoming a part of the legal profession. It's very hard from today's perspective to recreate the mindset. When we first started raising the issues about what was going on at Duke vis-à-vis the law firms, a lot of people initially reacted with indifference. It took some talking and some thinking for people to say well no, this really isn't right.

One of the things we studied in our women's seminar was the Federal Equal Rights Amendment to the Constitution that had passed out of Congress [but ultimately failed], I think in 1971. The ratification process was under way. So we read the record of the Congressional hearings on the Equal Rights Amendment. That turned out to be quite significant for me because shortly after I graduated in the spring of '71 I received an invitation from the North Carolina Legal Secretaries Association to come and talk to them about the Equal Rights Amendment. I spoke to them and as a result of that speech was recruited to work on the ratification effort for the Equal Rights Amendment in North Carolina.

When I graduated there was not a firm in that Triangle area [Durham, Chapel Hill, and Raleigh, N.C.] that would even interview a woman. The only women practicing in the area back then were women who were practicing in their father's or husband's firms.

Boalt Hall law students at the University of California (UC) began to attack issues of discrimination toward women two or three years before the women at Duke. Perhaps this earlier awareness can be attributed to the political activism that flourished at UC–Berkeley in the late 1960s, where it was difficult not to breathe in the lessons of rights consciousness and organizing on every street corner.

Wendy Williams entered Boalt Hall in 1967. Her class was 10 percent female. As she sat through her first classes Williams, now a noted feminist professor, thought, "[W]hen you are a woman in a male setting, you imagine that whatever the men have is magic because they've always had it and you're just a stranger in a new land." The term "women's liberation" wasn't yet being used at Boalt.

In 1969 the women faculty from different departments and professional schools at UC–Berkeley got together and resolved to have meetings with female students. According to Williams, the point "was to talk to them about women as scholars and professionals and equals to male counterparts." Herma Hill Kay, a Boalt professor and later dean, left the meeting, Williams said, "loaded for bear" and called the women law students together. So many came that they had to break the rules and hijack the men's lounge (with no men allowed). Kay told them that it "was really a woman's right to expect more from our institutions and to count on succeeding there and being able to go ahead and do what we were trained to do in school."[12] Thirty years later Williams still remembers the meeting as "inspiring. . . . It changed my life."

Following the meeting in the men's lounge, everyone agreed to work on the issues that Professor Kay had raised. Meeting attendees first founded the Boalt Hall Women's Association just as job interview season was to begin. A firm from Los Angeles, using practices seen at Duke and virtually every other law school, had, according to Williams, "posted a notice on the employment bulletin basically saying 'No woman need apply.'" Translating inspiration into action, Williams rounded up a friend and they each signed up for an interview with the firm. They told Assistant Dean Jim Hill about their plan. Hill, sympathetic, in turn told the firm's representative that if he wanted to interview at Boalt he would have to convince the women students that he should be able to do so. Williams recalls a meeting in the cafeteria where the women "raised holy hell" and the rep finally rushed off, swearing at Hill. It was, she said, "all very dramatic and very liberating." Subsequently, Williams filed an Equal Employment Opportunity Commission (EEOC) charge against the firm. She wanted it to agree to hire women, which the firm did, but not until several years had passed.

The Boalt Hall Women's Association also initiated a "breakfast with a judge" program. Williams said that the agenda for these meetings included polite confrontations about judges not hiring women as law clerks. Williams herself had applied for a clerkship with federal district court judge Alfonso Zirpoli, who always hired from Boalt, his alma mater. He granted her an interview (his first interview with a woman). As they chatted Williams said, "I heard that you really don't hire women clerks, and I was wondering if that was still true." His hands went to his face and he started mumbling about his secretary, and how secretaries didn't like to work for other women. She thanked him and left. Zirpoli subsequently hired a male student with a lower class ranking.

Ada Shen-Jaffe's experience with the administration at Suffolk University School of Law took a different turn:

Emboldened by the recent arrival on the scene of *Ms. Magazine*, three of us organized into "The Suffolk Women's Law Caucus," got letterhead printed up and started issuing a newsletter with a column entitled "Pig of the Week," in which a quote from an offending professor would appear alongside a cartoon of a pig, and the question, "Who said this?" On the back page, upside down, appeared the answer.

It didn't take long for me to be called up to the Dean's office and be ordered to apologize and cease and desist. I requested instead that the Dean send someone undercover to class to confirm whether the sexist behavior we reported was true, and then to take steps to sanction the professor. A few weeks later, the Dean called me in again and said the professor had been spoken to about his behavior and agreed to desist. I said that was not good enough, as without a public apology in front of the class, silence about his past behavior could be viewed as the administration's condoning of it. The following day, the professor apologized to the class. But we were denied official student organization status, and a budget. When the undergrads at the student union heard, they gave us access to their office in an act of solidarity I have never forgotten.

The women law students at Duke, Boalt Hall, and Suffolk were not alone in fighting the discrimination they were experiencing. At Yale Law School students persuaded the administration to approve women and law classes taught by female faculty. Wendy Williams says arming themselves with information followed with clockwork-like precision, with Barbara Babcock and Susan Ross teaching at Georgetown and Ross and Eleanor Norton following up with a case book, as did Babcock, Kay, and Ginsburg. In short order there was also a conference at Yale, in 1971, on teaching women and law. Trailblazer Sheila Birnbaum points to the importance of the growing number of women law students: "I got to teach in law school. . . . because the law schools were bringing in larger classes of women and the larger classes of women were demanding to see some women's faces in the front of the classroom, and this is when law schools began to search for women to teach. And I think that all this was the result of the Women's Movement."

By the early 1970s, women's law school experiences began to change, slowly, as quotas for women students were abandoned in the face of lower enrollments and Title IX of the 1972 Education Amendments, prohibiting sex discrimination in federally funded institutions. Women faculty members were hired, class curricula were rethought, and women's associations were formed, on and off campuses.

And women's response to the discrimination they experienced gained a name. On September 7, 1968, feminist members of New York Radical Women demonstrated at the Miss America pageant. Outside they threw false eyelashes, mops, and feminine products into trash cans along the Atlantic City boardwalk. Inside the contest hall, they unfurled a large banner bearing the words "Women's Liberation." Women, including women law students, now had the slogan, the catch-phrase that social movements seek. Together with the Title IX mandate and the empty seats created by the armed forces draft of men to fight in Vietnam, women law students and a new generation of women law professors created a space for themselves at American law schools.

Mentors and Role Models

Many Trailblazers spoke of their desire for female role models and mentors. They saw that the male students shared in these important relationships, that law school was far more than class work. Until the early 1970s, however, very few women taught at American law schools. Herma Hill Kay was at Boalt, Ruth Bader Ginsburg started her teaching career at Rutgers, and, preceding them, Soia Mentschikoff taught at the University of Chicago School of Law.

Professor Frank Zimring once said of Mentschikoff, his colleague, "She's the first woman everything."[13] In 1951, Mentschikoff, who with her husband Karl Llewellyn drafted the Uniform Commercial Code, started teaching at Chicago. Herma Hill Kay lists her as one of the fourteen "early women law professors," women in the United States who were full members of the regular faculty of their law schools.[14] As a result of her presence, women students who matriculated at Chicago in the 1950s and '60s had the unique experience of a female role model.

Mary Murphy Schroeder, later a U.S. court of appeals judge, studied at Chicago from 1962 to 1965. In her interview Schroeder spoke about the strategic advice that Mentschikoff gave her:

[She was] supportive to some degree of women. . . . I was not getting any decent interviews for summer jobs, and I went to her and asked what to do. I said, "When I go in, they look at my resume and they see my name is Mary Murphy, and they assume I am a good Catholic and that I will get married and have lots of children, so they stereotype me from day one. What should I do?" And Soia said, "First of all you go in and if you are asked a question you say, 'I do not plan to get married in the near future' and if they ask you if you want to get married, you say, 'I would like to marry eventually but I do not *plan* to marry and when I do marry I do not *plan* to have children right away.' You should keep emphasizing the word 'plan' and they will get the hint." It worked like a charm. I never got a job in a firm but I did get decent interviews, so it helped me and it sharpened my determination that sooner or later I was going to become a partner in a private firm.

Roberta Ramo came to the University of Chicago two years after Schroeder. She considered it a very unusual class, one that included Bernadine Dorn, later a leader of the Weather Underground, a domestic terrorist group ("our most famous outlaw because she became completely radicalized and went underground, and lived a story that's well known to everybody"); John Ashcroft (Republican politician and attorney general under George W. Bush); and Tom Gottschalk (later general counsel of General Motors). Ramo thought that Chicago had "a wonderful spirit that her friends at Harvard and Yale did not report."

Ramo also recalls that Mentschikoff taught an engaging first-year class that was basically a course in methods of thinking about the law. Was Mentschikoff a good mentor? Ramo answers that question with an intimate portrait of her teacher:

People always want to know if she was a great mentor to the women in the law school. It's very funny. Soia Mentschikoff looked like a woman Russian shop owner. She was a large Russian woman, and in an old-fashioned way she wore these jumpers she must have had made. She had beautiful blue eyes and wore her long white hair in braids in a crown around her head. If you gave her a wrong answer, she could hit you with an eraser from 50 feet and do serious damage. At the beginning of the year all the men looked at her and thought, "Oh great, Russian woman shop owner," and by the end of the year they were all in love with her because she was remarkable in every way. She did not go out of her way at all for women until after the first year because she wanted to see if you were smart enough. Her theory, I believe, was that it was so difficult for a woman to make it in the law that she didn't want to encourage anybody who wasn't going to be at the very top of their game because they would never get anywhere. As a result, she didn't pay much attention to me until my second year when I got the highest grade in the Constitutional Law class. Then we were able to chat a little bit. But she didn't really see it as her job. I think she felt—and I don't really blame her at all for this, this is the world in which she had grown up—that women had to fight to make a place in the law for themselves. And that her mollycoddling, which is how she would have viewed it, really wasn't going to give anybody much help at all.

Esther Lardent's years at Chicago coincided with tension and conflict—in classes as professors struggled to "deal with women," and outside the walls of the law school as opposition to the war in Vietnam expanded. The trial of the Chicago 8 (antiwar activists charged with crossing state lines with the intent to incite a riot during the Democratic National Convention) opened in that city in 1969 and, on May 4, 1970, four student antiwar demonstrators were killed at Kent State University.

Lardent, later head of the Pro Bono Institute, said that in this social and political climate, in which women were tolerated but not welcomed, the University of Chicago Law School women formed a Women's Caucus to use as a support network. The women used to joke that a woman could be on the Chicago faculty only if she had written some major piece of legislation (like the Uniform Commercial Code). Lardent found Mentschikoff brilliant, very soft-spoken but "very powerful," which was necessary since she was the only woman on the Chicago faculty, which Lardent likened to a "guy's locker room" with no place for a woman professor.

After the founding of the Women's Caucus, Mentschikoff asked to speak to Lardent and the other female students.

She gave what was in many ways a lovely speech about how wonderful it was to see more women at the Law School, how wonderful it was that more women were coming into the law. But then she said a couple of things that I think were very . . . upsetting. She talked about the fact that we needed to dress modestly, of course this was the time of miniskirts, and then she said that one of the things that was really important was that we had to be very careful in the way that we portrayed ourselves. And she said "so for example, if you're doing moot court and you get upset, you really shouldn't cry." And I thought, well why would I cry? I mean, why would we be more prone to crying? And the other thing she said was "and just remember, always remember that you're law students first and women second." And that did not go over well with our crew.

Herma Hill Kay, Ruth Bader Ginsburg, Sylvia Law, Linda Silberman, and Barbara Babcock, to name a few, were law school teachers and mentors of a different stripe. They belonged to the generation that followed Mentschikoff. They were the first generation of law professors, in the late 1960s and early 1970s, who were simultaneously aided by the women's movement and moving it along. Yale Law School professor Judith Resnik recalls that as a student she was impressed by Sylvia Law's unwillingness to look like a guy in a suit. Law, she said, favored blue jean shirts and knitted during meetings. In 1972, at Columbia University Law School, Lynn Hecht Schafran was among the women studying with Ruth Bader Ginsburg, newly hired from Rutgers. Schafran, later a litigator and gender rights activist, took several courses with Ginsburg, including one that examined sex discrimination law. She also worked for Ginsburg during one summer at the ACLU Women's Rights Project. Schafran described it as a very exciting time with several of Ginsburg's students working on different pieces of the forthcoming *Frontiero* case, a challenge to the use of gender by the U.S. military in the decision of which benefits to give to the family of service members.[15] A new area of jurisprudence was opening up, and Ginsburg, Schafran's mentor, was one of the lawyers pushing the door:

> She was a wonderful teacher and a wonderful person. She never says a word that is not thought-out with exquisite care; she is not afraid of dead air. She just is totally thoughtful and deep, so you feel that you must not utter any stupidity around her. She was solicitous. It's always disturbing to me when people misread her reticence, shall we say, as being coldness,

because that is absolutely not what she is about. I think one of the most important things about her is that, whatever the case is and even though, and perhaps specifically because, she started out working in the area of Civil Procedure and she did this whole project in Sweden on Civil Procedure Law, she never loses sight of the fact that there are real people in every case and that procedure is not just some abstract thing.

The Summer Intern Experience

Schafran had the good fortune to have an absorbing summer job that helped to shape her future legal career. No lawyer needs to be told the importance of good summer law school experiences. At the end of their second year, the Trailblazers, like their male colleagues, sought law-focused work that would help them test future interests, expand legal skills, network, earn money, and, perhaps, receive an offer for a post-graduation associate's position.

Some Trailblazers found summer work, even after their first year, with no greater effort than their male counterparts. Many, however, did not. Most leading law firms resisted making summer employment offers to women, in part because partners had no intention of hiring women after their graduation. In contrast, new poverty law and civil rights and liberties organizations often proved more welcoming. As the civil rights, poverty, and women's movements built momentum in the 1960s and 1970s, foundation and government money funded the expansion of rights programs and community legal services. New organizations were established, and older ones added initiatives such as the ACLU's Women's Rights Project. Law students already committed to using law as a tool of social change, as well as those considering a career in NGO work, flooded rights organizations with requests for summer employment.

Irma Herrera, later executive director at Equal Rights Advocates, never gave "one second of thought" to the idea that a large law firm position would interest her. In law school she was active with a Chicano group concerned with issues of women and fairness. After her first year at the University of Notre Dame, she worked in Michigan for Migrant Legal Services. She used her Spanish to speak to people about not receiving their wages or on-the-job injuries. The following summer she worked with Evergreen Legal Services providing representation to farm workers in the Yakima Valley. Staff member Mike Fox mentored Herrera. He encouraged her interest in laws affecting farm workers, which helped Herrera to decide that, after law school, she wanted to work on behalf of farm workers.

Antonia Hernandez's summer employment mirrored the path used by Herrera. After her first year at UCLA, she worked for the newly formed Mexican American Legal Defense and Educational Fund (she later became its president and general counsel). The following summer Hernandez signed on with California Rural Legal Assistance and began collaborating with farm labor activist Cesar Chavez. Her summer training created the beginning of the long, strong thread of a career in civil rights law.

Summer jobs during law school also provided the opportunity to test interests. Lois Schiffer eventually spent much of her career in the area of environmental law. As a student at Harvard, however, she was focused on becoming a poverty lawyer. At the end of her first year, Schiffer joined an NAACP Legal Defense Fund program in Mississippi, where she did research on civil rights cases. Back at Harvard she was also involved with the Community Legal Assistance Office (CLAO), an early clinical program. In her last summer Schiffer accepted a position in New York at the firm of Kaye Scholer. While still committed to poverty law, she thought, "I'll spend the summer working in New York and get big law firm experience."

Even as a college undergraduate, Ada Shen-Jaffe approached problems with the heart of an activist. During these college years she had identified her chosen career path, the use of law to create community justice. After her first year of law school Shen-Jaffe signed up for an internship with the Boston Legal Assistance Project and was placed at its Chinatown Outreach program. Most of the issues revolved around immigration questions, and wills, with an occasional dispute between neighbors and landlord/tenant issues. The following summer she obtained a grant from the Law Students Civil Rights & Research Council to fund her work as an intern at the Massachusetts Defender Association, assigned to Cambridge District Court. These summer experiences made her an attractive—and successful—postgraduation candidate for a two-year Reginald Heber Smith Community Lawyer Fellowship (a "Reggie"), a program that grew out of the Johnson administration's War on Poverty, and one that awarded fellowships to several other Trailblazers.

Judith Resnik had worked for the city of New York before entering law school, authoring a report on the issues associated with mentally ill criminal defendants. In 1973 she entered NYU Law School. With her past work history, during her first law school summer Resnik found a ready reception at the NYC Prisoner's Health Services office. In contrast, during her second summer Resnik chose to work in New York at the firm of Proskower, Rose: "I can remember being pretty clear that I learned not as much in my law firm summer as I had learned in these other settings." Very few women worked at the firm and, despite being made to feel welcome, Resnik feels firm members were not sure how to use the small number of female summer associates.

Resnik found a pleasant reception at Proskower even if her talents were not employed. Ten years earlier Barbara Robinson, later the first woman partner at Debevoise & Plimpton, had less of a welcome at the New York firm of Davis Polk. When she accepted the firm's summer associates offer she thought, however, that the experience would be better than one at another well-known New York firm, Sullivan Cromwell, where, in her campus interview, she was told that they would never let her see a client, "but you could work in our library, maybe."

And then there are stories of luck, including that of Dolores Sloviter, later a U.S. court of appeals judge. In 1955 Sloviter, a second-year student at the University of Pennsylvania serving on law review, realized that the male students were getting summer jobs while she was not. With opportunities slipping by, she applied to work in the city solicitor's office and, to her amazement, was hired: "They hired two other summer people, both men, both with political connections [the son of a judge and the son of a ward leader]. And I was the third, with no connection to politics or to an influential judge. Jerry Shestack just picked me out of nowhere."

And there were stories of love at first sight. Carolyn Dineen King chose to matriculate at Yale Law School rather than train to become a doctor, or study for a doctorate in philosophy. Still, at the end of her first year at Yale, King said she did not quite know why she was a law student. Summer work, however, brought her to the Justice Department's Tax Division (Appellate Section) and the Solicitor General's Office. King drafted a Supreme Court brief and loved the experience, later becoming a judge on the Fifth Circuit:

> All of a sudden that summer I found out what it was like to be a lawyer, and I just was smitten. You remember 1961 was one of the high points of the civil rights movement. The entire Justice Department was committed to the civil rights movement. I remember being—all of us being brought into Robert Kennedy's office when he was Attorney General—we all sat on the floor. He used the big office and we all listened to them talk about the civil rights movement and what was being done to secure equal rights for blacks. That whole summer told me what I was doing as a lawyer and convinced me beyond any doubt that this was a fabulous career that I was about to embark on. So it turned me into a lawyer, just in that one experience.

Conclusion

In her Trailblazer interview, Shirley Adelson Siegel, professor, public- and private-sector attorney, and the only woman member of the Yale class of '41, recounts a powerful story that suggests that the process of learning not to discriminate takes time.

> I had extremely friendly relations with my [Yale] classmates. We had re-unions of the class every five years. One year, ten or fifteen years out, I got a phone call from a classmate who was on the arrangements committee for the reunion. And he said, "Shirley, we have a good chance to have our reunion banquet at Mory's. And, you know the fellows would really like it. There's only one hitch and that is they don't admit any women at Mory's so we just wondered how you'd feel about it." And I said, that's okay, I don't mind [not attending].
>
> Many years later, in 1971, we were having a reunion. In 1971 they were more cognizant of woman's rights issues. At the end of the evening's pro-gram I was asked to speak. I spoke very briefly and very quietly. I said that now there are wonderful young women coming to the law. I have met these women and they are admirable and I really would be ashamed if they were to know that in the past, when asked by my class whether I would mind if they had their reunion at a restaurant that didn't accept

women, I had said I wouldn't mind, although the fact is that I was very disappointed. And I sat down. The program was then adjourned without comment. Everyone filed out of the room. They were just slinking out of the room. They did not want to be reminded of what they had done.

The reflections of Trailblazers on their law school experience and law school classmates reveal contrasting stories. Still, the dominant narrative is one of discrimination in various forms, with occasional frank attempts to humiliate. At Suffolk University School of Law three male law students backed Ada Shen-Jaffe against a wall and asked her, "How can you live with yourself . . . taking away a breadwinner's ability to support his family." Elsewhere, during the war in Vietnam, Trailblazers were told that they were taking the place of "some guy dying in Vietnam." Other women were asked if they came to law school to find a husband, or told that they were just there on a lark. Professors only called upon women to analyze rape cases or to act out the part of the victim.

But alongside these accounts of ugly harassment and prejudice were examples of women handling unwanted attention and insults with aplomb and with humor. And there were encouraging, supportive husbands, at least one of whom pushed his reluctant wife to join law review though he understood that work at the review would take all her time and attention.

These women law students knew they were pioneers, and felt the pressure of newcomers to prove their right to be present. There were few full-time women faculty members. The few who held these positions— Soia Mentschikoff, Dorothy Nelson, Herma Hill Kay, and, later, Barbara Babcock and Ruth Bader Ginsberg—became important mentors. And so did a number of male faculty members. One Trailblazer reports that Professor Phil Kurland "wrote me like 500 recommendations."

For a number of Trailblazers law school, beginning in the late 1960s, became the institution they would use in critically examining the gendered nature of law, and the gendered teaching of law. A handful of schools responded to the demands of women students for courses on women and the law. Xeroxed materials used in these seminars morphed, with considerable work, into the first textbooks on the subject. Wendy Williams on the west coast, Nancy Gertner and Lynn Hecht Schafan in the east, were among the many women students who participated in these courses and then went on to careers built around, or highly sensitive to, women's issues.

Until the mid- or late 1970s, U.S. law schools mirrored most of the gendered values of American culture. This included the view that the profession of law was a guy's game, with law schools training men, but not women. New civil rights law, the Vietnam War, and the women's movement challenged, and changed, the patriarchal culture that ruled law schools. Some Trailblazers carry negative views of their law school experience—or aspects of it. But one said, "No blame; they were from a different era." And yet another told her interviewer, "Law school gave me the career I've loved."

4

Work Profiles

The Post–World War I Generation

Trailblazer Shirley Mount Hufstedler, U.S. court of appeals judge and, later, secretary of education, tells this story about the start of her legal career. She and Warren Christopher, later Bill Clinton's secretary of state, were members of the Stanford Law School class of 1949. Each graduated ranked fifth. Their class, swollen in size to accommodate veterans returning from World War II, numbered three hundred.

Hufstedler and Christopher both served on law review. In their third year each of these star students began the traditional search for a post-graduation job. What difference did gender make? The dean recommended Hufstedler for a position as legal secretary in a Santa Barbara firm. Christopher received the law school's backing to go to Washington, D.C., in order to interview with U.S. Supreme Court justice William O. Douglas with the hope of becoming his law clerk. Christopher was accepted and said yes. Hufstedler turned heel and said, "No, thanks," the job was not exactly what she had in mind. Three years later two other Stanford Law standouts, each later justices of the U.S. Supreme Court, played out the identical scene: Sandra Day O'Connor and William Rehnquist, graduates of the class of '52, sought jobs. Supreme Court Justice Robert Jackson hired Rehnquist to clerk for him. O'Connor, who unsuccessfully applied for associate positions at private California law firms, was offered work as a legal secretary. Like Shirley Hufstedler, she said no thanks, and eventually was hired as a deputy county attorney in San Mateo.

Shirley Hufstedler had held down part-time jobs since the age of thirteen. After college she obtained a position in Hollywood as secretary for Paramount Studio movie stars Paulette Goddard and her then husband, Burgess Meredith. Hufstedler's enchantment with the entertainment industry was short-lived, but the job permitted her to establish a law school tuition nest egg. She worked hard at Stanford, perhaps thinking that women had won a new place in American society during and after World War II:

> What may startle people today is that nobody would hire a female lawyer. Nobody. Of course, the profession at that time was far more segregated in every way than one would imagine now. There was no lawyer of color in a public law office, the only women in any law office were those few that were hired during the Second World War, when the men were gone. None of them was ever made a partner no matter how good they were. And, of course, Gentiles were not in Jewish law firms and the other way around; so, it was just completely segregated. As nearly as my friend and I could ascertain, there were seven of us females in the State of California who were admitted to the bar in 1949.

Hufstedler went on to say, "Nobody would hire me, so I just created my own job. I went to see a very fine lawyer who was a graduate of Stanford Law School, a solo practitioner named J. E. Simpson, and I started just working for him doing legal memoranda, and then I graduated quickly to writing briefs. Ultimately, I had a lot of lawyers for whom I wrote briefs. I wrote briefs anonymously so many times I thought I was made out of ectoplasm—I spent a lot of time at the County Law Library, and eventually I became very well known for brief writing."

The opening wedge for Hufstedler occurred when a former Stanford professor, handling a major water rights case at the state attorney general's office, asked her to help with research memos. She began writing briefs for the case, *Arizona v. California*, and preparing expert witnesses' examinations. In time she was made special legal consultant to the attorney general of California, Edmund G. Brown. It had taken Hufstedler nearly ten years to establish herself as a successful solo practitioner, and suddenly she had the good fortune to be working for a man who was about to become a political legend as Governor "Pat" Brown. Hufstedler joined Brown's team in 1958, months before he won election as California's governor. Between 1961 and 1968 she served as a judge on the Los Angeles Superior Court and, later, the state court of appeal, each appointment made by Brown. As the only woman judge on the Superior Court—"119 men and me"—she did not feel any hostility from the male members but believed that they thought of her presence "as like having a strange pup in with their litter." During her five years on that court (1961–1966), she did try to persuade her colleagues "that it was inappropriate to call female lawyers who showed up in court as 'honey' or things of that kind." During these years she and Judge Mildred Lillie were the only women in the southern divisions of the state appeal court.

During his six years in office, President Lyndon Johnson had no female cabinet members. He did, however, successfully nominate two women, Constance Baker Motley and June L. Green, for U.S. district court positions. Shirley Hufstedler was Johnson's choice for a seat on the U.S. court of appeals' Ninth Circuit. She believes that the president's wife, Lady Bird, influenced her husband: "Lady Bird was vigorous in her defense of women, and I think she thought it would do a great deal of good in the justice system to have more women."

Hufstedler recalls her nomination in 1968 being greeted elsewhere with "about as much enthusiasm at the court as if I had been nominated as the Typhoid Mary for Dairy Queen." Nevertheless, ten years after joining Pat Brown's team, she became the highest-ranked female jurist in the United States (Florence Allen retired in 1959): "I remember vividly my experience when I first met Dick Chambers, the [Ninth Circuit] presiding judge. We met in chambers and I had never seen a man more nervous. He had no idea what kind of a freak he was going to have to deal with. He was so nervous during the time he was interviewing me I had to fight down the tendency to go over and put my arm around his shoulders and say, 'There, there, Dick, I'm not going to do the court over in chintz.' His announcement to the Ninth Circuit Conference of my appointment had been that he was going to have to build a bathroom for females."

Hufstedler said that she participated in "legions of significant cases" in her eleven years on the Ninth Circuit and then, in 1979, she received a phone call from then vice-president Walter Mondale. He told her she was being considered for a post in President Jimmy Carter's cabinet and needed to fly to Washington ASAP. Hufstedler arrived at the White House only to discover that there was no short list, no consideration— that she "was the list," and the agency was the newly reconfigured Department of Education (DOE). In selecting Judge Hufstedler, Carter surprised the pundits. As the first head of DOE the president chose what journalist Robert O. Boorstin called "the wisest and most politically expedient course—nominating an effective, respected public figure whose background was solid enough to arouse interest but vague enough to seem fair to all concerned."[1]

> It was a pretty heavy decision to make to walk out on my lifetime job as a Federal Appellate judge to turn into a cabinet officer, but my husband and I talked it over and, after all, when the President of the United States asks you to do something for the country that's honest and needed, you have to be pretty pusillanimous if you're going to say no. During my confirmation hearing more than one Senator asked me about what I was going to do, how soon I was going to resign to go on the United States Supreme Court. As I pointed out to them, I knew the members of the Supreme Court, and I didn't know anybody who was planning to resign, so I was finally confirmed.

Hufstedler was a natural choice for the Supreme Court. However, when Republican Ronald Reagan defeated Democrat Jimmy Carter in November 1980, Hufstedler's shot at becoming a member of that court went the way of partisan politics. Yet western women prevailed: On July 7, 1981, Reagan, who had vowed to appoint a woman to the high court, announced Arizona native and Stanford Law graduate Sandra Day O'Connor as his choice to fill the vacancy left by the retirement of Justice Potter Stewart. She was sworn in as the first woman Supreme Court justice on September 25, 1981.

On the east coast, Shirley Adelson Siegel, born in 1918, faced many of the same problems and made several career decisions similar to Judge Hufstedler's. After graduating from Yale Law School in 1941, Siegel built a distinguished career in the public and private sectors. She became an expert on housing law, argued at the U.S. Supreme Court, and served a term as New York State solicitor general.

Siegel began the search for her first job, as was usual, while in her last year at Yale. She was a law review editor who ranked very high in her class. She thought she had cause to be optimistic. In the autumn of 1940 the dean's office gave all of the third-year students a list of law firms in Manhattan. They were encouraged by the dean and the faculty to stop at any one of the firms for an interview. Siegel had that list and one of her own making, a kind of spreadsheet:

My list, dated January 9, 1941, spelled out "Firms I've been to where prospect is hopeless." 23 names. Then, "Letter asking for appointment not even acknowledged," one name. Then "Wrote for appointment but couldn't get it," another name. Next, "Where I was told no interviewing at present," eight firms. Wrote on the top of the right hand column, "This side of sheet is brighter." Then, "Keeping my name," eight firms. Then, "Prospect is excellent, Proskauer Rose & Paskus." Then "Prospect is pretty good." Office of Cahill, U.S. Attorney. Then, "Nothing doing at the Corporation Counsel's office but I am going to pull strings to meet Mr. Tretter, head of their legal division at the New York City Housing Authority." And then, "I'm still planning to get an introduction to Rex Tugwell [member of President F. D. Roosevelt's administration] somehow." I never did get that introduction.

By the Spring of '41 word was getting around [at Yale] that I hadn't yet got a job despite making the rounds at forty law firms. Professor Arthur L. Corbin, a giant in the field of contract law, stopped me in the hall and asked how I was doing. He then gave me a list with the names of half dozen firms. He said that he had written personal letters to them, they would certainly grant me an interview. I was later shown a copy of the letter. It read, "Here is a girl for whom I hope you can do something. . . . She is *one of our best* in industry, in mental power and in personality. Anyone who employs her in legal work will have reason to be thankful to us. . . . [S]he needs help to get a starting job first because she is a girl, and secondly, because she is Jewish. There is no reason for the slightest hesitation on *either* ground. Anything you can do for her will be a special favor to me."

Corbin was not the only Yale faculty member who, on his own initiative and without an approach from Siegel, reached out on her behalf. In the end Proskauer extended an offer. Siegel accepted and became the first woman attorney at the firm. One of the partners wrote that hiring Siegel would "break down a precedent of many years' standing." As she was introduced to staff and partners, Judge Proskauer said to her, "You will be the rose in Proskauer Rose and Paskus."[2]

Proskauer had a policy of giving associates a very diverse experience. Siegel assisted in litigation, worked on certiorari proceedings (appellate proceedings for the reexamination of actions of a trial court, or lower appeals court) to review tax assessments, and carried out some estate planning. She plunged into labor law issues as soon as World War II got underway and the U.S. War Labor Board was reestablished. In court with Proskauer one day, in the Appellate Division First Department, holding his papers while he argued, Siegel noticed that the person who was holding all the papers for his opponent was Soia Mentchikoff.

The war created opportunities for Siegel. She had job offers from the Department of the Interior and the Foreign Economic Administration at the Department of State. When a Proskauer associate was drafted into the armed forces, she asked that he recommend her for his volunteer's position with the lawyers' panel of the ACLU. She was the only woman and the youngest person on that panel, which was chaired by future state senator and U.S. attorney Whitney North Seymour. Working pro bono, with the approval of the firm, she wrote briefs and legal memoranda about President Roosevelt's 1942 executive order permitting the establishment of military zones within the United States and, in particular, challenging the internment of Japanese Americans. And, at another time, when noted lawyer Dorothy Kenyon planned to take legal action against the city of Boston for the dismissal of married women teachers, Siegel made certain that the senior members of the Lawyers Panel were paying attention. With several former Yale classmates, she also organized an ACLU committee to make legislative proposals concerning the lack of civil rights enjoyed by members of labor unions (principles and provisions that were later included in the 1959 federal Landrum-Griffin Act).

Siegel also joined New York City's Citizens Housing and Planning Council (CHPC). After college she had studied affordable housing in England and Sweden. In New York City, again working pro bono, she wrote legal memoranda on proposed amendments of the city's zoning regulations. In 1943 she became deeply engaged in the issues surrounding the proposed massive residential development plans of the Metropolitan Life Insurance Company. The project-in-planning was called Stuyvesant Town. CHPC opposed the plan because the proposal to house thousands of families (including many returning veterans) included no schools or other community facilities. In addition, the head of Metropolitan Life conceded that there would not be any Negroes admitted once the apartments were built. Siegel worked on appeals attacking each issue.

Housing had been an issue of interest for Siegel for some years. In 1943 Leon Keyserling, then general counsel to the National Housing Agency, offered her an opportunity to work in Washington on plans for postwar community planning and rehabilitation. She turned Keyserling down, staying at Proskauer. Two years later, however, she accepted the position of executive director of CHPC. She left Proskauer, where she was on a partnership track, on good terms and with a letter from Norman Goetz, one of the partners, saying, "[T]he latch is always off the door."

In Siegel's subsequent career as a litigator she divided her time between the private and public sectors, with seven years at the firm of Rosenman & Colin during the 1950s followed by positions as New York State assistant attorney general in charge of the Civil Rights Bureau, New York Mayor John Lindsay's general counsel at the Housing and Development Administration, and New York State solicitor general.

Miriam Wolff, born two years before Siegel in 1916, graduated from Stanford Law School in 1939. She recalls faculty giving her the tired line that she was taking the place of a man. Wolff stopped interviewing for jobs when her father was diagnosed with cancer and she went home to Los Angeles to help out. She recalled that her failure to complete interviews "changed everything." It was still the Depression and she was a woman. Job hunting in Los Angeles, she was told "there is no way [my firm] can take a woman lawyer," when she could even get by the receptionist to speak with a firm member. A series of small ad hoc jobs convinced Wolff that "if I really wanted to practice law, the thing to do was to go into public service." It was not, she found, a difficult decision to make, and it resulted in an illustrious career:

> It was evident that if you wanted to really practice on a high level and do things that were really productive in practicing law and still be an independent woman—that was the route to take. It seemed to me it didn't take a genius to figure that out. I took the civil service exam for junior counsel, placed number one, and accepted an offer from the California Department of Employment in Sacramento with the promise of trial work. Stanford had not had any kind of trial work for law students and I felt that I was putting a client at a disadvantage if I went into court, that I really couldn't do that to a client and that I needed trial work experi-

ence. The department administered unemployment insurance and I tried something like two cases a week, all over the state. And as anyone knows, once you learn in court, you learn. I mean you're very soon a relatively sophisticated lawyer. And generally I was given respect in the courtroom; I was the representative of the State of California.

San Francisco was Wolff's idea of the place to live. When the Stanford placement service called in 1944 with an offer of a position as chief law clerk at the district court of appeals, she said yes. Her family situation now permitted the move. The decision marked the beginning of a long legal career in the City by the Bay that included twenty-three years in the California attorney general's office, criminal law appellate section. And in a state known for its car culture, she joined the ranks of Palo Alto residents commuting by train to San Francisco. She became a regular, for years, in a game of bridge organized by a group of male lawyers.

Wolff observed that her life was not "particularly impacted by the prejudices that existed," but in 1946 she was turned down for a mortgage by Wells Fargo because she was a single woman. She also confronted discrimination at private clubs used by lawyers that did not admit women or, in Wolff's case, insisted that she enter through the back entrance and service elevator.

In 1964, when the Port of San Francisco was transferred from state to city control, Wolff was asked by its board to come to the port as chief counsel. She left the attorney general's office thinking, "[T]here's seldom an opportunity like this." It was, in fact, a first: No woman had ever been the port's chief counsel. Here, in her interview, Wolff pauses and says, "And I love this story. There was an organization called Municipal Executive Employees. They met a couple of times a year with the Board of Supervisors." One hot day her secretary told Wolff that she had a call from a city chief executive. They were connected and he said, "I sent you a letter asking you to join the Chief Executives organization, but we didn't realize you were a woman. And we don't have any women—and we have to withdraw that offer. . . . but we understand that your assistant is a man and he can join."

Wolff said that it was one of the very few times that she ever lost her temper: "I excoriated him." Then she hung up and called her colleague Agnes O'Brien Smith, chief deputy district attorney in San Francisco.

She relayed the story to her and asked, "Have you put up with this all these years?" And Smith said yes. And then Smith told her, "Oh, forget it; you know it's not worth it—it's just not worth getting worked up about." Wolff cooled her temper that day but did get involved in organizations such as Advocates for Women.

Wolff was courted for a number of federal jobs. In 1970 she had accepted the position of chief counsel for the Federal Maritime Commission and had rented an apartment in Washington, when the commissioners of the Port of San Francisco Board offered her the job of port director. It was a position, she said, that couldn't be refused, and she took it. She became the first woman director of any major port in the world. Yet when she stepped into that position, in 1970, she and other women were still excluded from lunch (and, therefore, business meetings) at the World Trade Club—which happened to be one floor above her office. Women's exclusion from men's social and professional clubs was a near-universal practice in those years. As the women's movement gained strength in the 1970s, and different aspects of professional discrimination became the topic of discussion among career women, this was one aspect of exclusion that was attacked—successfully

* * *

Catherine Roraback, born in 1920, was the only woman to graduate as a member of her 1948 Yale Law School class (several started). She came from a family of well-known Connecticut lawyers. Her father was a minister. Being the offspring of a locally known and respected family helped Roraback when it came time to interview for a job. She had little trouble meeting with partners, although obtaining a decent job was another matter. She quickly learned in which firm she would sit in a back office doing research, out of sight of clients, or where she would be nothing more than a glorified bag carrier for a partner going to court.

Through Fowler Harper, her former Yale teacher and friend, Roraback was connected to Harry Grandy, a New Haven lawyer who had a general practice heavy on bankruptcy work. Grandy hired the recent graduate and was quite willing for her to try her hand at everything. He gave her trial cases in her first year. Roraback said, "[H]e was probably a pre-feminist . . . and he was always very protective and nurturing and stuff." This played well to her progressive politics and social thinking.

She was active in the Progressive Party, supported candidate Henry Wallace, and had become a member of the liberal National Lawyers Guild, founded in 1937 as an alternative to the American Bar Association. In 1948 she helped to found the Connecticut Civil Liberties Union.

Roraback stayed with Grandy for five years doing a little bit of everything, including bankruptcy and small criminal cases. She called it "moving up the line on the level of cases." She was also acquiring a reputation as a committed civil liberties attorney willing to represent individuals with dissenting beliefs, among them several people prosecuted under the Smith Act, legislation that established criminal penalties for advocating the overthrow of the government. Later in her career, beginning in 1970, Roraback would gain fame representing political radicals. These included Black Panther Party member Ericka Huggins, accused of conspiracy with intent to commit the murder of a man thought to be an FBI informant (Huggins was freed in a mistrial after a ten-to-two vote for acquittal), and Susan Saxe, an anti–Vietnam War activist accused of a Pennsylvania bank robbery.

In 1953 Roraback opened her own law firm in a room one floor above Grandy's office. Five years later she was asked to join the locally based New Haven legal team associated with the Planned Parenthood League of Connecticut (PPLC) as it began to shape a new challenge to the state's nineteenth-century statute prohibiting the use of contraceptives. Roraback, still in her thirties, had been approached by Yale faculty members Fowler Harper and Tom Emerson, who respected her progressive politics and, needing a local lawyer, knew she was a member of the Connecticut bar.

Roraback said that her association with PPLC began with simple legal work. She wrote an office lease for PPLC executive director Estelle Griswold as well as a memo concerning insurance questions about the women who were volunteering and driving people to New York to obtain contraception. Concern over Connecticut's 1879 contraceptives law was a longstanding matter, as Roraback described:

> There was this [1879] statute in Connecticut that prohibited the use of contraceptives and although everyone knew, it was not exactly enforced as such. The problem was contraceptives were sold in Connecticut, doctors saw patients and they prescribed to that kind of patient. . . . There were birth control clinics in Connecticut that had been opened. . . . But

when they opened the clinic in Waterbury, the police raided it and shut it down. They arrested the doctor and several nurses. . . . and prosecuted on the grounds that the people in that clinic were aiding and abetting the commission of a crime which was incidentally, a misdemeanor. And the case went to the first, oh, I guess the judge in the lower court, may have just referred it up to the [state] Supreme Court . . . which upheld the constitutionality of the statute. There was a long history before this of attempts to repeal this statute.

Roraback participated in two challenges to the Connecticut law in the late 1950s and early 1960s. She became one of a handful of lawyers crafting legal strategies that would ultimately result in the landmark case of *Griswold v. Connecticut* in which the U.S. Supreme Court was asked to determine whether a state could criminalize the use of contraceptives.

The legal strategy established by Harper, Emerson, and Roraback was to bring cases involving married couples, a conservative approach that, if successful, would later permit an all-out attack on laws criminalizing the use of contraceptives by anyone.

Roraback briefed and argued what came to be known as the *Poe-Hoe-Doe* and *Buxton* cases at the Connecticut Supreme Court. Roraback and the rest of the team expected the court to uphold the 1879 law, which would then permit an appeal to the United States Supreme Court. They guessed correctly, and after their "defeat" the team quickly moved to organize an appeal. Roraback's colleague, Fowler Harper, argued *Poe v. Ullman* in March 1961.

Rorabach credits the ACLU's then assistant legal director Melvin Wulf with proposing that, in their brief and argument to the U.S. Supreme Court, the New Haven team members consider a strategy that would more aggressively assert a constitutional privacy right. Roraback had referenced the privacy concept in her brief to the Connecticut Supreme Court but had not made it the centerpiece of her argument. Before the U.S. Supreme Court, however, Harper pressed the right to privacy far more forcefully. In the *Poe* brief they wrote that the Connecticut statutes unlawfully "invade the privacy of the citizen" and "regulate the private sex life of all married people."

On June 19, in a five-to-four vote, the U.S. Supreme Court justices dismissed *Poe,* citing the "lack of immediacy" of any threat of prosecution.

Estelle Griswold, supported by PPLC and PPFA, immediately moved to eliminate what the Court considered the abstract nature of the challenge by establishing a birth control clinic in New Haven. On the morning of November 10, 1961, chief circuit court prosecutor Julius Maretz called Roraback, telling her arrest warrants had been issued for Griswold and Lee Buxton. They should, he said, surrender to police that afternoon. This action prepared the way for what became the landmark case of *Griswold v. Connecticut*. In the ensuing months, Roraback handled the briefs and argument for the hearings and trial. In early January, 1962, Griswold and Buxton were found guilty and each fined one hundred dollars. Roraback immediately filed an appeal and in October, after submitting a forty-two-page brief, argued the case before an appellate panel. On January 17, 1963, the three-judge appellate division panel affirmed Griswold and Buxton's convictions. Months later, Roraback again argued on behalf of the two before the Connecticut Supreme Court, which, in the spring of 1964, affirmed the convictions, opening the way for an appeal to the U.S. Supreme Court.

After the high court agreed to hear the case Roraback and Fowler Harper began work on a new brief, one that Harper expected to draw upon when he argued *Griswold*. Cancer made that impossible. Fowler asked his Yale colleague Tom Emerson to take over, which he did. Roraback never commented in public on that decision and whether she had hoped to argue *Griswold*. She did, however, sit next to Emerson at the counsel's table on the day of Supreme Court oral argument. Later, when Emerson was thanked for his work by PPLC, he replied that "the basic work on the case had already been done by Fowler Harper and Catherine Roraback."[3]

On June 7, 1965, in its *Griswold* decision, the U.S. Supreme Court ruled that the Connecticut statute violated the constitutional right to privacy of married couples. Roraback reported waiting for the announcement of the Court's decision with her law partner at a Connecticut restaurant. She ordered a second martini on hearing they had won.

The Early Generation: Children and Career

The question of marriage and children emerged as a natural issue as women Trailblazers began to establish careers. Most did not ask "Do

I want to marry?" but rather, "When is the wedding?" Several of these early women lawyers, including Shirley Siegel and Shirley Hufstedler, folded family into sustained work lives; others started legal careers and then withdrew, several for a decade, before resuming full-time work and establishing illustrious reputations. And still others married and reached the age of thirty with no thought of a career, legal or otherwise.

Betty Roberts, born in 1923, did not make it through college until she was thirty-two. Her Texas childhood was marked by hardship. Roberts's mother would say "we are white and poor [but] . . . not white trash." In 1942, at the age of nineteen, Roberts had married a serviceman who later worked for an Oregon bank. Between 1943 and 1952, they had four children. By 1962 she had divorced, obtained an undergraduate and a master's degree in political science, and married a man who was also interested in a career in elective office.

In her memoir *With Grit and by Grace*, and in her Trailblazer interview, Roberts pinpoints the "aha moment" that turned her toward a career in law:

> I went to talk to Burt Wingert, the chairman of the political science department at the University of Oregon, about working on a Ph.D. I felt I could be a good college professor. So I went to see Wingert with high hopes and grand plans. But when I asked his advice on how I should start my Ph.D. program, he gave me this stunning reply: "Betty, I can't let you do that. You're thirty-nine years old. By the time you complete a doctorate you will be forty-five and you'll only have twenty years to repay the taxpayers of Oregon for their investment in your education." I don't know what shocked me more, his twisted reasoning or the casual air with which he made his remark. Title VII did not yet exist. On the drive to Portland I stacked up in my mind the many times a man had told me, "You can't."
>
> But I did begin to think about the fact that I am not through learning and I remembered that I had heard about a law school, a night law school that had been established for many years in Portland by some local lawyers and judges. Northwestern College of Law.

Roberts started law school in August 1962, teaching high school during the day and taking law classes at night. Three of her children were still at home; she also served on the school board. In 1964 she campaigned for a seat in the state legislature and won. She took a leave from teaching, started her legislative term in 1965 while finishing her law degree, and late in that year decided to end her second marriage. In 1966, law degree in hand, she won another term in the Oregon House of Representatives.

Solidly established as a citizen of Oregon, Roberts started her own practice in Portland while teaching part-time at Mt. Hood Community College. In 1968 she returned to the legislature as a state senator, and made the decision to go into practice with her third husband, legislator Keith Skelton. Together, in 1971, they initiated a pro bono Oregon-based challenge to the criminalization of abortion (decided by *Roe v. Wade*). Later, she supported the Equal Rights Amendment and, a year later, in 1974, ran for governor, losing in a tight race. In 1976 she served as Oregon cochair of Jimmy Carter's campaign for the presidency. One year later, the Oregon legislature approved adding four judges to the state court of appeals, and the governor announced his intention to name a woman to one of the positions. Roberts got the nod, becoming the first woman to serve on that court and, later, the first woman judge to serve on the Oregon Supreme Court. As she was being sworn in as a member of the court of appeals, Roberts recalls thinking, "My decision to go back to school had carried me a long way, further than I'd ever expected."[4]

Unlike Roberts, Betty Binns Fletcher began to focus on a legal career as a young girl when her lawyer father would take her to his office and, occasionally, let her miss school if he had a good trial.[5] She did a year of law school as a Stanford undergraduate, and when she married in 1942, she intended to finish law school as quickly as possible. World War II and the birth of four children kept her from the law degree she had begun working for in 1944, but in 1954 the University of Washington accepted her as an advanced student. Her youngest child was nine months old and the oldest one was ten. Her parents supported this decision by moving in with the Fletchers to take care of their grandchildren. Their daughter thrived at law school, made law review, and graduated first in her class. With these sterling credentials, at the age of thirty-three, Betty Fletcher set out to find a job.

> Only when I got out of law school and was looking for a job, prejudice came down on me like a ton of bricks because the professor who was

supposed to get interviews for graduating students, never got one for me. At all. I knew that that was the end of any help there so I pounded the pavement with my resume and would just go in cold and say I wanted to see the hiring partner and the receptionist always thought some secretary was getting sacked. So I would get in and get the interview.

But you know, they would look at my resume and say "What a lovely, wonderful record you have, but I suppose you're going to want to spend more time with your children." Nobody sparked any interest except the Preston firm.

Preston, Thorgrimson was a firm of seven lawyers that liked to hire the University of Washington's top student. The Seattle-based firm made Fletcher an offer only after one of her law professors set up a meeting at a law review dinner with the holdout partner. The partner asked her maiden name and discovered that her father had been instrumental in his obtaining a Rhodes scholarship. Years later Fletcher was still telling people, "I hate to say this, but it was kind of the old boy network that got me my job." And that holdout partner, Charles Horowitz, became her mentor:

He worked my head off. He was a perfectionist, and I learned a great deal from him. I worked hard for him and thrived. He had two daughters, and he saw them really in roles as housewives or secretaries or things like that. In talking with them in later years, they were just amazed that I had thrived under their father.

At first, the firm was a little touchy about having me meet clients, so I was doing briefs, drafting contracts, doing this stuff, and giving it to the partner. Then they would get busy and I would have to see a client for them. Of course, I realized that my future lay in getting along with clients, so I would do whatever they wanted as quickly as I possibly could, always returned their phone calls. Pretty soon, the firm realized that I was an asset and not a liability. It was kind of a plus to be a woman. The clients thought, well, they wouldn't have a woman unless she was good.

By the 1960s Fletcher had become a partner in Preston, the first woman to make partner at a Seattle law firm. She had U.S. Supreme Court Justice William O. Douglas as a long-time client, taking care of his personal legal work. Fletcher was very involved with women's rights issues, including a state equal rights amendment. After twenty years at the Preston firm, Washington's governor approached her:

> Governor Evans had asked me [earlier] if I was interested in being a judge, and I had said at that time, "I can't, no." I had children I had to put through college. I was prospering at the law firm, and judicial salaries were pretty bad at that time.
>
> Still, it tweaked my interest. Every lawyer, there's part of him, or her, that wants to be a judge. Anyway . . . Carter put out an executive order saying that he wanted to change the complexion of the federal judiciary, he wanted women, he wanted minorities. . . . he wanted people who had already shown a commitment to justice. I was thinking that was kind of interesting, but my law practice was thriving. I had just acquired several Japanese companies for the firm as clients, people who were doing joint ventures with the Boeing Company, and I was made general counsel for Seattle Trust. And also, I was going to be nominated to be president of the state bar. So I had kind of mixed feelings.

In the end Fletcher put in an application to the Carter White House and won the nomination, although it was temporarily sidelined when a senator from Alaska tried to work a deal, offering votes on certain key issues if the president would appoint an individual from Alaska. Crisis averted, in October 1979 Fletcher took her seat on the Ninth Circuit of the U.S. court of appeals. She had no previous judicial experience:

> I had had two conversations with a few judges but I really got no clear sense of what I was getting into. I had this naïve notion it was going to be a job which would be quite contemplative, time to think about policies, a lot of time to kind of take a step back and take a look at the law. Of course, it turned out that wasn't the case at all. My [private practice] venue had basically been in state court. There was much I did not know. I'd had no criminal law in practice. I knew no Indian law, I didn't do environmental law, just the whole world was there to be learned. It was pretty frightening in that you realized that so many people's fate can depend on a ruling of the federal court.

Fletcher spent more than twenty years on the federal bench. In those two decades she wrote seven hundred opinions. Very early in her tenure, she served on panels hearing important cases concerning Native American law. In 1984 Fletcher wrote the majority opinion in the women's affirmative action case *Johnson v. Transportation Agency, Santa Clara City*, a landmark ruling upheld in 1987 by the U.S. Supreme Court.

The rules of the federal judiciary permit a judge, after the age of sixty-five, to elect a reduced caseload by taking senior status. Fletcher did this in 1999 but continued with a heavy schedule of cases. In 2009 a Seattle journalist described the eighty-six-year-old jurist, who had influenced many areas of law with her opinions, as "a high-powered icon of liberalism, the likes of whom may never again get the nod for a federal bench. She's a holdout from an unprecedented era of left-wing judicial appointments under President Jimmy Carter."[6]

Prior to her nomination to the court, Fletcher had been active in abortion reform, part of the work that earned her this reputation as an icon of liberalism. She had, however, served on the ABA Ethics Committee with Republican Clare Nelson, who went, unbidden, to Senator Orrin Hatch and other Republican judiciary committee members. Nelson knew and liked Fletcher's family and told the senators that he wanted to make sure that there was no unfavorable comment directed at her when her nomination was considered. On the day of her Senate hearing no Republicans appeared and so nobody spoke against her.

Judge Fletcher won confirmation of her Ninth Circuit position months after Democrat Patricia Wald endured a controversial Senate Judiciary Committee hearing in the summer of 1979. Fletcher and Wald were two of the several women nominated to the federal bench following passage of the 1978 Omnibus Judgeship Act, which established 158 new federal judgeships.

Wald had been tapped by Carter to serve on the U.S. Court of Appeals for the District of Columbia. If confirmed, she would be the first woman to serve on that court. Her confirmation experience could not have been more different from Fletcher's.

In the spring of 1979 Wald learned that the Congressional Republican Policy Group had decided to oppose her. Their position surprised Wald. She was then the Justice Department's assistant attorney general for legislative affairs, and in her oral history said that she was working under the assumption that she had "pretty good relations with the Republicans." In 1970, however, she had authored a chapter on drug education for the Ford Foundation that suggested there should be drug education in the schools. Despite her being the mother of five, the Republicans went after her as "antifamily."

New Hampshire senator Gordon Humphrey called her "wild and wooly." Ronald Reagan, not yet president, also attacked Wald as a "wild" activist. Republicans called Bob Jones, of the Bob Jones University, to testify. He had never met Wald, but this did not stop him from calling her an "instrument of the devil." His judgment prompted Democratic Senator Birch Bayh to ask Jones if he had ever met Mrs. Wald, and to look behind the nominee where her sons and daughters sat. After the Judiciary Committee voted to confirm her, a reporter went up to her high school–aged son. "Well, how did you feel when they called your mother an instrument of the devil?" to which he replied, "Well, she burns the lamb chops, but otherwise she's okay."

Jones's "instrument of the devil" was born Patricia McGowan in 1928. She grew up working class in Torrington, Connecticut, with an absent father. The women in her family, many of them factory workers, encouraged her. They said "go for it," not "you're a girl, you can't do that." Scholarships, waiting tables, and a Pepsi-Cola fellowship permitted her to attend Connecticut College and Yale Law School, class of 1951. A high class ranking and a position on law review won her the support of three Yale faculty members as she set out to begin her legal career. Wald said simply, "[T]he law school professors . . . were instrumental in getting me a federal clerkship."

In 1951, Second Circuit judge Jerome Frank accepted Wald as his second female clerk, but while she was waiting for the offer, Wald looked for other jobs. She was unmarried, had a stellar record, and like most of her sisters in law was gobsmacked by discrimination:

> Gender . . . I think my first encounter with reality was when it came time to get a job. Jodi Bernstein, my best friend at Yale, and I got on a train—cold—no prior appointments and we went down to Wall Street. And we just started knocking on doors of major firms. I ended up getting an offer from Chadbourne & Park, a securities firm. My law review work had been

on securities. A good friend of mine from Law Review, Dan Freed, also got an offer from them. We were both unmarried and had similar records but they offered him a salary of $500 more than me. And in those days that was a big difference. So I did not take the job. I took the clerkship.

I was the only woman clerk in the whole circuit. Frank was very, very pro-women—ahead of his time. He had worked closely with women lawyers during the New Deal. It's not as though the dawn of creation for women came only in the 1960s and 1970s. Abe Fortas' wife, Caroline Agger, had worked with Frank in one of the agencies. The wife of Frank Shea was also a New Deal lawyer he had worked with. Women in law, there was a middle ground where it could—it didn't happen a lot but it could happen. It wasn't outside the realm of reasonable ambition.

The clerkship was one of the defining experiences in my life. I had a very, very intense working relationship with the judge. I worked on his correspondence and speeches as well as the actual drafting of memos and decisions. Frank was noted for his dissents. He was way ahead of his time in terms of identifying several problems in the justice system. . . . problems of poverty and their relationship to the criminal justice system. He was 20 years ahead of the Warren Court in terms of legal rights for criminal defendants.

Frank was the only Jewish judge on the Second Circuit Court of Appeals. During the year that I worked for him the Rosenberg case came up [Ethel and Julius Rosenburg were accused of conspiracy to commit espionage]: The first of many rounds of that notorious case. After oral argument Frank said to me, "I know that they are going to assign me this opinion because I am Jewish." And they did. Frank felt strongly that the death penalty was inappropriate. He wrote a long and passionate opinion urging the Supreme Court to review the death sentences, which ultimately of course didn't happen.

In 1952, just as she was finishing her clerkship, Wald married a Yale classmate. And as she tells it, "[T]his is where my personal life begins to have a real effect upon my professional life." She moved to Washington, D.C., to be near her husband with a recommendation from Frank that said, "She is the best law clerk that I ever had." Arnold Fortas & Porter hired her. Wald left in less than a year to have her first child. The door was open if she wanted to return, but she did not—"I was really taken up by motherhood." Between 1953 and 1960, Wald had five children and did not work as a lawyer. She did not go back to work until all of her children were in school, a career break of ten years: "My mother had to work all the time. There was no welfare. We were living in an extended family. And I could see how much she wanted to give me more time. So when I had the option, the economic option, of being at home with my children—I took it."

Wald eased herself back into legal work part-time in the early 1960s, aided by male friends from Yale, "now in their peak years as lawyers," who started sending her work: "[T]hey persuaded me with part-time opportunities." These opportunities were many: Following race riots in the United States in 1967, President Lyndon B. Johnson established the Kerner Commission. Wald was hired to write the chapter on the performance of courts during the riots. In the same year Wald asked not to be considered for a vacancy on the D.C. juvenile court, feeling, she told her interviewer, "that I did not have enough experience or practice behind me to be a judge."

Instead, in the late sixties and early seventies she worked for the Vera Institute of Justice in New York on bail issues. She also joined the Neighborhood Legal Services Program, successfully arguing a case at the U.S. court of appeals that upheld the program's provision of free divorces to poor women. The opportunities of this period also included one to author a report for the Ford Foundation on drug treatment and education. And in 1972 Wald became affiliated with the Mental Health Law Project, an offshoot of the Center for Law and Social Policy, and what Wald called "a sort of shadow government for the upcoming Carter Administration." Five years later, in 1977, President Carter named Wald assistant attorney general for legislative affairs in the Department of Justice.

The experience and respect garnered in these years of work landed Wald in the Senate Judiciary Committee's hearing room, "the instrument of the devil" who was confirmed as the first woman to serve on the U.S. Court of Appeals for the District of Columbia.

Wald was not alone among those women born in the 1920s who decided on a time-out to have and raise children before relaunching themselves as attorneys. In the Philadelphia suburbs Norma Shapiro, later a U.S. district court judge, stayed home for nine years to raise her three children, drawing up wills and doing probate work and name changes out of her house. Jodie Bernstein, Pat Wald's friend from law school, also stepped off the career track for a decade to raise three children. Bernstein sums up the issues of her day as compared with the culture of the current moment:

> I think our choices were—it was really foreclosed for us. I mean not only did everybody say you must be home with your children, but the employment opportunities were foreclosed. They were just foreclosed. If you didn't have any choice, you didn't have any choice. Today, I think there are many choices in some senses and fewer choices in others. By that I mean I don't think that I would advise anybody to stay out for ten years or 12 years like we did. I think it would be almost impossible to come back and to be able to have any range of choices. And that's why I say I think in some ways there is more choice and in some ways less choice. It may turn out to be the same kind of foreclosure on the opposite end that we had. That is, you better not take more than a very short period of time or you will put yourself at a tremendous competitive disadvantage.
>
> I think Pat [Wald] and I hit it, Pat and I and others. [It was an easier period for professional women to stay home]. . . . We went back at the same time. . . . [I]t was extraordinarily important to me, and critical to my courage to try to do it, personal courage, personal confidence to try to do it again, [and] that she was trying to do it again too. And the other factor was that it did become quickly a time of real opportunity for women who had any training. . . . [W]e both were wonderfully positioned for the Carter administration. There was hardly anybody [female] who was trained and had experience. In fact, there were some disasters because they put women into jobs that didn't have sufficient experience really. So I think we kind of lucked out in that sense. We hit it at a time in which there was demand for lawyers. And the other, I think, significant factor for me, probably for Pat as well, is we did know people. There were a lot of Yale people here [Washington, D.C.]. Many of them were already partners. . . . assistant attorney generals. So that kind of thing kind of hurt, but they were more than willing to help.

Bernstein received help from Yale classmates in reestablishing herself, first as a member of a small practice and then at the Federal Trade Commission (FTC). She had long been interested in government and politics, and had engaged in political party precinct work years before while raising her family in Chicago. In Washington two male friends helped her to make connections. Bob Wald had worked years before at the FTC. He gave her resume to former colleagues while conversations with lawyer Matt Watson confirmed Bernstein's belief that she needed to find a fairly new field of law in order to avoid playing catch-up. Savvy, Bernstein asked herself, "What's new, what's happening where I could sort of be on the ground floor?"

Matt Watson mentioned a couple of things, and one of them was the Bureau of Consumer Protection at the FTC. It was 1970. Consumer advocate Ralph Nader had released his report on the Federal Trade Commission the year before. His so-called Nader's Raiders had described the agency's many problems and called for a bureau that would stop unfair, deceptive, and fraudulent business practices. Nader's report led to a round of hiring. Bernstein started at the FTC in 1970, launching a renewed career in which, in short order, she served as director of the Bureau of Consumer Protection, general counsel in the Environmental Protection Agency, and general counsel of Health and Human Services, where her office was "the principal architect of Title IX stuff." Following these years at federal agencies Bernstein became a private law firm partner, and later vice-president and general counsel at a private corporation.

Conclusion

Trailblazing woman lawyers born before 1930 almost to a person wanted to practice law in a private firm. A small number eschewed what then passed for large firms, or private-sector work of any kind. Most, however, graduated from law school hoping to be hired by a prestigious firm, an ambition more than consistent with their outstanding credentials. Several women won first-rank clerkships, at a time when clerking for a judge was still not common, but most found gender and, occasionally, religion, to be a rigid barrier. As New York State judge Betty Ellerin, herself a Trailblazer, has said, "[L]awyers and the Bar and all of its constituent parts hate change." And, of course, what these women requested was change, what was perceived as the radical opportunity to compete equally with their male counterparts.

Women Trailblazers of this generation who were hired at private firms found that partner status came late, or not at all. They therefore took their career ambitions to other legal institutions. Tamar Frankel, Marygold Mellis, and Dorothy Nelson developed careers at law schools. Katie Roraback, Cornelia Kennedy, Norma Shapiro, and Judith Vladeck spent part or all of their adult lives in solo or family firm practice.

For this early generation, lawyering for government provided both initial career prospects and capstone career opportunities. Local, state, and federal governments hired women lawyers when private firms would not. The culture of the public sector differed from that of law firms and corporations. To be sure, public sector cultures varied one from one another; some regions of the country and some agencies were slow to accept women. Still, a democratic ethos, local connections, and many women's willingness to accept lower salaries opened the door to public-sector employment. Trailblazers took these positions to get a foothold, learn the ropes in local courts and agencies, and have less grueling work hours. Because of their outstanding credentials and the high professional regard in which they were held, many of these women became state and federal judges. They, like a number of the Trailblazers of the next two generations, benefited from changing times and, in particular, pressure on the White House to bring women into major government positions.

ENTR'ACTE

Tales from the Clothes Closet

Every woman lawyer has her favorite story about hair and clothing. Trailblazers are no exception. Some of their recollections are full of humor, but other memories are painful, meditations on having to cope with bias toward their sex, race, or ethnicity as it was reflected in their appearance.

* * *

Before these modern Trailblazers, in the last quarter of the nineteenth century, members of the Equity Club, an organization of pioneering women lawyers, exchanged letters about professional issues. They struggled with the public perception that they were mentally and physically inferior and required special treatment to do their job. But, happily, certain professional questions elicited their sense of humor. Chief among them was the implicit women's dress code. In 1876 a wit styled "E. Quality" wrote to the *Chicago Legal News* to ask if women lawyers should not "remove their hats, and address the court with head uncovered, as the gentlemen members of the bar are compelled to do."[1] Washington, D.C., lawyer Belva Lockwood always removed her hat, presenting herself as equal to her brother members of the bar who, of course, removed theirs. Other women attorneys objected to abandoning contemporary nineteenth-century etiquette and, in court, kept theirs on. The male model of dress would not define them.

In the twentieth century, clothes became an ongoing source of struggle between men in the legal world with seniority and power, and women new to the profession. In 1947 the *Los Angeles Herald Express* covered the story of a visiting judge who told a colleague of Trailblazer Selma Smith to "take off your hat."[2] Smith reported that the lawyer, Nadia Williams, was absolutely nonplussed: "This had never happened before, and none of our Los Angeles County judges had ever raised this issue. She said, 'Well, may I speak?' And he said, 'After you take off your hat.' And I happen to know that she had a hat pin that was holding it on, and that when she would take it off, her hair would be down in a different arrangement. That hat was holding it in a certain place. At any rate, she had to take off the hat. This was a disturbing thing to everyone in the courtroom, except to that judge."

And then, in the 1960s, Ruth Abrams, a lawyer with the Middlesex County district attorney's office, was told by a hostile judge that she could not be in his courtroom *without* a hat and white gloves: "I was stunned. I didn't say anything. I mean what was I going to say? I said there was nobody else who could try the case. I think the court officer told him to back off, or the court clerk. [In those days] women were wearing dresses and skirts in the courtroom. Women were wearing short skirts in the 60s so one of the judges had green curtains made for the jury box so that the lawyers would not look at the women jurors' legs. . . . Occasionally women would wear pants, but some judges would object to pants suits."

New York City lawyer, feminist, and congresswoman Bella Abzug took on the increasingly crazy issue of hats and owned it. Abzug began wearing hats when she was young and one of the few women lawyers in practice. When interviewed later she would say, "Working women wore hats. It was the only way they would take you seriously. After a while I started liking them. When I got to Congress, they made a big thing of it. They did not want me to wear a hat. So I did."[3]

Most women made it through law school without thinking about wardrobe choices, but that was not true of everyone. In *Pinstripes and Pearls*, Patricia Schroeder, Harvard Law class of 1964, told the story of walking into Langdell Hall in Bermuda shorts and knee-highs with a sweater tied over her shoulders. Several people came up to her to say that she was not dressed properly "for the most prestigious law library in the country." Schroeder, later a member of Congress, recalled thinking, "Who are these people? There was no dress code for studying in the library as far as I knew."[4]

In fact, a few law schools, including NYU, the University of Pennsylvania, and Louisiana State, did have dress codes for men and women, but at Harvard one was, apparently, just supposed to know what was proper. Elsewhere, according to Barbara Babcock, Yale class of 1963, everybody dressed up: "Well, dressed up by today's standards. . . . This was before pantyhose. . . . I mean, people didn't wear pants. [And the men] wore sports jackets and Chinos . . . [S]ometimes they wore ties, often they wore ties. And sometimes they even wore suits. And shirts with collars, I mean, people did not wear t-shirts."

And, occasionally, there were wardrobe malfunctions. In 1964, Roberta Ramo, later the first woman president of the American Bar Association but then just out of college, toured the east to visit prospective law schools and sit interviews. For her last one, at Yale, she had purchased "this fabulous dress":

> It was when they were first making suede thin enough that you could have a dress made. So this was a coat dress. It buttoned all the way down the front. I went to the fanciest hair dresser in New York. . . . Got on the train to New Haven. I was greeted by the admissions director, who I thought then was 850 years old. . . . And he had a 17-piece suit on and invited me to come into his office and sit down. And as I sat down. . . . [f]rom the ride on the train my suede dress had stretched—And almost as though it were a comedy that had been prepared for years each button. . . . [o]pened up—doop, doop, doop—leaving me sitting [laughter] in front of him. And I said to him without thinking, "Does this mean I get in?" And I didn't. When he didn't laugh, I knew it was not a good sign!

In the late 1960s and 1970s, as the number of women at law firms increased, there were virtually no women mentors, no reliable authority to suggest and approve wardrobe choices. Judith Resnik, reflecting on a 1975 recruitment lunch with men from Prokower, Rose, neatly summed up the new woman lawyer's dilemma:

> So, they took me out to lunch. I was sitting at a table, but I was the only female with seven or eight guys, two partners and the associates, all talking about who they'd seen that morning to interview at the law school. And, somebody said, "God, somebody came in really badly dressed" and I said, "Oh, like blue jeans or something?" He said, "No, he only had a sports jacket." And, I said, "What else could he have worn?" Until that moment, I actually didn't know about the idea of a suit.

Only then was I told that if a man had walked into that firm in that summer as a summer associate and had worn only "a sports jacket," he would have been taken aside and told what to wear. Well, I was a female there and nobody ever took me aside and told me anything about clothes. I thought I was really, you know, spiffy because I didn't have blue jeans on and I had little pants suits, a vest and a pair of pants. It was before people had dress codes for women because there weren't enough women to be able to say: wear a blue suit and look like them [the men].

African American women lawyers had different experiences and choices. At the end of law school in 1974, LaDoris Cordell, later Judge Cordell, interviewed for jobs wearing a big afro. At one large firm an older white male quietly told her that the firm just was "not ready to hire a Black woman." Cordell was shocked but said that she did not have the sense to file a lawsuit. She did not mention changing her hair style.

Peggy Quince, later chief justice of the Supreme Court of Florida, approached racism differently:

Let me tell you about the first time I ever went to court. This is in Virginia. When I first finished law school, I used to wear my hair in an afro and I decided after law school to straighten my hair, because a lot of people didn't like that style hair dress. I decided I didn't want to do my clients any kind of disservice by having my hair in an afro, so when I went into private practice I straightened my hair and cut it into the style of every other woman. [I went into court] and the case was called and I was thinking I looked very professional, started walking up to the bench and the judge looked at me and said, "Who are you, the defendant?" I was very upset but I just said, "No, your honor, my name is Peggy Quince. I'm an attorney at law and I'm representing . . ."

In Mississippi, African American civil rights attorney Constance Harvey took yet a different approach. She was very comfortable in pants and wore them when other women did not. She also liked short skirts and boots. It was, after all, the early 1970s:

Jack Young is the attorney who moved my admission to the United States District Court in the Southern District. He stood before Judge Harold Cox, who was a renowned racist judge, who professed to be ultra conservative and who indicated that he did not like white people coming to Mississippi trying to help black people. Jack Young made a motion before Judge Cox to have me become a member of that bar. Judge Cox refused to let me be sworn in because he didn't like what I had on. I had to leave and go to Vogue on Capital Street and buy me a red, white, blue and yellow dress and a pair of red and white shoes and come back and be sworn in before Judge Cox by Attorney Young. . . . When I initially appeared before him that morning, I had on a brown skirt and a brown vest which were just alike, same material, brown and green. I had on a green turtleneck, and some brown boots. The skirt was short but appropriate. He just said he was not going to swear me in looking like I'd come from a honky-tonk. . . . In order to get into his court, I bought that outfit and I wore it just when I went before him. I think I wore it every time I went before him to remind him that I had to buy that dress and he was going to see it every time he saw me.

The Pants Suit

In those years the question of whether to wear pants, and where they were permitted, was constantly discussed. Harvey just swatted the issue away, obeying a judge's order not to wear them for a few years and then insisting on changing the rules: "I made it permissible for women to wear pants in court. Some judges would tell me not to wear pants and I wouldn't wear them in his court. One judge told me that if you want to win a jury, you wear what women wear; women don't wear pants. The juries were all white and all men so it really didn't matter. As long as I wore an Afro, it really didn't matter. [But now] if I have a jury that looks conservative, I won't wear pants, I'll wear a dress or suit."

In the 1970s the pants suit was radical fashion because it crossed gender lines. Women wanted the comfort and, ironically, the modesty that pants offered. Men, and quite a few women, however, saw the wearing of a pants suit as a statement of want-to-be female power, as the usurpation, through clothing, of opportunities available only to men. And, not to overlook the obvious, many men liked women in skirts because they wanted to see a little leg.

The wearing of a pants suit became an item of discussion at support groups. When Marcia Greenberger arrived at Caplin & Drysdale in 1970, she began attending lunches that were set up by young women associates in other Washington firms "to provide each other with support":

> One of our big issues at the time was whether women could wear pants suits to the office. They were quite stylish at the time, but the whole idea of coming to work in pants suits was pretty revolutionary. And there was no such concept as dress down anything. . . . I dutifully raised the issue with my firm and the leadership agreed that women working at the firm, including secretaries, could wear pants suits to the office but they had to have matching jackets and they had to bring the jacket to work. . . . It had to be a real suit. That was one of our first successes. Of course, the whole concept of arguing a case in a pants suit was never something that anybody thought to even put on the table. This was a pretty progressive response, and I did wear pants suits.

Senior partners established dress codes, but judges had even more authority to set the rules. Professor Myrna Raeder argued the obvious when she said, "[You] didn't want to do anything that would offend a judge because you knew that the judge wouldn't go against you, the judge was going to go against your client and so that was always a very delicate balance."

As women became judges, change occurred. Male judges took their cues from female colleagues on the bench and let their female clerks wear pants suits. Miriam Wolff became a California municipal court judge in 1975: "One of the first requests I had from the chief clerk was, she came in and said, the women want to know whether you would permit them to wear trousers to court, and I told them I was sure you would not. And I said oh yes I would. And she said, 'Well!' She said I assume it has to be something like a pants suit and I said yes that would be fine. . . . Actually I had for a while an all-female court . . . court reporter, first woman bailiff."

The Bow Tie

During the 1970s and 1980s, women lawyers continued to search out wardrobe choices that would satisfy senior partners and judges. As with the issue of hats in the nineteenth century, women often had to choose whether or not to mimic maleness with feminine garb. Enter the floppy bow tie, described by Oregon lawyer Katherine O'Neil: "The mid-80s were an interesting time for women lawyers. The number of women law students was increasing and increasing, but of course it takes a while to get through the pipeline. There were more and more young women lawyers around, and they were trying to get their bearings in so many different ways. I was reminiscing about how we all dressed in the mid-80s. I never succumbed to the floppy bow tie attire, but many women lawyers considered that as a way of asserting the same formality of dress as the men lawyers did with their ties."

As one of the few women in the Missouri attorney general's office in the late 1970s, Ann Covington recalled a formal, highly professional dress code:

> We wore suits and we wore suits with skirts. At that time, and probably into the 80s after I had left, in the practice women were many times trying to look a bit like men in terms of attire. Now, that was not overdone, but by that I mean that it was more common to have some kind of a white blouse with a jacket and a matching suit, and some women would have what I laughingly call "little tielets" even, that were certainly not little miniature men's ties, but somehow subconsciously evoked that kind of look or effect. I could never quite bring myself to do that, but then I've never accessorized very well anyway.

As a young Boston lawyer, Rya Zobel observed this search for an outward identity:

> There was also . . . the whole issue of dress. There was a kind of uniform for men, but the uniform for women had not yet evolved. When it did begin to evolve, it evolved into a female version of what the men were wearing: loose suits or black suits. That was it. And the big bow ties on the blouses. And what really amuses me is the various ways in which the women then ultimately broke away from that. Nancy Gertner tells the story of how she used to go to court carrying her stuff in a shopping bag. And she always wore red. So it came out in various ways. I used to wear

a hat all the time. I loved wearing hats until I started wearing glasses, and then I decided hats looked sort of funny on glasses. And of course, nowadays, nobody would wear a hat anyhow.

Color

The world of law is generally not a place for fashion peacocks. An expensive Italian silk tie for men, a pair of cannot-help-but-be-recognized pricey pumps for women, along with carefully selected bling—all this may be acceptable. But walk around large law firms or go to court and what you see is what one *New York Times* reporter observed while covering new lawyers at the federal courts in New York: "They arrived at the United States Court of Appeals for the Second Circuit, in Manhattan, on Thursday in similar shades of gray and black suits, posed to continue their training in a new program to help represent immigrants. . . . a sea of monochrome suits that belied a spectrum of diverse origins."[5]

According to her biographers, pioneering Mississippi lawyer and legislator Lucy Somerville Howorth learned the color lesson in the early months of what she called "hustling the law": "When she first appeared in court, her bright print suit drew snide remarks from the men at the bar. 'I never made that mistake again,' she said. 'After that I always wore something plain, like navy blue serge.' Initially she wore a hat in the courtroom, but as one judge recounted, 'She may have come into court with a hat but when the argument gets hot, that hat flies across the table.'"

Virginia attorney Anne Marie Whittemore described a lack of tailored clothes for professional women when she started her legal career: "Women's clothing at that time—you were either a hippie or you were a preppie . . . [S]o, my compromise generally was to find a dress in a solid color and wear a jacket or a sweater with it. I do recall that one of the first days I was at Arent Fox I was in the law library wearing a mauve sleeveless dress and white pumps, and one of the lawyers came up to me and said, 'You look like you are going to a party.' I did not take that as insulting at all."

Black, of course, was safe. In the early days of the Reagan administration, Zona Hostetler argued an age discrimination case before the U.S. Supreme Court on behalf of State Department employees who were subject to mandatory retirement at the age of sixty-five:

The argument was held during the first snowfall of the season, and my old friend and mentor, Erwin Griswold, came to the argument. He was quite elderly. . . . When the case was over Erwin Griswold came up to me and said he had two things to say. One was to compliment me on how I dressed. Let me back up. When I was getting ready for this argument I spent a great deal of time preparing for the argument of course but I also spent a great deal of time figuring out what I was going to wear. (laugh) I scoured the department stores and found a very severe looking black pin stripe suit. It was not a pants suit because women were not supposed to wear pants suits to court at that time. I came home with this black pin stripe suit, and my husband looked at it and said, "That is the most God awful outfit I have ever seen and I hope you burn it after the argument." After the argument, Erwin said to me, "Zona, I want to complement [sic] you on how well you looked. It is just disgraceful how women lawyers are dressing to argue in the Supreme Court these days." (laugh) The second thing he said was "You gave a fine argument and your brief is excellent, but you know you will lose. It has nothing to do with the merits. It has to do with the system." And I did lose, although Justice Thurgood Marshall wrote a wonderful dissent in my favor.

Lois Schiffer also thought long and hard about what to wear in 1998 when she argued a Superfund cleanup case for the Justice Department before the U.S. Supreme Court:

I will tell one funny women's story about that argument. At some point a couple of weeks before the argument, I had been working a lot of late nights. . . . So I went upstairs to the Solicitor General's Office . . . and there was a lovely woman lawyer there and I said, you know, we haven't really talked about what to wear, but I'm planning to wear my navy blue suit. Well you'd think I had said I was planning to wear my red cocktail dress. She said you absolutely can't do that. I said I can't? No, she said. Actually there's a dress code that grows out of the fact that I, meaning she, had gone to Court one day in a taupe suit, taupe-colored suit, and that Justice Rehnquist had thought that was a little dicey and not befitting the Solicitor General's Office and so a dress code had been negotiated and basically what women could wear were either black suits or black dresses or an outfit that was made for them that looked like morning coats that the men wore. I certainly wasn't going to do the latter, and I didn't have a very good black suit, so I thought, oh my God, I have to go shopping. At first I said, can I wear a black dress. She said no, that's for people who are pregnant. You really have to wear a black suit. So in the midst of all this preparation, I had to . . . spend one of my evenings out shopping to get a new black suit.

Justice Ruth Bader Ginsburg is only one of several women who favored tailored suits, conservative in color, "because my idea in court was always to dress in a way that wouldn't be distracting. I wanted the Court to concentrate on what I was saying and not on what I was wearing." But some women had different statements to make with color. Defense lawyer and, later, federal judge, Nancy Gertner joined this camp early in her career:

> I still felt like an outsider, cavorting around in someone else's skin. Lani Guinier describes it as having "insider privileges" and "outsider consciousness." Insider privileges accrue to lawyers as professionals, and now, in a fashion, to me. I "seemed" successful. "Outsider consciousness" involves that "peculiar sensation of always looking at one's self through the eyes of others."
> I fell back on Professor Gary Bellow's advice. Gary [taught a trial advocacy course at Harvard Law School]. . . . Being a lawyer, he told his class, was like being an actor or an actress. It is a role; the courtroom, a stage. You put on a costume in the morning—for me, [Gertner said,] it was the fire-engine-red-suit—but importantly, you take it off in the evening. You decide the range of parts that you could conceivably play—within the limits of age, appearance, audience, and yes, gender.[6]

Waterways law expert Carol Dinkins also thought about clothes from the perspective of an outsider—with humor. In 1979 she was elected partner at the Texas firm of Vinson & Elkins: "I went out and bought a red designer suit and had in my mind that I was going to look so different anyway from the rest of the partners, just by virtue of wearing a skirt, that I would make a very bold statement in my red suit. And I had a good time buying that suit, but I had an even better time wearing it."

Judge Ruth Burg also had a definite philosophy of style:

> I never succumbed to the fact that you had to dress like a man. I probably wore more tailored items but in the early days I couldn't afford to buy a lot of clothes. . . . As I became more involved professionally and reached a level where I became respected as a person, I always thought it was important never to lose my femininity in order to be successful. . . . [On panels, often the only woman,] I made it a point to wear a bright-colored outfit rather than a dark suit. I always felt it was important to not play down the fact that I was a woman and I was proud of the fact that, as a woman, I was able to reach a certain level of achievement. On the bench I wore a scarf (often colorful) not a jabot.

I'm Pregnant and Other Tales

Nancy Gertner loved being pregnant: "After all the years of squeezing yourself into what seemed to be a male role, literally and figuratively, there was something wonderful about being openly, irresistibly female. Although I was only a few months pregnant and hardly 'showed,' I sported huge dresses. And I worked out hand signals with the judge to let me sprint to the bathroom when I had to."[7]

When Zita Weinshienk was a county judge, she found her judicial robe a helpful cover-up for her pregnancy, because it was so unusual in the 1960s for people to see a pregnant woman in the workplace. People did not even know that Weinshienk, mother of three, was pregnant. A decade later Christine Durham, pregnant with her fourth child, also knew that a pregnant lawyer in court was pretty unusual: "I remember going to a hearing in federal court in a fuchsia maternity dress. It was very dressy but the general effect was that of a pink balloon in the middle of all the suits. I kind of enjoyed that."

Christine Durham's good humor, her pleasure in looking a bit like a colorful balloon, typifies the insights and strength of personality that helped to carry these women through endless professional challenges. Marna Tucker could only laugh when she arrived for a meeting at the White House wearing a pink ultra-suede suit with grape jelly spots down her front, an early morning gift from the four-year-old she had just dropped off at nursery school. And Antonia Hernandez had to look twice when, being courted by Ted Kennedy's Senate Judiciary Committee, interviewer David Boies greeted her in a "rumpled seersucker suit, which he's notorious for, and lots of rumpled hair." She, of course, had gone out and taken great care in her selection of a proper interview suit. But returning home she told her husband that she had had "the most interesting conversation about immigration, about civil rights, about the type of cases I've taken." Days later she was offered the job.

The late Shirley Hufstedler, feminist, federal judge, and U.S. secretary of education, saw it all. As a young woman she had worked in Hollywood and knew how to size up a costume. She described the changes that occurred during her career on the west coast:

[Pants] were not appropriate at any time I was on the bench. We had given up wearing hats and gloves every day, but one wore skirts and a coat for most things, and in the summer time we wore dresses. That carried through to D.C. [By 1981] the dress code in L.A. was beginning to loosen up. It was permissible for women to wear pants suits as long as they were very dignified pants suits, and now it's become even more informal, because casual Friday has turned out to be casual every day, which shocks New York lawyers, I think.

Tax attorney Joanne Garvey completes these tales with a twenty-first-century recollection. In 2003 she was among the women chosen to receive the Margaret Brent award given by the American Bar Association's Commission on Women in the Profession. Describing the event during an interview, she paused to make a "sartorial" comment:

How times have changed. Our group, when it was inducted, every single one of us was in a pants suit. And I was thinking . . . ordinarily in the past, we would have been uncomfortable in our spike heels and whatever else, but this was very nice needless to say . . . that sartorial advance has arrived. . . . With the advent of business casual, I think most of the women are better dressed than most of the men these days in the offices. Brighter colors . . . a sea of color as opposed to the rather drab black and brown.

5

The Next Generation

The Path to Private Firm Partnership

Interviewing for a job is an art form, a performance, a test of quick wits. It is impossible to repeat too often that in the 1960s and early 1970s, women law graduates could not even obtain interviews. "Our firm does not hire women" is a phrase they came up against time and time again. In some instances outside supporters, firm specialization, family connections, or local culture helped to open a partner's door for an interview. As with male applicants, of course, not every interview led a firm to extend an offer. With women, however, gender was an ever-present issue; it was the elephant in every interview room.

In the early 1970s, when federal judge Betty Fletcher was still in private practice, she received a friendly telephone call from a partner at a local Seattle firm. He wanted to chat about her oldest daughter. Susan had recently graduated first in her law school class at the University of Washington, a ranking that generally led male job seekers to win associate positions at local firms. But this call, Fletcher said, was not intended to signal that his firm would extend an offer to her daughter: "You know I just want to tell you how proud you must be of your daughter—not only beautiful, but brilliant and charming, but of course, we're not ready to hire a woman."

Fletcher acknowledges that it was "part of the culture then." Nonetheless, Trailblazers repeatedly said that as young law graduates they were surprised that firms refused to interview them, or to hire them. These women wore their abilities and ambition proudly. Since childhood, they had successfully maneuvered around economic, racial, and patriarchal obstacles meant to defeat their aspirations. Somehow, in the 1960s, they did not expect to encounter gender discrimination in a country that had been led by the young president, John F. Kennedy, who, in his 1961 inaugural address, electrified the nation when he admonished, "Ask not what your country can do for you—ask what you can do for your country."

Perhaps the 1960s generation of law graduates had not heard the stories of the women who went for interviews in the genial 1950s era of President Dwight D. Eisenhower. In 1952, during a job interview, Betty Weinberg Ellerin, later an associate justice of the New York State appellate division, was asked, "Oh, why should we hire you, after all you'll get married and you'll have children and you'll leave." Ellerin, a noted wit, thought to herself, "Gee, I wish you'd tell that to my mother." At this interview, and elsewhere, she "was not flooded with offers." Six years later Zita Weinshienk was also told by interviewers that they would not take a chance on someone who might get pregnant. "So I absolutely could not find a job." If a graduate went cold calling at law firms hoping for an interview, women receptionists barred her way or, ironically, because the Trailblazer was female, let them through, assuming the job seeker was answering an ad for a secretarial position.

In the late 1950s, Carla Hills, later secretary of the U.S. Department of Housing and Urban Development, interviewed for a private firm position in New York. Her experience was not uncommon: "As soon as I walked in, they'd say, 'What we believe is the appropriate specialty for women is trusts and estates or marital law,' and those were not my interests. So I went and interviewed in San Francisco and Los Angeles, and found LA more progressive."

Still, even in LA, the county Bar would not let women lawyers into Junior Barristers (its "youth group" for attorneys under the age of thirty-six), and Hills was able to network only through her lawyer husband, who was active in the all-male group.

Joanne Garvey, one of two daughters, was brought up in the Oakland-Berkeley area of California. When she was three, her dad handed Joanne a baseball glove and started pitching to her. Sports became a lifelong interest. As a lawyer, Garvey, who stood nearly six feet tall, could be found in courts of law as well as on basketball courts. Later, she played center on a team that won a silver medal in the Senior Olympics.

Garvey entered the University of California's law school, Boalt Hall, in 1958 with eleven other women. She was the first woman whom the school sent on the so-called law review interviews (an early opportunity given members of law review to interview with law firms). As Garvey described the experience,

They figured I would be "okay." I could get through the interviews. So I go out, and I had some very interesting interviews. I would walk in, and one guy said, "But you're a woman." Because it was "J. Garvey," and I would say, "yes." I remember one interview with a firm out of San Diego. And the guy said, "Well, you know we do a lot of community work like Little League, and I don't know whether you could do that." And I said, "I was a Playground Director, and, you know, I think I probably know more about Little League baseball than most of the people you've got playing there."

I got an offer from a firm down in Santa Barbara [Caveletto, Webster, Mullin & McCaughey]. I accepted that offer, though I also had an offer for a clerkship with Justice Dunaway. That I turned down, because my goal was to be a "real" lawyer and this was my opportunity. I was hired to do tax. I found out I liked the practice area. I liked problem solving because that's what we were doing. We were doing big ticket planning because this is the time [early 1960s] when Santa Barbara farmers who had bought their land for pennies on the dollar were now swapping it for downtown Los Angeles [real estate]. You couldn't afford to sell it, so what you did is you did tax free exchanges. So they were swapping farm land for L.A. office buildings. It was a very sophisticated, very interesting practice but I was let go when the firm ran out of work for me.

So I called one of my friends in the Bay Area and asked, is anybody looking for tax associates? He said, yeah there are a couple of firms that are looking for tax associates. So when I went to his office I decided to walk across the street and see if I could get an interview with the Managing Partner, Aylett Cotton, at Kelso, Cotton, and Ernst. Aylett did not like women lawyers. In fact, he hated women lawyers. The fact that he had never met a woman lawyer did not especially bother him but he was a gentleman of the old school. So when I arrived without an appointment, he decides he will give me a courtesy interview. So, I walk in—we start chatting and he finds out that I'm a tax associate and they have been desperately looking for a tax associate for months. I have a rather sparkling resume, and so he decides he'll talk a little further. Well, I notice his desk and office, I saw the Stanford diploma, and I think he had some other memorabilia around, and he also had some books on archeology. And one of the things in my dim dark past was that I wanted to be an archeologist to prove Schliemann was wrong in his discovery of Troy. So, I sort of gently steered the conversation to Stanford football, cause I was Cal of course, and we talked Stanford-Cal, and we talked about archeology. So, by this time he's thinking, well they really had been looking for a tax associate. I have all the credentials that they ordinarily look for, and I knew something about Cal-Stanford football, but of course he's not going to make this decision, so he passes me on to the tax partner. Before the day is out I meet every attorney [about twenty partners and associates] in that firm. When I got back to Santa Barbara on my desk was an offer. So I joined the firm.

Quick-witted, Garvey clearly understood the art of interview performance. While at the Kelso firm, she also proved effective at finding a place for herself in the local Bar:

Lou Kelso encouraged the associates to go to educational classes which the firm paid for. The only thing around was programs put on at lunch by the Bar Association. And so we found out as associates that since the firm would pay for all these, this is the way to get a free lunch. So we [associates] all signed up as a group, and we went to every darn educational program that was going on in order to eat lunch free. At some point somebody looked at the expense accounts and decided this had to stop. You were only supposed to go to educational programs in your area of practice. So we looked around to try to find a program where we could justifiably all go, and we found the Barristers Club Continuing Education of the Bar Committee. So we all signed up for that . . . something like ten of us, and we show up at a meeting, and there are nine members of the Barristers Continuing Education Committee there. And they had just lost their Vice Chair and were going to have an election to select a new Vice Chair. Well we outnumbered them, 10–9, and everybody thought it would be a great idea if I was the Vice Chair. So I was elected Vice Chair of the Continuing Education of the Bar Committee of Barristers. And about a week later the Chair resigns, so now I am the chair. So you wonder how I ascended in the Bar, there is my start.

She made partner in six years, the first woman partner of a downtown San Francisco firm. Later, Garvey learned that when she had been hired, the partners discussed what would happen if a client didn't want a woman to work on a case: "And they decided they would tell the client essentially the client could go fly."

Garvey stayed at the firm for twenty-five years: "And just toward the end of my tenure there, we had sort of had a discussion as to whether my name should go in the firm, but there was a concern about having four names in the firm, so I traded it for more points, which is the smartest move I ever made."

Out of Bounds: Supreme Court Clerkships

Brooksley Born chose a career in law after an all-too-familiar late 1950s experience with an academic counselor:

> At the beginning of my sophomore year I went to the counseling service at Stanford [University] which gave vocational testing, and I asked to be vocationally tested, which they thought was a little strange—that a woman would want to have vocational testing. There were two tests . . . one for men and one for women. I took the one for women but then I said I wanted to take the one for men, which they really thought was strange. But they allowed me to take it. Then they analyzed the results. . . . I had scored very low in the women's test on being a nurse. . . . And I tested very high on being a doctor on the men's test. The counselor sat me down and said that the difference in my scores for nurse and doctor showed that I didn't want to be in medicine for any compassionate reasons, that this was just purely greed on my part and bad motives that I would want to be a doctor. That made me very upset, but nonetheless I quit pre-med. I was indignant [at the counselor] even in that era. I was a member of that society then too, and I largely bought into its values, but I knew he was wrong.

Late in her senior year, Born made the decision to apply to law school. It was a career choice that Born had also flirted with, influenced by her mother's best friend, Trailblazer Miriam Wolff, director of the Port of San Francisco, who, unlike the counselor, was encouraging: "[Miriam] made it obvious to me that law was an okay career path for a woman. She was very supportive."

Wolff arranged for Born to meet with Sam Thurman, Stanford's acting law school dean. He encouraged her to apply but told Born that she would have to score higher on the LSAT than if she were a man. Born was accepted, one of the ten women who entered Stanford in 1961. She was apprehensive about going to a male-dominated school, but "absolutely loved it. I found it enormously challenging. I think I really became intellectually engaged academically for the first time."

Born found a number of the male faculty to be open minded although she had also received "a lot of subtle signals all year long from various sources, some professors, some other classmates that a woman couldn't really succeed well in law school." When the first-year grades came out, however, she was first in the class of 165, and was invited to work on the law review. A year later she was elected the first woman president of the *Stanford Law Review*: "A couple of days after the election Dean Emeritus Spaeth called me into his office. I had never met the man and so I was a little bewildered why I was being called in. I went in to see him, and he said that he just wanted to tell me that the faculty stood ready to take over the law review if I faltered. And I said, 'Well, I am going to do the best I can not to falter.'"

At graduation, Born received the U.S. law school honor society Order of the Coif and the Outstanding Senior awards. She had ranked first in her class at Stanford each of her three years as a law student. Like most Stanford graduates, Born interviewed with many law firms, although she was excluded from some campus interviews because of her gender: "If they [the firms] told the placement service that they didn't want to interview a woman, we were told not to sign up. However, I did sign up for O'Melveny & Myers because I had not been told that the firm would not hire women. Interviews were held at the law school in small offices. Of course, my name was ambiguous in terms of what gender I was."

When Born walked in for her appointment, the interviewing partner from O'Melveny, presumably pleased to receive an applicant who was first in the class, took one look at her, stood up, turned white, pointed at the door and said, "Out, out, out!" So she turned around and left.

Five private firms did extend job offers to Born, who had hoped, however, to spend her first year after law school clerking.

> I very much wanted an appellate clerkship. In that era, that was the most popular thing for top students to do, to have at least a one-year clerkship

at the appellate level. I very much wanted to be a law clerk on the U.S. Supreme Court. There had never been a woman law clerk on the Supreme Court, and at some point, maybe early in my third year, Justice Arthur Goldberg, who was on the Supreme Court, had visited the law school. I had met him and said that I was interested in being a law clerk on the Supreme Court, and he had said something that I took as encouragement. [In 1944, during World War II, Lucile Lomen served as clerk to Justice William O. Douglas. Her service was ignored by historians until late in the twentieth century.][1]

There was a faculty committee that would decide who the faculty would recommend for the Supreme Court clerkships. Stanford was more or less entitled to two clerkships on the Supreme Court. One was for Chief Justice Earl Warren who had been the Governor of California and always took a California clerk. The second was for Justice William O. Douglas, who was the Ninth Circuit representative on the Supreme Court and was from Washington State and usually had a Stanford clerk. The faculty clerkship committee called me in during the fall of my third year. Gordon Scott, the Corporations professor, was the head of the committee. He said that he was sure I would understand that it would be unseemly for a woman to clerk on the Supreme Court, so they were recommending two of the men in the class. . . . I was utterly crushed. I don't think I said anything. This was a problem of that era—you didn't protest. Interestingly enough, I found out years later that my father had protested. . . . So I then wrote to two of the justices and decided to apply on my own to Arthur Goldberg and Potter Stewart. [When Bayless Manning became permanent law school dean the following year, he arranged for the law school to put Born up for Chief Justice Warren's clerkship, which Born described later as "heartening." Warren did not interview her.]

One of my professors, my Labor Law professor Keith Mann, wrote a recommendation to Arthur Goldberg for me. Goldberg had been a labor lawyer in Chicago. I actually saw that letter sometime in the last few years when I was going through things and was startled to see that the letter began, "Even though she is on the distaff side . . ." [an archaic reference to Born being a woman]. I met with Potter Stewart who was certainly perfectly gracious to me and served me tea, and we had a nice talk. He later wrote to me saying that he had chosen two men as law clerks.

And then I met with Arthur Goldberg. . . . He didn't tell me that he was not interested. However he gave me a note that he wrote while I was in his chambers and told me to go to the U.S. Courthouse in Washington and go to the U.S. Attorney's Office and give the note to Sylvia Bacon who was a woman lawyer [there] whom he knew. And so I did. And it turned out, Sylvia told me later, that the letter said, "Dear Sylvia, Brooksley Born has applied to me for a clerkship. Of course, I can't possibly have a woman law clerk. But please take her and introduce her to Judge Henry W. Edgerton." Judge Edgerton was at that time the only judge on the U.S. Court of Appeals for the D.C. Circuit who had ever had a woman law clerk.

Sylvia took me up and introduced me to Henry Edgerton whose current clerk then was Barbara Babcock, who was later the first woman law professor at Stanford. Judge Edgerton was absolutely charming and grandfatherly. He was a very strong feminist and had had four or five women clerks over the preceding 10 years. He looked at my credentials, and he offered me a job. Steve Breyer, who is now a Supreme Court Justice, did get the job clerking with Arthur Goldberg.[2]

According to Born, Judge Edgerton was

enormously welcoming and a lot of fun to work with. He was a great liberal. He was really a free thinker. [He agreed to officiate at my wedding.] I'll never forget the wedding ceremony that he gave: he took the Book of Common Prayer of the Episcopalians, and every place it referred to God, he put in "the Congress of the United States," which made for quite a funny service. In fact, [Judge] Skelly Wright, who was there, laughed out loud at one of these references to the Congress: "the Congress of the United States blesses this union," or something like that. Judge Edgerton also said that I should not wear a wedding ring—which I ignored—because it was a symbol of chatteldom, and a woman should not be treated as chattel.

When faced with Stanford's refusal to nominate her for a Supreme Court clerkship, Born distinguished herself by making her own arrangements for interviews. She was not alone in facing unequal treatment. A decade earlier, Ruth Burg graduated first in her George Washington University law class. The dean called her in and said that normally they would find a good position or good clerkship for their first-in-the-class graduate but that, in this case, it was not possible.

Barbara Paul Robinson reports her name being sent to two justices of the U.S. Supreme Court for a clerkship before she graduated from Yale in 1965. Robinson, later the first woman partner at Debevoise & Plimpton and the first woman president of the Association of the Bar of the City of New York, was not selected: "It was just a combination of the Justices perhaps not being too receptive and the law professors not necessarily wanting to push too hard." Indeed, two decades after Lucille Lomen had clerked for Justice Douglas during World War II, no other woman law clerk had been selected. The women who were turned down included Ruth Bader Ginsburg, a future justice of that Court.

In a 1998 speech at Wellesley College, Justice Ginsburg related her experience while attempting to obtain a clerkship: "In 1960 one of my law teachers, who selected clerks for Justice Frankfurter, suggested that I might do. The justice was told of my family situation—I was married and had a five-year-old daughter. For whatever reason, he said no."[3]

Ginsburg went on to teach at Rutgers Law School and then Columbia Law for most of the 1960s and 1970s while also playing a critical role in the establishment, in 1971, of the Women's Rights Project (WRP) of the American Civil Liberties Union. She developed a national and international reputation in the 1970s litigating a series of cases for the WRP. The outcome of these cases, beginning with *Reed v. Reed*, solidified a constitutional principle against gender-based discrimination.

The story of these four women is that they were among the fortunate individuals who survived the rampant discrimination of the period, and thrived in their legal careers. Following her year clerking for Judge Edgerton, Born plunged into the world of private legal practice. While she was serving her clerkship, several firms, including Covington & Burling and, later, Arnold & Porter, tried to recruit her. In 1965, Born accepted an offer from Arnold & Porter, a firm she later described as "really quite wonderful and unique then in terms of the place of women. . . . a tremendously open-minded place [that had] the premier pro bono policy of the country." Born spent many decades there as a partner with time out in the late 1990s to serve in the Clinton administration. She combined a stellar legal career specializing in financial market transactions with extensive contributions to the women's movement and the American Bar Association.

Would You Like to Work in the Library?

Dolores Korman Sloviter, born in 1932, reported blatant discrimination while attempting to land her first job with a private law firm. Sloviter's parents were Jews from Poland. As a young child in Philadelphia, she spoke Yiddish before she spoke English. Sloviter attended Temple University, where she majored in economics in an attempt to get away from the 1950s stereotype that "bright young Jewish girls" became teachers. A chance meeting with a young woman who was prelaw, and the influence on Sloviter of attorney Clarence Darrow's biography, led her to apply to law school. In 1953, she entered the University of Pennsylvania, the first step in a career as a private firm partner, law professor, and U.S. court of appeals judge:

> I had no idea that there would be discrimination. I didn't know any lawyers. I just decided that's what I wanted to do. I went ahead and did everything I could do to do it. I applied to NYU and got an offer of a scholarship. I was dying to take it, but it didn't cover room and board and I couldn't afford to live in New York City. I wanted to go to Penn. I remember I was interviewed by W. Foster Reeves. He said to me, "Why should we let you into the law school? You'll only take a seat for a man and you will make no contribution to the law school and the legal profession." I don't know what I answered, but I got into the law school. It was a slap in the face. By the second year I was on Law Review.
>
> It was in my third year that I began to job hunt, and I had my first recognition of pervasive refusal to accept women as equals. After all, I had a very good academic background, and was third or fourth in the class. [As we started looking,] the guys got jobs right away. All the guys got jobs. There was no formal employment office at the Law School. The Assistant Dean, Ted Husted, did everything.
>
> I remember going to Ted and he said go through the book that lists the law firms, Martindale-Hubbell, and see which law firms you want to apply to. I knew by then that more than half of the law firms in Philadelphia wouldn't take a Jewish person. It turned out that all of them except for one wouldn't take a woman.

Sloviter interviewed at Dilworth & Paxson, one of Philadelphia's more diverse firms, which did not need a new associate. At another firm, where Sloviter felt the interview "wasn't going anywhere," she spelled out her job philosophy:

> I said I wanted to be treated the same as everybody else. I wanted to go into court with other lawyers, wanted to be just an associate, didn't want to be limited to writing briefs. How I was so bold I don't know, but I was. I went to some of the big firms in New York and some of the big firms in Washington and I got the same story that you've heard Justice O'Connor and Justice Ginsburg tell. I graduated the same time as Ruth but after O'Connor. I was told, "We would be very happy to have you but our clients wouldn't know what to do with a woman lawyer," or, "Would you like to work in our library?"
>
> By the spring of my third year, I realized that the only place for women lawyers to get jobs was the government. And I wasn't going to go to the federal government because I still remembered the [1954] McCarthy hearings [a Senate investigation into conflicting accusations between the U.S. Army and Senator Joseph McCarthy]. After some discouraging interviews with state government officials, I went back to the Dilworth office and reminded them that they told me that I should come back in the spring. That firm was my first choice, and I said, "Well, here I am." So I had another interview. They were about to go to trial in a big antitrust case, *Eastern Railroads Presidents Conference v. Noerr*. I was told if this case goes to trial, we'll need another associate and we'll hire you. Within a couple of weeks they called and said you better come aboard.
>
> The job hunting affected the rest of my life because I became absolutely aware of the depth of discrimination against women in the law.

Working primarily on antitrust matters, Sloviter spent thirteen years at Dilworth, making partner in 1964 at the same time as a male associate who had also joined the firm in 1956.

Sloviter remembered a case against the *Daily Racing Form*. The work required that she travel to Oklahoma to handle the motion for summary judgment, which she won. Afterward, she had lunch at a local club with the firm's local counsel: "The judge was eating there and I saw him and he said to me, 'Miss Korman, you did a wonderful job! Why don't you consider settling here?' I thought to myself, living in Oklahoma? But I simply said, 'Thank you very much, Your Honor.'"

Changing Careers

Rosemary Barkett, later judge of the U.S. Court of Appeals for the Eleventh Circuit, grew up in Miami, where her Syrian-born parents ran a small grocery store. In the late 1950s, after graduating from high school, Barkett joined a convent. She liked her religious vocation but, slowly, realized that aspects of the life did not make sense to her, "rules that were based on customs that had originated in the middle ages and had never been changed." With a college associate's degree, Barkett began teaching at various parochial schools and completing courses for a BA degree, while continuing to consider whether she would stay in the convent:

> Things were happening all over the country then. We're in the 60s, there was much social upheaval, nuns and priests marching in Selma, speaking out about social injustice and we couldn't go. We couldn't participate. Like many others during that period, I began to question the relevance of religious life. . . . I wondered if, in fact, more could not be accomplished outside of the confines of a religious community. . . . I left in 1967. . . . [I]n a quiet way, I do believe I am a person who wants to control her own life. . . . At the same time, it was my religious upbringing that I credit with my social conscience.

Barkett attended the University of Florida Law School in the late 1960s, having decided that teaching did not give her sufficient autonomy. Law school, she discovered, also had its conservative side. Male students, for example were still following the practice of "shuffling" when she attended. It was, she said, "a silly custom that if a woman walked into a classroom or the library or any other common room in the law school, all the male students would start shuffling their feet against the wooden floors."

The former nun graduated in December 1970, having done "pretty well." She had been on moot court, and loved the trial advocacy class where she and a partner won their case. Although she later said, "to be honest I didn't have a clue about the interviewing process," Barkett's years of teaching, outgoing personality, and desire to stay in Florida made her job hunt quite easy. A friend from law school recruited her for a small trial firm in West Palm Beach, Farish & Farish:

> I was a trial lawyer. And it was great, because it wasn't one of these stodgy firms where you had to carry someone else's trial briefcase or sit second chair to anybody. You immediately got to try cases. Six months after I was out of law school, I was arguing a case in the Florida Supreme Court. One of our senior partners had a civil habeas case, seeking the return of a child. And I worked on the brief. And then he got tied up, and the next thing I knew, he was telling me I had to go to Tallahassee to argue the case in the Florida Supreme Court. . . . I woke up at 5:00 in the morning in the Tallahassee hotel room throwing up. I used to tell that story after I was appointed to the Florida Supreme Court.

Barkett's strong conscience influenced her evaluation of the good she could do as a lawyer, as well as the kind of cases that she *hated*:

> I also had to conduct my first jury trial within the first six months. It was an absolutely horrible case. A three-year-old child had crossed the street and crawled under the defendant's car in his own garage. Of course, the defendant did not see him under the car and backed over him. The firm had sued him for negligence and that's the case I was supposed to try! It was terrible. My first case, my first loss. Amazingly, the child recovered. [I tried] plaintiffs' cases and a lot of family law cases. A lot of divorce cases. . . . wealthy divorce cases. I hated them. People were always unhappy, no matter what you did.
> I liked trying cases where I thought we could right some wrong—whether a tort case or a contract or a family law matter. I also liked trying cases before a jury because it brought to bear all the same skills I used to have as a school teacher. You have a blackboard you can use and you must try to make the jury understand your side of the story and then persuade them you are right.

Barkett stayed at Farish & Farish for nine years, working twelve-hour days. While there, she came to understand the differences between a trial firm and a corporate firm with respect to gender issues:

Trial lawyers seemed much more willing to take a risk, perhaps because they didn't have to worry about a continuing client-base where they would be afraid, in those days, of some corporate client reacting negatively to a woman lawyer. . . . The other thing is, again, in a personal injury practice or a trial practice, people are so concerned about their own problems, and they just want to tell it to a sympathetic person.

We would be trying cases in front of the same few judges. So, it was like a small comfortable family kind of thing. I really don't have a recollection of ever being treated badly; on the contrary, I have a very clear recollection of being treated kindly and certainly evenly. . . . I always thought that discrimination worked in your favor because everybody was nervous about appearing to be a big bully. . . . [L]itigating against the very same people over and over makes a difference. . . . And so, you were going to see them again and again in court and then these were also the same people whom you would gather with after work to have a drink with.

When Barkett left Farish & Farish, it had nothing to do with gender and everything to do with examining the firm's books: "Plaintiff firms are a very unique kind of place . . . [B]ack then you had this very strong dominating individual who ran the firm. And you never asked questions and you were expected to just accept whatever he said. So at the end of the year he would simply say, 'okay, your share of the partnership is 11 percent.' And that net amount works out to be X amount. And for a few years one just accepted it."

Finally, Barkett and two others left. She started her own trial law practice, but she was so successful, and so overworked, that in 1979 she accepted an appointment as a trial judge on the Fifteenth Judicial Circuit of Florida (Palm Beach County). After a decade in private trial practice, she moved permanently to the other side of the bench, eventually retiring from the U.S. court of appeals.

The Power of Judges

Rosemary Barkett's positive experience with judges as a "repeat player" trial lawyer in a small community of legal professionals mirrored that of many Trailblazers. Others, however, recounted grim stories about male judges who engaged in egregious courtroom behavior while the women were arguing cases. Several judges openly turned their backs on a Trailblazer for reasons of gender or race, or both. While practicing in Mississippi in the early 1970s, Constance Harvey was, she recalled, repeatedly referred to as a "nigger" by Judge L. B. Porton. Harvey had nowhere to file a grievance and speaks of the pain that resulted from that treatment.

Maryann Saccomando Freedman reported a similar experience in court as a young Buffalo, New York, attorney in the late 1950s. Both her and Harvey's encounters underscore the power of individual judges:

Another experience that I had was also very typical of what young women lawyers who were going into the courtroom to actually try cases were up against with the bench at that time. There was no place that you could go to file a grievance, unlike today, where I think almost every state has something comparable to our judicial conduct commission. There were no rules about equality, diversification and treating women equally. [One day] I had to go to Special Term in front of Judge Rowe. . . . [L]awyers would be hanging from the rafters and it was always a long calendar and my case was finally called and I walked up to the bench and when I started to speak, he looked up, got very upset, "Who's this little girl here?" and there was some back and forth going on between us. His final words were, "Girls do not practice in my courtroom. Bailiff, escort her out of the courtroom," and the bailiff did. Of course, I'm but, but, butting and that meant I couldn't deliver for my client or for my firm. Personally, I was insulted . . . [T]hat incident has stayed with me all these years. But as I was being escorted out and sitting down out in the hall and carrying on with the bailiff, Judge Noonan was walking down the corridor and saw all this. He stopped and said, "What's the problem?" and I explained. He told me to just sit there for a little while . . . and went into Judge Rowe's courtroom. I don't know what he did. . . . [W]hen he came back out, he said, "Wait about ten minutes, go back in and your case will be called again." That is exactly what happened.

Freedman's experience highlights the limits of even an ambitious, successful woman's power when faced with discrimination. It also underscores, like it or not, their reliance on the intervention of men at certain times to get jobs and to do their jobs.

Freedman had graduated from law school during a recession and was fortunate to be asked to stay on at the Saperston, McNaughton & Saperston firm where she had clerked during her third year. She was not certain that staying on was her best opportunity: "[S]o [I] pounded the pavement, going from law office to law office, saying I'm looking for a job. I had any number of lawyers who were thrilled at the prospect of hiring me as a secretary because they wouldn't have to explain anything and they would have another lawyer's brain very cheaply. That is the same thing that Sandra Day O'Connor has talked about. I know exactly what she was talking about. It happened to me."

Freedman took the job at the Saperston firm. She had interview experiences that had left her wondering whether she would spend all of her time being chased around a desk. The large firms were not hiring during the recession and, she said,

> [T]hey certainly were not hiring Italian-Americans: I had done a good job as a clerk, I knew I would have to work hard, I knew I would have to be better than any male. They never had a woman in that office, and I think, to some extent, when the offer to stay on was made to me, I think part of the thinking that went on in making that offer was that, "It will be kind of cute for a little while. It will be fun and interesting to have this little girl running around the office for a while."

Like many women, Freedman found that she had to produce more work and better work than anybody else. She also determined that the men hired after her were paid more because, she was told, "they had families to support and she did not." And she also experienced resentment from the female secretaries and suspicion from the wives of the firm's male lawyers:

> I don't know what the hell they thought went on during the day in those law offices, I really don't, but they clearly thought something was going on. I learned, very quickly, that I had to make a point of making those wives my friends, which meant, at social functions, I would have much rather been with the lawyers talking about lawyer things, but I would make a point to spend time with the wives and was sympathetic to them

and cultivated them as friends. Now, that sounds very Machiavellian, and it probably was, but that was the way I could survive.

Dealing with the wives of colleagues marked one aspect of how women like Freedman had to consider domestic issues in their workday situations. Freedman's own domestic situation, her marriage four years after she joined the Saperton firm, precipitated her break with the firm when the partners made it clear they feared she would send her clients to her lawyer husband. She quit, and developed a very diverse career that included a partnership at Freedman & Freedman, a decade as law clerk to New York State Supreme Court judge William J. Ostrowski, and, in 1987, selection as president of the New York State Bar Association.

The Power of Partners

Before becoming a judge on the Fifth Circuit, Carolyn Dineen King practiced corporate law. Domestic issues shaped many of her early career experiences. In 1962, after graduating from Yale Law School, she followed her husband to Houston. With a letter of recommendation from a mentor at the Department of Justice, King interviewed with Woodrow Seals, the U.S. attorney in Houston. Decked out in cowboy boots, white Stetson, and large belt buckle, Seal, a Texas liberal, put his arm around King and said, "'Now don't get me wrong ma'am,' . . . [H]e had 'hired him' an African-American and he 'hired him' a Mexican, but he wasn't up to 'hiring him' a woman yet."

Failing to become Seals's first woman assistant D.A., King used her father's professional network to arrange an interview at the Houston firm of Fulbright, Crooker, Freeman, Bates & Jaworski. Leon Jaworski, a prominent Texan and later Nixon-era Watergate special prosecutor, offered her a job doing collection work at half-pay—half of what they were paying the men. The firm had one other woman on staff, a former member of the law review at the University of Texas. She also did collection work at half the pay of the male associates:

So the theory was that I would be her assistant and I would be paid half. I remember not being too sure what to say, but I finally said that I appreciated very much the fact that they had made a place for me because I knew that they really didn't have any job openings. But I concluded that I did not want to work at half what they paid the men, and I also didn't want to do collection work. And I remember thinking to myself, when I managed to get those sentences out, that this was probably the dumbest thing I'd ever done. So there was a long pause, and finally [Jaworski] looked at me and he said, "Okay. We'll hire you. We'll pay you what we're paying the men, and you can do anything you want to do here. You don't have to do collection work. Would you like that job?" And I said, "Yes! I would love it!"

I worked there for ten years. The first year I was put in what they called the "pool," a group of lawyers who were available to anyone in the law firm. I wound up doing a lot of work in the litigation section.

King tried tax work but eventually asked to be assigned to the corporate section, where she worked for partner Pat Marshall. She charged clients for between twenty-five hundred and three thousand hours of work a year, far more than other members of the firm and, in general, a high number for most American lawyers in the 1960s. She also stood out as a woman doing corporate work—public offerings, private placements, mergers, and acquisitions—at a time when many firms put women only in estates work or blue sky law (state law regulating the offering and sale of securities to protect the public from fraud):

> The clients were marvelously accepting of me. I think the firm was somewhat apprehensive that the clients would not want a woman working on their business, but the clients were the most egalitarian of all God's children. They were perfectly happy to have a woman lawyer working on their stuff, particularly if the woman lawyer was going to put their work first and get it done fast and well.
>
> I'm a workaholic. Every year I would get the maximum increase in pay and the maximum bonus, and I would get an excellent review. My compensation was ahead of the men.
>
> In 1968 I had my first baby and worked right up until the end and was back at work in maybe three weeks. I had another baby 16 months after the first one. [After the baby was born,] Pat Marshall arrived at my house at 10:00 in the morning, which was a shock. He hadn't told me he was

coming. I showed him the new baby and the old baby. We sat in the living room, and he said to me out of the blue, "You are not going to make partner." And I said, "Why not?" And he said, "You're just not going to make partner, I can tell you that now."

Marshall's pronouncement was "a bolt out of the blue," but King was not about to be put off. She absolutely loved what she was doing, "was addicted to being a lawyer," and had no reason to think that she was not going to make partner based on any of the treatment that she had received up to the time of Marshall's visit. That night King's attorney husband said, "You know what they're going to do, they are going to discriminate against you because you're a woman." King replied, "Absolutely not, they are not going to do that. They have never done it and they are not going to start now." But three years later, despite a tremendous career and superb relations with clients, King learned otherwise:

[In 1972] when the partnership decision making process was almost complete, this same partner told me that I would not make partner, and he wouldn't say why. It was the early 70s and everybody made partner at Fulbright.

So I decided to go see Leon Jaworski and find out why I wasn't going to make partner. I asked him whether the firm was in any way dissatisfied with my work. He said, "Oh, no. Your work is excellent. You work harder than anybody else and you've been very profitable for the law firm." And then he said, "But we thought you'd get pregnant and quit." And I suddenly realized that I had spent ten years working for a law firm that treated me very well, but the premise was that I would get pregnant and quit. And I'm pretty confident that, when that partner came out to see me that day, what he wanted was for me to do what everybody expected me to do, and that is stay home and take care of these children.

So I had spent ten years of my life completely committed to the law firm, but they were operating on the unspoken premise that I was going to just have a baby and leave and obviously I wasn't going to make partner. So I quit. Right there in Leon Jaworski's office. I said, "What you're doing to me is unlawful and it's immoral, and I don't work for lawyers who are unlawful or immoral or inhumane." He didn't say a word after that.

So there I was at the age of 34 with no job and no prospects.

King's good reputation and excellent relationship with clients came through for her when Fulbright did not:

> I was [immediately] offered a job at Childs, Fortenbach as a partner (a smaller firm that did corporate work), and they paid me plenty . . . more money than I was making at Fulbright. The other thing that happened—talk about another surprise—several of my clients came with me to Childs, Fortenbach. One of them was a listed company, Digicon, on the American Stock Exchange. The chairman of Digicon went and talked to Leon Jaworski and told him exactly what he thought about him in no uncertain terms. It really was thrilling. I was just amazed.
>
> But it took me two years to emerge from the emotional devastation that being passed over for partner at Fulbright resulted in. It took me many more years simply to accept the fact that a decision had been made for me that was different than the decision that would have been made for a man. . . . You blame yourself. One of the worst results of discrimination is that it leaves you thinking that you failed. That you were measured up and you were found wanting. The damage to your sense of self-worth is very heavy, and to some degree it's permanent.
>
> I used to think, like a good Yalie who came of age during the civil rights movement, that I understood what discrimination meant. What I found out was that I'd never really understood what it did to its victims. But don't forget, what happened to me was a one-time experience. For people who are black, for many other women, for people who are Hispanic, that kind of discrimination happens every day of their lives and I can't imagine the damage that that must do to their sense of self-worth. On the other hand, imagine the triumph that it is for people who can overcome that kind of daily experience and succeed in this world.

New Theories and Areas of Law

In 1965, recent NYU Law graduate Sheila Birnbaum, in search of a job, sent out resumes. In response to her queries, she found "a closed world of job opportunities" where, if a woman lawyer was hired, she did trusts and estates. Birnbaum did interview at the small personal injury firm of Berman and Frost after being told at a United States attorney's office that she could do appeals and indictments, but could not handle a homicide case. Birnbaum related that the interviewer asked her rhetorically, "How could you send a woman out to interview witnesses in a homicide case?" There were other gender concerns. Again, the interview became all-important:

> Partners asked me questions like: "Would your husband let you work late." I didn't think that was a question that was hard to answer. They also asked: "Do you intend to get pregnant?" I told him I had no plans at the moment. Questions like that, of course, nobody would ask today.
>
> When they offered me a job, they told me that they would be paying a male associate at that point $6,500 a year, but they were only paying me $5,500 a year. And, that this was really a test, that I shouldn't think I was really an employee until three months went by. . . . So I took the job and I said to them (and really, to this day, don't know how I had the guts to do this): Well, let's make a deal. I'll take the job, but if I am still here in December and I passed the "test," you will pay me a bonus of what you would have paid me if I was a man, $6,500. They said, sure because they didn't think it was going to really work out. I was there in December and they did make up the difference.

A month later Birnbaum passed the Bar. She went back to the partners and said, "I understand when you pass the Bar, you are supposed to get a raise. They said, we just gave you a raise in December. No, I said, you gave me what you should have given me to begin with. Now I want a raise. So, I got the raise."

Four years later, Birnbaum became a partner and, in her words, had many, many opportunities to practice law at a very high level despite the fact that, when she was offered the position, the partners' expectations of this first woman hire were nonexistent. She felt they did feel there was some risk of sending a woman out to represent them:

> But it soon became an asset rather than a liability. I have told this story before. One of the times I went to court, the Judge said to me: "Miss? Where is your lawyer?" And, I said to him: "Your Honor, I am the lawyer." They just had no experience with women lawyers, especially litigators. It became clear to me that the Judge's expectation level was so low, that when you put together a coherent argument, they thought you were a

genius. You were just pretty good [but] immediately I started getting rave reviews. The Judges would tell my boss: "Oh, Sheila did this great argument." It sort of became something that I could use as a sword—their low expectation levels made me look better than I think I was certainly at that point.

Birnbaum understood that everyone initially figured she would fail and then would cry. It was a learning experience for the partners who came around quickly, and recognized that she would be an asset. In 1969, their estimation of her only improved when the firm became counsel to Syntex, one of the drug companies involved in national litigation involving an oral contraceptive:

> Having a woman became an asset because most of the firms didn't have a woman arguing from a defendant's point of view. So, I became, very quickly, a very important part of the defense of these cases and began defending, with the senior partner, these cases all over the country. . . . We didn't know it at the time but I think that was the first really mass tort in the personal injury business. We didn't have the word for it, but the defendants, a number of defendant corporations, they organized themselves and created a national defense. . . . It was a joint effort. Some of the procedures we used are very commonplace now.

Such was the career of a woman who dared to bargain and ended her career as a partner at Skadden, Arps, a law school professor, and special master of the September 11th Victim Compensation Fund program.

Sheila Birnbaum, dubbed the "Queen of Torts" by the press, developed an expertise in product liability strategy early in her career. In Texas, while still in law school, Carol Dinkins, later the first woman partner at the Houston firm of Vinson & Elkins, similarly saw the professional possibilities of becoming an expert in an emerging field of law. At the end of law school, Dinkins accepted a position at the newly created Texas Law Institute of Coastal and Marine Resources. Each of these women, like Jodi Bernstein at the Federal Trade Commission, succeeded because she acquired expertise in new theories of the law.

It was 1971 and Dinkins accepted the Law Institute position because she loved property law, loved the coast, and appreciated, as a mom, that the job would be family friendly. She took the job specifically because "I really want[ed] to learn a brand new area of law so that it [wouldn't] be so easy for a law firm not to take a hard look at me. . . . I had a clinical program in conjunction with the D.A.'s office because they were trying to get started with environmental and pollution prosecutions. I ran that clinical program and I put together conferences. And I worked on the Texas Coastal Zone Management Program. I published a very lengthy article on Texas seashore boundary law."

Dinkins was on the cutting edge of developing the environmental law of Texas property, coastal, and water law, integrated under the umbrella of new and revised federal statutes (the Clean Water Act; the Clean Air Act; the Endangered Species Act). After two years at the institute, she was asked to interview (again) at Vinson & Elkins for a position in its public finance section. When offered the job, Dinkins told A. Frank Smith, the managing partner,

> "What I really want to do is what I'm doing now, which is working [in] the area of coastal and marine law." He thought it over, and he said, "Well, Carol, we don't have a practice in that area." I said, "That's okay, Mr. Smith. I believe you will get one."
>
> I came to work the day after Labor Day in 1973. When I reported to A. Frank Smith's office, he said, "Oh Carol, we're so glad you're here because since you accepted our job offer, we've had three of our firm's big clients need help on coastal issues." The following Monday, I got on a plane and flew to Austin to meet with state agencies about one of those client's problems, with nobody with me. You know, a second year lawyer, my first week with the firm, and they sent me up there. So one of the things I immediately liked about Vinson & Elkins is the fact that they give you a lot of responsibility very early. . . . I did endangered species, historic preservation and archaeological work, and wetlands, and other coastal matters. I did lobbying before the Texas Legislature as an associate.

In January 1980, Dinkins was admitted to partnership at Vinson & Elkins. A woman making partner was sufficiently rare that *Texas Monthly* magazine ran an article about it. And in the same year, the year that Ronald Reagan was elected president, Dinkins, a Republican, began receiving calls asking whether she had any interest in a federal appointment.

In the first years of the 1980s, she served as assistant attorney general for land and natural resources and, later, as the first woman deputy attorney general at the Justice Department. The importance of her appointment as deputy AG did not go unnoticed: "The day after the swearing in [carried out by Justice Sandra Day O'Connor], I was getting into my car outside the Attorney General's entrance at the Justice Department to go to a meeting at the White House and a woman stopped me and she said, 'I'm so and so and I'm a lawyer in the Antitrust Division and I just wanted to tell you how much it meant to all the women in the Department yesterday to see you sworn in.'"

Start with a Mentor

By the mid-1970s, some women lawyers found that discrimination toward them was beginning to ease up. The career of California native Mary Cranston suggests that a bright, self-described "high energy" woman lawyer could take advantage of opportunities not necessarily available twenty, or even ten, years earlier.

Cranston grew up in California and graduated from Stanford Law School in 1975. She had a strong role model in her mother, who had taken a Stanford degree in economics, and a lifelong competition with her "best friend" twin sister (later the first certified female vascular surgeon in the United States). The sisters attended an all-girls' Catholic high school where Mary began to see women's potential as leaders: "It was in that high school that women had to absorb all of the leadership roles that there were, and I think it was quite subtly, and maybe not so subtly, important for how I saw the world and I saw what women could do, going forward."

In law school Cranston met Professor Barbara Babcock. She describes her as "one of the Earth's wise women." Cranston studied the law "as the tools that I was going to need to work in the business world and to help people." And then she was ready to get a job: "I was very interested in economics antitrust at that time and I asked a couple of lawyer friends of the family which firms in San Francisco would be the best at that and they said Pillsbury. . . . And I was lucky enough to get an interview . . . [and] was hired . . . along with one other woman. And at that point there were two women partners, and there were a few women associates, one in litigation."

When interviewed, Cranston said that the presence of those women, two of whom became important mentors, was one of the reasons she signed up with Pillsbury, a firm that "has always been on the forefront with women." It did not hurt Pillsbury's chances of recruiting her that, while interviewing at other firms, she had experienced "partners drinking too much and hitting on me."

She started at Pillsbury (now Pillsbury Winthrop Shaw Pittman) in 1975, the beginning of a thirty-year career with the firm that culminated in her election in 1998 as chair. Along the way, Cranston took risks and analyzed how best to use her interest in leadership. At a time when few women chanced having children before making partner, as an associate she had her first child. Pillsbury did not have a maternity policy. She had colleagues draft one that established six weeks of paid leave, and got the firm to accept it, one of the first such programs in the United States.

Cranston was initially an antitrust litigator. She handled big antitrust cases. Her personal need for autonomy was great:

I always go for the job where I can lead and be in charge. . . . I had a little extra expertise [in economics]. So I would always work to get onto the part of the case where you're developing the economics. And I'd worked with the consultants. And it was a kind of an independent thing you carve out. And I really avoided most of the document work and a lot of the schlock because of that. Then, as a fourth-year associate, I saw this, it was a 20-year, multi-class action antitrust case, and there was a counterclaim that was pretty big and I sort of grabbed that. . . . Just did it on my own. . . . So I got a lot of good experience early on and a lot of it was because of this need I had to be in charge.

Cranston appreciated the power of leaders and developed strategies to become one. She sought out male and female mentors among the Pillsbury partners—something, she argues, many women are slow to do. In addition, Cranston mentored younger associates, which brought her to the attention of the partners: "As I got more senior, they realized that I would take administrative responsibility and I would do it and I would do it well. I always had an ever-increasing load of that in the firm. But it made me happier because I had my career stuff, I had my professional stuff, I had firm administration, I had my community, and I had my kids."

She balanced all of this with the help of a live-in housekeeper as well as her husband, and her sister and mother, who lived nearby.

Cranston was on a seven-year partner track, which she made, the first woman partner in litigation. While she was waiting to make partner, the head of litigation told her, "This was not a game for women," and that she ought to think about doing something else (although she was getting top reviews). She went to her mentors and said, "'You know what this turkey told me?' And they took care of him." It was a gutsy thing to do, but she was not the inhibited type: "I think women just have to learn to kind of put the verbal communication out there, even to hold their place at the table."

After making partner, at the age of thirty-four, Cranston did something completely consistent with her personality:

> I was completely thrilled and happy for about three weeks . . . but I kind of woke up and I realized, "You know, I'm not that happy. Now what do I do?" I mean, this has really driven me for many years, and it's gone. And I was kind of depressed, and that sort of sent me on a little journey to study how people have made, how they've developed their lives. . . . And so I decided I was going to practice [setting goals]. . . . And I looked around myself, and I said, "Well, you know, the successful people here are the big-in-demand trial lawyers and they have big books of business. So that's what I want. That's going to be my goal." . . . So I would every day make myself take a couple of baby steps. I mean, it might be taking somebody my age at Chevron to lunch.

Cranston revealed that the hardest part was fear:

> So I had fears that women would not have an opportunity to do this. I had never seen a woman stand up and successfully lead one of these cases in court. I had fears that I'd get out there and be crucified by all these men. I had a lot of fears. . . . I learned to not try to push them away, but let them come in, sort of give them a name, pat them on the head, and

go for it anyway. . . . [I]f you don't set the goal, the whole chain just never gets started.

By the time Cranston was forty-four, in the early 1990s, she had a $10 million book of business. As Angela Bradstreet, her interviewer, said, "Very, very few women, back then, had $10 million books of business." Eight years after being elected chair of Pillsbury, Cranston described her greatest achievement in that role:

I would say, overall, it was taking a 150-year, 140-year-old San Francisco-based law firm and, with the use of vision and a cohesive strategic plan, step by step transforming it into a national and international firm that it is today—we have more lawyers on the east coast now than we do on the west coast—with offices in London, Tokyo, Shanghai and Sydney. So that was a very conscious forced march . . . and it required quite a bit of facilitation to get the partners to see the vision and to go along with it and to vote for the mergers. And to make the investment. . . . You know . . . I looked out at the marketplace and I saw where our clients were going. They were globalizing. . . . [T]o me . . . the status quo was a very risky strategy. And this was less risk. We did not have risk-free options.

Conclusion

In the late 1950s and 1960s, many Trailblazers attempted the nearly impossible: to break the prevailing law firm tradition of neither interviewing nor hiring women as law associates, nor promoting them to partnership. The degree of discrimination varied. In 1963, Sylvia Walbolt graduated first in her University of Florida law class. Although the partners at the firm of Carlton Fields had not expected to hire a woman, they interviewed Walbolt because of her class standing, and made an immediate decision to hire her. She says, with a laugh, the high level of her tennis game sealed the deal.

But when interviewing in 1969 as a third-year Harvard student, environmental law expert Lois Schiffer was told, "We hired a woman once. We may never hire another one." Roberta Karmel, law professor and private firm securities regulation attorney, recalls that her NYU Law classmate Judith Kaye, later chief judge of the New York State court of appeals, wanted a job at a big law firm, and in 1962 went on twenty or thirty interviews. Karmel said to her, "Judy, why are you doing this? They don't want us." Kaye, however, persisted and was hired at the Manhattan firm of Sullivan & Cromwell.

The stories of Trailblazers who graduated from law school after 1964 suggest that newly enacted federal government laws—Title VII of the 1964 Civil Rights Act and the creation, in 1965, of the Equal Employment Opportunity Commission (EEOC)—had not affected most of the private law firm male lawyers who were in a position to hire women associates. The job-interview and work stories recounted by the dozens of Trailblazers who approached private firms affirm the more casual accounts that a significant change in attitudes and hiring did not begin to occur until the mid-1970s. Mary Cranston's experience demonstrates how one woman used this change in law firm culture to shape an extraordinary career.

Even before the 1970s, however, walls did begin to crumble. Women like Joanne Garvey, Brooksley Born, Constance Harvey, and Carolyn Dineen King pushed, or, in the now iconic words of Sheryl Sandberg, "leaned in."[4] Fifty years before Sandberg caused something of a cultural firestorm by suggesting that women had not taken sufficient risks, or demonstrated a sufficient will to lead in the workplace, these Trailblazers had faced down gender discrimination with courage and their wits. They did not always prevail, but they most definitely had a will to lead. They put their reputations, and their ambitions, on the line time and time again, determined to have meaningful positions in a profession that they loved. On their own, but also with the aid of sympathetic mentors and receptive clients, they brought change to the world of private law firms.

6

Breaking New Ground

Law Schools and Public Interest Law

As we have seen, some Trailblazers leaned in on private law firms. Beginning in the late 1960s, others pushed to expand the opportunities available to women at law schools, at public interest organizations, and in state and federal government. Bringing change to these institutions, and through these institutions, also became part of the story of defeating gender discrimination and providing women with significantly expanded opportunities, in this work, to influence law students and to shape public policy.

Law Schools Bring in Women Faculty and Deans

In 1986 Barbara Aronstein Black became the dean of the Columbia Law School, from which she had graduated in 1955. She took up the position as the first woman dean of an Ivy League law school with strong recollections of her years as a law student:

> My memories are much like the memories of other women who were here in the thirties, forties, and fifties. And that is to say very good, favorable memories. We had a wonderful experience at this law school. The intellectual challenge, the friends we made. I do not think of my law school experience as a time when discrimination was rampant and we were the victims of discrimination, although discrimination was rampant and we were the victims of discrimination. The point is, it didn't feel that way at the time. And the reason for that, as I have said in numerous places, is that we tended to accept the world as it was. Even though we were active on behalf of racial justice and were very sensitive to racial injustice, we never took the next step. We were not the people who launched the feminist movement, by any means.

When Black graduated from Columbia Law School, she became an associate in law, which was a one-year teaching fellowship. She and three men had been granted the fellowships. When they met with the dean, he said that if "you" (meaning the men) were interested in an academic career, this job was the first step on the ladder. Telling the story decades later, Black was clear that she should have "raised hell [but] I guess I thought, well, that's the way things are."

Shortly thereafter, like Pat Wald, Jodie Bernstein, and others, Black stepped off the career track, raising three children in New Haven, Connecticut, with her husband, the eminent law professor Charles Black, later caring for her bedridden mother, and only easing back into legal work after nine years by helping colleagues with brief writing, teaching part-time, and earning a PhD in legal history. She became an assistant professor in the Yale History Department in 1976 but was also courted by Yale Law School, now under pressure from its growing number of women students to bring women onto its faculty. The University of Chicago Law School offered Black a faculty position, one she turned down because of her mother and her husband. In Black's words, she "let the personal dominate the professional" and, with regrets, took an offer from Yale Law. When she was fifty, her Yale colleagues voted her tenure. The same week Columbia Law School offered her a named professorship. On July 1, 1984, she became a member of the Columbia Law faculty. A year and a half into her new position at Columbia, Black was confronted with an extraordinary request: her law school colleagues asked their new colleague to let them put her name forward to replace Dean Benno Schmidt, who was leaving to take up a position at Yale. After much soul searching, Black, who loved teaching, said yes. She attributed her decision to the opportunity to become a public figure, the request of her colleagues, and the "woman, or feminist, question." She believed that her appointment would give encouragement to women, and she was correct. Black reported one letter that said, "I read about your appointment and it made me feel that I might succeed as well; I work twice as hard now and I feel that I really have something to strive for."

* * *

When Rutgers Law School hired Ruth Bader Ginsburg as a faculty member in 1963, there were, she believed, not more than a dozen women teaching at law schools in the United States. Although she had hoped to join a private New York law firm, Ginsburg also planned to teach at some point and took the position fearing that another offer might be years off. She brought to Rutgers a newly acquired consciousness of women's situation, awoken while conducting research in Sweden: "The Swedes were already at the stage where it was accepted that families should include two earners. I had never really thought about being treated differently. I accepted it as something you had to contend with. That's the way it was. Not until I was in Sweden did I start to think, 'It doesn't have to be that way. It can be changed.'"

By the end of her first decade of teaching at Rutgers and, next, at Columbia, Ginsburg had joined with a small group of activists to address the issue of "being treated differently." In 1970 she cofounded the *Women's Rights Law Reporter*, the first law journal in the United States to focus entirely on this issue. Two years later, she cofounded the Women's Rights Project (WRP) at the American Civil Liberties Union (ACLU) and became its lead litigator. And, she read Simone de Beauvoir's book *The Second Sex*.

By the late 1960s, as the women's movement exploded, students at Rutgers asked Ginsburg for a course on women and the law. She had not taught such a class and was hampered by the fact that no law casebook on the subject yet existed. Then she met Boalt Hall law professor Herma Hill Kay, who had the idea of compiling a casebook about sex-based discrimination. Kay asked Ginsburg to join her, along with Buffalo University law professor Kenneth Davidson. In 1974 the three published the first casebook on this subject.

Ginsburg, Barbara Babcock, and Sheila Birnbaum were among the small handful of women faculty who began teaching classes on women and the law in response to pressure from the new generation of women law students. Ginsburg's experience at Rutgers was not unique. Several other Trailblazers were also beginning to develop courses, and course materials, at the request of students.

In 1970 in Washington, D.C., Yale Law School graduate Barbara Babcock was heading the Public Defender Service when students at Georgetown came to her:

I said, "what is that about?" knowing nothing. They said, "oh, there was this course that started at NYU and it's a great course and it's about women in the law, in all areas of the law, how women are not in the curriculum and nobody ever talks about women and women are so unequal in the profession." And so I said . . . "of course." I'd been reading *The Second Sex* and Betty Friedan, though I didn't resonate to it. But I thought, "well, I'd better find out about this; this sounds like something I ought to know about." Then Yale asked me to come teach it. So I flew up once a week from Washington, D.C. to Yale. At any rate, at one point I began to get it, to be aware of the movement—the women's movement. But I think I just truly marked the beginning of it—my consciousness—to these students coming to me and asking me to teach.

Babcock found that these women students, only ten years behind her, were completely different. They wanted to know why women's issues were not covered in their law courses. They asked why women were not teaching at law schools, and why there were no women judges. Babcock felt that they were going to change everything. Even though her abiding interest was criminal procedure, she got on the bandwagon:

> I really saw that this was just a huge thing. What had happened is I taught the course at Yale and there was a young woman who had been instrumental in getting me hired there and getting the course started named Ann Freedman. And she and Dru Ramey and Janice Cooper were in the class, and a woman named Leonore Weitzman, who wasn't a law student but wrote a book on divorce, and Nancy Gertner. . . . And these women at Yale were just amazing to me. I really can't get across to you. They were so different and it had been less than a generation. . . . [T]hey were teaching me as I was teaching them.

Ann Freedman told Babcock that after graduation she did not want to clerk; rather, she wanted to write a book for the course Babcock had been teaching. Or, at least that is what Babcock recalls. Freedman remembers that it was Babcock who suggested the need for a standard text that would help women's legal studies succeed as a field.[1] Babcock went to the Carnegie Foundation, obtained funding, and brought Eleanor Holmes Norton and Susan Ross into the project. In 1975, shortly after the Kay, Davidson, and Ginsburg book appeared, Babcock and her colleagues published *Sex Discrimination and the Law: Causes and Remedies*.[2]

Babcock was gone from Washington by the time the casebook was published. In 1972 she moved to California to take up a faculty position at Stanford Law School. She is frank in explaining how that bastion of male power came to make its first-ever offer of a tenure-track position to a woman: "There was a sudden influx of women into law school, and it suddenly became apparent that although many women had graduated from law school, there were almost no women law professors—almost none. Many, many schools, Stanford included, had never had a woman law professor on the tenure track. So, I saw that this little window of affirmative action was open. They wanted, they all wanted, to hire a woman. One woman. And I could get a job that I wouldn't be able to get a few years later."

Babcock, who subsequently served as assistant attorney general for the Civil Division of the Justice Department during the Carter administration, was voted tenure and settled in at Stanford as its first woman professor. She uncovered the story of nineteenth-century California lawyer Clara Foltz, whom Babcock calls "the inventor of the public defender," and wrote Foltz's biography. Simultaneously, she created a unique women's legal history course in which students were required to write a paper about a pioneering woman lawyer, which was then posted on a Stanford Law website.[3] And she mentored women students across the country. Babcock's hiring signaled the beginning of the impact of Title IX of the Education Amendments of 1972. That statute prohibited sex discrimination in both admissions and hiring by educational institutions. Babcock took "the little window of affirmative action" and became one of the most important law professors of her time.

* * *

Wendy Williams came to law school teaching after an early career clerking, serving as a Reginald Heber Smith Fellow in Poverty Law (at San Mateo Legal Aid), and cofounding Equal Rights Advocates, a public interest law firm, with a clinical teaching component focusing on women's rights. Mentored by Herma Hill Kay, who taught the importance of women's equality, Williams was always on the lookout for pathbreaking cases. Early in her clerkship she wrote the memo that convinced the California Supreme Court to hear *Sail'er Inn*, a case arguing women's right to be bartenders. She argued that sex should be a suspect classification and that the state law prohibiting such employment violated Title VII of the 1964 U.S. Civil Rights Act. The court accepted the case and declared that sex was a suspect classification, making California the first state in the union to do so (*Sail'er Inn v. Kirby*).

In 1975, having made the decision to move to Washington, D.C., Williams applied for a job at Georgetown University Law Center and was hired: "The reason I got the job, I later found out, was because Georgetown's women students had founded a women's collective, as they called it, and began pressing the school administration to hire more women on the faculty and, specifically, a woman with my expertise in women and law. They had been getting along by importing adjuncts to teach women and the law."

Williams began teaching in the fall of 1976 at a time when the U.S. Department of Health, Education, and Welfare was going after colleges and law schools for sex discrimination in faculty hiring. In her oral history Williams said, "Ruth Ginsburg calls 1972 'the year of the woman' in law schools, because they were all scurrying to hire women. Columbia made her its first woman on its regular faculty that year and Stanford hired Barbara Babcock as its first woman. Georgetown hired Judy Areen, a Yale Law grad, in 1972, and Patricia King, a Harvard Law grad, in 1973."

King and Areen, who was later Georgetown's dean, welcomed Williams. Williams describes a triad that they formed, "keeping each other afloat for several years while Georgetown was still a wilderness for women." The three colleagues were, Williams says, "just scared and struggling to find our way in an alien environment." The male faculty could be sexist and so were many of their male students, a situation reported by a number of women faculty:

> Pat and Judy and I had similar experiences, which was that the men in the class would challenge our authority in some way. Some male student would come forward to challenge you the first week. If you survived that, good. If you didn't, you'd have to struggle because then the wolves would really come out. It was fascinating, that psychology. The three of us actually consulted an expert in—I don't know what the expert was in exactly—but the point was that she could describe how we could set things up so that we could diminish that kind of behavior.

At Georgetown Williams taught courses on women and law and feminist legal theory. She joined the team that produced the second edition of the Babcock-Freedman women and law casebook. She served as associate dean. She also helped to draft the Pregnancy Discrimination Act as an amendment to Title VII, as well as the Family and Medical Leave Act, and testified against the nomination of Robert Bork for the U.S. Supreme Court. In 1983 Williams cofounded an initiative at Georgetown called the Women's Law and Public Policy Fellowship Program (WLPPF). Graduates of American law schools (and, later, African schools) committed to women's rights were brought to Georgetown, where faculty conducted a seminar for them, and placed them with organizations in the area where they would work on women's issues of various kinds. In 2010 Williams said, "If you go and look at the super structure today of lawyers and law professors doing women's rights work, a large percentage of them have come through our WLPPF program. And they do great things."

New women law professors not only often found a tepid welcome— Babcock wrote that "the university welcomed me mainly for my gender";[4] they also discovered that some male colleagues did not think much of their research and teaching when it focused on issues involving women. In a 1991 article Judith Resnik, later a professor at Yale Law School, told this story: "In the late 1970s, when I first started teaching large law school classes, a colleague gave me what he took to be very kind advice. He said: 'Be careful. Don't teach in any areas associated with women's issues. Don't teach family law, don't teach sex discrimination. Don't teach trusts and estates. Teach the real stuff, the hard stuff: contracts, torts, procedure, property—and don't be too visible on women's issues."[5]

At the time Resnick, who was teaching procedure, federalism, and constitutional law, was doing research on women in prison as well as "procedure, habeas, and a whole bunch of other things." Resnik has written that her experience was "in no way idiosyncratic, nor is it a tale of any particular law school in the United States."[6] Looking back on that 1980 conversation, she felt this way about how things worked out: "So, I have been fortunate in that unlike women a decade ahead of me, some law schools by the time I was teaching thought that they'd like to have a woman. The fact that I wasn't 'only doing women's things' was good, but that I did a little wasn't bad either. Thank you is due to law students. Students are an important part of how we all have jobs."

Resnik's story is interesting in light of Trailblazer Dorothy Nelson's long history with the University of Southern California's (USC) law school beginning in 1957. USC hired Resnick just as Nelson resigned as dean in 1979 to become a federal appeals judge.

Nelson was hired as a USC law professor in the late 1950s at the request of students who had taken her course on judicial administration. This made her one of the very few women faculty members at a West Coast law school. Younger lawyers have said that it was "thrilling" to have a woman role model at a California law school.

Nelson, born in 1928, became an expert in court reform. In 1962 she was asked to become an assistant dean, a position that ultimately led, in 1970, to her being appointed dean of the USC law school. This promotion made her the first woman dean of a major, accredited American law school, highly visible and much sought after. In a 2005 interview, Nelson said she was well treated and well paid as a woman dean, "welcomed and valued."[7] In the 1960s and 1970s she helped to initiate affirmative action programs at the law school as well as a center on conflict resolution. According to USC's oral histories, Nelson is recalled by women alumni as a caring and practical dean who guided several to graduation in the face of daunting family responsibilities.[8] Resnik's experience with male faculty at USC suggests, however, the limits of the change that was possible even under deans committed to women and women's issues. The first generation of women deans could only hope for a slow erosion of entrenched biases against bringing women and the law courses into the curriculum. The fight against women professors who were visible as researchers on women's issues was often even fiercer.

Public Interest Law and the Shaping of Public Policy

In the 1960s and 1970s, men and women began to call certain legal work public interest law. Members of this movement sought to advocate for underrepresented individuals, people facing poverty, displacement, and various forms of discrimination. Some Trailblazers report enrolling in law school so that, as graduates, they could practice public interest law. A number made their mark starting up and leading public interest law initiatives. Their public interest law careers varied in focus—racial rights, housing, immigration, poverty, consumer protection, environment—but many of the Trailblazers who committed their careers to public interest law work focused on, or intersected with, women's rights. And the women dedicated to using law to bring change in women's lives were, according to Wendy Williams, connected institutionally:

> For example, Ruth Ginsburg not only headed the Women's Rights Project of the ACLU, she served on the board of the Cleveland Women's Law Fund and for a while, was on the NOW LDEF Board [National Organization for Women Legal Defense and Education Fund]. I was on the board of NOW Legal Defense Fund and chaired the ACLU Women's Rights Project Advisory Board. I also served on the Women's Legal Defense Fund litigation committee. We were all interlocked in many ways. And, of course, we'd all show up for the annual National Conference on Women and Law. So the women's legal movement kept evolving from something serendipitous to a coherent national interwoven group of women working on these cases, and a couple of good men, too.

The Women's Legal Defense Fund (WLDF) (later the National Partnership for Women & Families) started in 1971 as a Washington, D.C.–based volunteer-lawyer effort founded by a dozen women attorneys, including Trailblazers Brooksley Born, Sally Determan, Gladys Kessler, Lois Schiffer, and Marna Tucker. In its first years the founders, sophisticated members of the civil rights legal world, organized the work of WLDF around specific concerns, including providing pro bono services for people experiencing credit discrimination, employment discrimination, and family law issues.

In 1974 Judith Lichtman became WLDF's first executive director, hired with seed money raised by Born from the Junior League of Washington, D.C. Lichtman inherited a public interest law organization that took the best of what existing models—the ACLU, the NAACP Legal Defense Fund, the Lawyers' Committee for Civil Rights under Law—offered.

Lichtman, a 1965 graduate of the University of Wisconsin Law School, belonged to a new generation influenced by the fight for civil and economic rights. She said, "I went to law school because being a lawyer gave me a license for activism." After an early career at the Department of

Health, Education, and Welfare, the Urban Coalition, and the U.S. Commission on Civil Rights, she landed the job at WLDF. She brought a consciousness on matters of gender discrimination that had not taken shape until, when she was pregnant, her boss at the Civil Rights Commission said he could not hold her position while she waited to give birth. After that he denied her a promotion that was due. At the commission she also began to make the connection among poverty, race, and gender: "I said before that had we been in any other city [but Washington], we would have stayed a local direct service organization. Importantly, I think most nonprofits are made in the image of the people who lead them. So I wasn't the litigator. I understood lobbying; I understood administrative advocacy; I understand how administrative agencies worked. I knew a little bit about Congress; I knew a little bit about putting together coalitions from my days with the Urban Coalition, Civil Rights Commission. . . . so I played to that strength."

In leading WLDF, Lichtman, considered by many of her colleagues to be brilliant at strategic planning, did draw upon her strengths. She also appreciated the unfolding realities of women's rights activism: other public interest law groups and individuals had already begun to shape litigation strategies to further gender rights, and had cases ready to be argued. At the ACLU's Women's Rights Project in New York, Ruth Bader Ginsburg was preparing a ground-breaking litigation strategy to challenge gender-based discrimination. Labor unions were also litigating. At the International Union of Electrical Workers, lawyer Ruth Weyand was working on a case arguing that General Electric Company's exclusion of pregnancy-related disabilities under its health plan violated Title VII of the 1964 Civil Rights Act (*Gilbert v. G.E.*).

And, in Washington, D.C., in 1972, the Center for Law and Social Policy (CLSP) hired Trailblazer Marcia Greenberger and gave her the go-ahead to start the Women's Rights Project (WRP) within the center.[9] Greenberger, soon joined by lawyers Lois Schiffer and Margy Kohn, began with a focus on employment, education, and reproductive rights and health issues. She put litigation at the center of WRP's early mission, quickly challenging the government's failure to enforce Title IX.

Greenberger came to CLSP from Caplin & Drysdale, a private D.C. firm that had been supportive of her interest in serving vulnerable and underrepresented populations. She represented the firm at the Lawyers'

Committee for Civil Rights, an organization started in 1963 at the request of President John F. Kennedy, and served on the executive committee of the Washington Lawyers Committee. She took on pro bono law cases. Working at the firm also provided Greenberger with the opportunity to learn the law from former Supreme Court Justice Arthur Goldberg: "I had this unexpected and really unique opportunity to work with Arthur Goldberg and he was fabulous to me. He was a wonderful teacher and advisor. Never for a minute did I feel as if he was less interested in me because I was a young woman lawyer, or that he took my career any less seriously than any of the other young lawyers in the firm."

Goldberg had agreed to help the Center for Law and Social Policy get started. He chaired its board and helped to obtain funding from foundations. The center, says Greenberger, was created to provide representation for interests where "each individual person didn't have enough of an economic interest, or the capacity, to hire a lawyer in the way that a company would" in areas such as consumer protection or environmental problems. She interviewed for her position at CLSP at the suggestion of Pat Wald and Goldberg.

Thus, by 1974, Washington had two public interest law projects with a law and gender mission. Should they merge? Some observers felt that they should, but they did not. Instead, each organization thrived with Lichtman and Greenberger, joined at WRP a few years later by Nancy Duff Campbell, leading the two groups for several decades. (The WRP became the National Women's Law Center—NWLC—in 1981.) Campbell came with an expertise in poverty and welfare law. She had spent six years at the Center on Social Welfare Policy and Law (CSWPL) in New York City and for several years had taught courses on welfare law. She guided the expanded focus at WRP on poverty-related issues.

The leaders of these two organizations describe the decades of the 1970s, 1980s, and early 1990s as years that included major achievements, as well as dispiriting defeats—ongoing negotiation and litigation involving Title IX, passage of the Pregnancy Discrimination Act, the Family and Medical Leave Act, and the 1991 Civil Rights Act (targeting employment discrimination); a role in mapping strategy over the contentious nominations of Robert Bork and Clarence Thomas for the U.S. Supreme Court; action on numerous tax code issues as they concerned women, including tax treatment of dependent care and single-headed households; and the evolving debates over health care coverage and health care reform.

The cooperative relationship between the two organizations has been long and productive. Lichtman summed it up in her oral history: "Both thrive, and the organizations have two voices, with great syncopation."

* * *

In 1963 President John Kennedy asked lawyers to volunteer to go to the American South to help people denied their civil rights. The president's request resulted in the founding of the Lawyer's Committee for Civil Rights under Law (LCCRUL). One branch of this public interest law organization was located in Jackson, Mississippi. This is where Trail-blazer Constance Slaughter Harvey, who had been mentored by Medgar Evers, found herself after law school.

Harvey says that she went to law school "to try to bring about changes in the legal setting and the legal environment." She had no immediate African American women lawyer role models in Mississippi, but she knew about the professional contributions of two African American women lawyers who lived in the North. Constance Baker Motley had successfully represented James Meredith before the U.S. Supreme Court in his 1962 bid to become the first black student to enter the University of Mississippi. Two years later Marian Wright (Edelman), a 1963 gradu-ate of Yale Law School, traveled to Mississippi to work with lawyers from the NAACP Legal Defense Fund who were representing activists during the Mississippi Freedom Summer.

The chief counsel for the Lawyer's Committee in Jackson recruited Harvey to work at LCCRUL immediately after graduation. With her law books barely closed, she was handed provocative cases:

[I did] *Morrow v. Crisler* against the Mississippi Highway Safety Patrol. We knew that there were no African American highway patrolmen so we sent a young African American man out to get an application. They said they had no applications. We then sent out a white guy to get an applica-tion and they gave him one. There were also cases where young black students were stopped at roadblocks and their afro haircuts were cut off. I took those kinds of cases. I was the only attorney serving with the Lawyer's Committee licensed to practice in the state. There were white lawyers coming down from all over the nation. They could not practice in Mississippi so I had to sign all of their pleadings in order for them to be able to go to court. I handled redistricting lawsuits, boycott lawsuits that were filed by the NAACP down in Natchez. Discrimination lawsuits against black people not being able to work for state government.

I knew that the system was not about to correct itself. It had to be prodded and even pushed to make certain that justice was in fact blind. So I nudged, I pushed, I forced the doors open. The Sixth Amendment guarantees that persons shall be tried by a jury of his or her peers. Now when I got out of law school, black defendants were being tried by all white juries. I had to file at least 40 lawsuits in various counties in the state to make certain that that Amendment had meaning—that you are tried by a jury of your peers.

But Harvey experienced complicated strategy issues with her committee colleagues, as well as salary discrimination, and stayed for only two years: "I knew I couldn't stay at the Lawyer's Committee any longer because I was having serious problems with white men telling me what priorities were for black people. I didn't know what priorities were for black people so I didn't feel that they had any expertise to determine what black people needed."

Harvey was one of several Trailblazers committed to working at public interest law organizations to fight the unequal treatment of racial and ethnic minorities. Chicana Irma Herrera attended the University of Notre Dame Law School, where she never thought about building a resume designed to attract an offer from a large law firm. Instead, after her first year of law school, Herrera worked for Migrant Legal Services in Michigan. The following summer she worked with Evergreen Legal Services in Seattle, which was providing representation to farm workers in the Yakima Valley. Two years later, in 1980, Herrera became a member of the Mexican American Legal Defense and Education Fund (MALDEF) staff in San Francisco, making education law her area of expertise. She helped draft the Supreme Court brief for *Plyler v. Doe*, a landmark case that established the right of undocumented children to free public education. Earlier, she was involved in a late phase of the equally important *Keyes v. School District* desegregation case, intervening on behalf of Spanish-speaking children who, according to MALDEF lawyers, were not adequately represented in the desegregation efforts ordered by the Supreme Court.

For Herrera, and others, MALDEF served as an anchor and launching pad. She stayed two years and then, despite her earlier no-private-firm work philosophy, took a position working under a partner with a commercial law practice. Here, as in her public law positions, she enjoyed the help of a very committed male mentor.

Herrera returned to public interest law in 1991, and in 1995 became executive director of Equal Rights Advocates, an organization advocating for women's economic and educational rights. By this time, she had quite different, and positive, feelings about the importance of spending time at a private firm:

> I encourage young people to get some firm experience if they can. I know it's controversial in public interest circles. Often times they look down, we look down, on people who had been at law firms. If you're committed to public interest why were you at a law firm making money? I find it short sighted and unfortunate but it is a very common view. . . . that you're not really committed to the cause. . . . that you will not be as strong an advocate as you need to be because you will be analyzing a case from a defense standpoint.

* * *

Public interest law work was liberating and self-chosen at a time when discrimination or affirmative action often determined job options. Trailblazers described participation in public interest work as tied to personal worldviews, experience, and political leanings. Unlike most private law firm experience, public interest work brought power and responsibility, including organization leadership, quite early in the careers of these women. This included initiating public law projects or organizations. Nancy Duff Campbell explained an aspect of the public law culture that existed when she, as a 1968 NYU Law grad, joined New York City's Center on Social Welfare Policy and Law (CSWPL): "It was a very different time when we started practicing law. We went to work in organizations where we were thrown immediately into very high-level work because the people who were our bosses were only a couple of years older than we were. . . . [W]e were all just young kids, and there wasn't a cadre of people above us or below us. . . . [W]e all got very interesting work to do . . . [T]here was a certain headiness because there weren't that many people doing it and within each office there weren't that many resources. We each had a lot of responsibility, but at the same time, we wanted to exercise that responsibility in a way that was going to be effective and as strong as possible."

Part of the excitement, and challenge, of this public interest law was the introduction of new theories of law, ideas that were introduced because, as Nancy Duff Campbell emphasized, there were finally lawyers interested in bringing cases that hinged on new jurisprudence. At the ACLU's Women's Rights Project, Ruth Bader Ginsburg devoted nine years to litigating cases about "the constitutional principle of the equal citizenship stature of men and women."[10] At CSWPL, Campbell helped with the development of a new body of welfare law that began with *King v. Smith,* the so-called man in the house challenge. Constance Harvey filed at least forty lawsuits in various Mississippi counties to make certain that that the Sixth Amendment had meaning—that the accused were tried by a jury of their peers. Irma Herrera participated in several landmark U.S. Supreme Court education cases involving undocumented and Spanish-speaking children.

Pro Bono, the Bar, and Private Law Firms

Until she retired in 2015, some colleagues called her Ms. Pro Bono; others preferred "the Queen of Pro Bono." Esther Lardent, the child of Holocaust survivors, was brought to the United States in 1951 at the age of four. Lardent told her interviewer that her commitment to the civil rights struggle was firm by the time she was in high school. As a scholarship student at Pembroke College (now Brown), from 1964 to 1968, Lardent participated in a VISTA (Volunteers in Service to America) program, assigned to work on a project in the Roxbury neighborhood of Boston. Influenced by the "power to do right" of the VISTA lawyers, she applied to law school intending to become a civil rights lawyer. She graduated from the University of Chicago in 1971.

Lardent does not speak of leaving law school with a fixed notion of how she would marry her political ideas with her new profession. Her resume, however, reflects the steps by which she developed the expertise and networks to reshape and dramatically expand the legal profession's participation in pro bono work, an area that also flourished through the work of male practitioners.

She began at HEW's Office of Civil Rights, working on a major discrimination suit filed by women against the University of Michigan. By 1973 she was staff director of the ABA's Section on Individual Rights and Responsibilities (SIRR), which was then, she said, "the liberal conscience of the ABA."

> The leadership of the section was incredible—Brooksley Born, Sally Determan, Cecil Poole, Mona [Marna] Tucker. Unbelievable people who were creating public interest law . . . [I]t was great. And the division of the ABA that I was in had a number of men who were also staff directors, who were also younger, and they were great to work with. We were working on all kinds of interesting issues. Chesterfield Smith, who became one of my beloved mentors—was just an amazing man. All the issues about the Nixon impeachment were raging, and Chesterfield had testified and supported the impeachment in court, and Bert Jenner who was the counsel for the Democrats in the impeachment, was one of the leaders in the section. It was the legal education that I never got at law school being around these amazing people . . . and it taught me what the law could be and how you could be a really good, effective lawyer. . . . that if you were a good lawyer, you cared about these larger issues, you could really make change. It's this amazing sense of potential, and the power of it all. They were such empowering experiences for a young woman.

After her work for the ABA, Lardent was hired as the first director of a newly funded program to establish a local pro bono program under the auspices of the Boston Bar.[11] Lardent had observed volunteerism while heading the ABA's SIRR: "It really made me believe in volunteerism and the impact that volunteers could have because the work that people did with the Section was all volunteer work on top of very demanding full-time legal jobs."

Under her leadership the Volunteer Lawyers Project took shape. There was, she said, "no roadmap." The existing pro bono initiatives in the Boston area were mostly tied into the old Legal Aid Societies that had been founded at the beginning of the twentieth century. Lardent thought of them "as Hey Joe Programs where somebody's secretary would call up and say 'hey Joe, would you take a divorce?' You know, very noblesse oblige, very informal":

> I thought this is the time where we could do something different. So we put together a program that married volunteerism with the best practices in public interest law. We recruited more broadly, we had a broader range of cases that we would handle, we provided training and manuals and support and we did quality control on volunteers and we fired volunteers if they didn't do what they were supposed to be doing. The Board and the staff of the Legal Services Corporation in Washington watched this all happening and they thought, "wow this is really great." So they funded five more pro bono programs in the second year in New Hampshire, San Francisco, Los Angeles, New York and Washington D.C. The people who were running those programs contacted me and we became the Pro Bono Six. We felt like we had found something pretty incredible and very powerful and that there was a huge promise to this delivery method.

There was excitement but also pushback because some lawyers in the legal services community saw these programs as alternatives, rather than supplements, to what they were doing. They feared that the legal reform aspects of legal services would be abolished if these experimental pro bono programs succeeded. Lardent and her colleagues had to argue that while pro bono was a powerful tool, it could not exist on its own. It was supplemental and complementary to the work of full-time legal services lawyers.

The Pro Bono Six refined their models. The ABA became interested in these projects and joined the Legal Services Corporation in funding even more programs. In 1980 the directors of the original six programs were told that they would be permanently funded. It was, Lardent recalled, "a big moment with great coverage in the media." But in the same year Ronald Reagan was elected president: "Reagan, who, as governor of California, had tried to destroy California Rural Legal Services which represented migrant workers, and he came damn close to doing it. He and Ed Meese. And when he came in, of course he was trying to create smaller government, and so his recommendation for Legal Services was zero funding. The idea was that, if every lawyer in America would just do one case, it would be fine. It was devastating."

Lardent next describes what could only be called making lemonade out of lemons. Reagan's action, she recalls, was "to be really a blessing," one that made the ABA more supportive of the programs, made it "own this issue," along with many state and local bars. In her view, as the result of this crisis, the leaders of legal services programs across the country came out of their self-imposed isolation and began talking to the leaders of the profession, judges, and others. Lardent argues that this new culture of communication broadened the range of supporters as well as the number of people who understood the importance of these legal services. In the end, the Legal Services Corporation survived with its budget cut 25 percent. And between 1982 and 1984, the number of pro bono programs across the country skyrocketed, in part because Lardent and her colleagues participated in a "pro bono roadshow," in which they explained the mechanics of pro bono.

After these intense years of work, and a farewell party where Lardent remembers respected members of the Boston Bar dancing to *Material Girl*, she left her work in Boston and struck out for New Mexico, where for several years she consulted and taught at the state law school. Then Trailblazer Sally Determan, the new chair of the ABA's Section on Individual Rights and Responsibilities, made a phone call to Lardent.

Determan persuaded Lardent to move to D.C. in order to become a consultant attached to the association's Post-Conviction Death Penalty Project. Lardent worked on assistance of counsel and training issues. It was, she said, "a tremendously exciting time, but she missed some of the pro bono stuff."

Robert Raven, president of the ABA in the late 1980s, gave Lardent the opportunity to reconnect with pro bono work when he asked to her to write speeches for him. He wanted to provoke colleagues, and give them a new perspective. In a short while she was again in the thick of pro bono advocacy:

> He was very worried that the increasing pressure for large law firms to be business-like was negatively impacting pro bono, and he pulled together a conference of people from law firms to talk about pro bono. Mary McClymont, at the Ford Foundation, attended, and then came to me and said, "I'm hearing from all of the groups, the Inc. Fund, the civil rights groups, the ACLU, that use these large law firms that they are becoming more

resistant to taking on really big cases, really controversial matters because it's not business-like." And she said, "I wonder whether I could convince you to work on a project to strengthen law firm pro bono work." And I said, "That would be fun." And so they came up with a $40,000 grant [run through the ABA Pro Bono Committee]. . . . Sally Determan was the inspiration in many ways for what we decided to do on the law firm project because she was doing pro bono at Hogan. Nobody knew what most of the law firms were really doing. Nobody was writing about it because it was pre–*American Lawyer* [the profession's trade magazine] days.

After signing on to the project, in an effort to shape the goals of their work, Lardent put together what she called "regional listening tours." She brought people from law firms together to talk about whether, and how, they were participating in pro bono work. After one of these tours she told Determan, "I wonder whether it would make sense to give billable hour credit for pro bono. And she looked at me and she said, 'oh, you're so Pollyannaish. That's so sweet, but firms will never do that.'"

But Lardent knew that the D.C. firm of Arnold & Porter was encouraging people to spend up to 15 percent of their time on pro bono work, counting it in the same way that billable time was counted. Determan's response reinforced Lardent's realization that there was a huge vacuum of information on best practices, and so "that's where we went with the project."

She began just as big firms were, in her words, "giving a whole new meaning to big and as they were becoming increasingly the sort of power center, dominant force and exemplar in the profession." Lardent began collecting data on law firms nationwide and found that, in good times and bad, even with changes in managing partners, "pro bono was a constant." The time was right, she felt, to expand participation in pro bono legal work at private law firms and corporate legal departments—to provide pro bono legal services to low-income and disadvantaged individuals and families and nonprofit groups.

Encouraged by colleagues at several leading law firms, Lardent spent two years collaboratively drafting what became the Pro Bono Challenge:

I don't think any of us would have ever imagined that it would become the industry gold standard and how much it would drive firm behavior.

People said to us, three or five percent of billable hours, are you crazy? And now, it's considered, you know, entirely feasible and doable and everybody strives toward it—it's just amazing. The people on the advisory committee literally just picked up their briefcases, and they were like the Willy Lomans of pro bono. What we did as a strategy, before we unveiled the Challenge, we got 48 charter signatories and we got geographic diversity. We got highly respected firms. John Pickering of Wilmer Cutler Pickering was very close friends with Justice Brennan who had just retired and was not in great health, but very excited about this, and Justice Brennan agreed to write a letter on his Supreme Court Justice stationery to all the firms. It went to about 500 law firms inviting them to participate in the Challenge.

With these efforts, pro bono commitments became larger and more institutionalized. Lardent suggested that the *American Lawyer* start using the project's definition of pro bono, and it did. The Pro Bono Institute (PBI), which received no federal funding, was founded in 1996, and Lardent became its head. Law firms signed the Pro Bono Challenge, as did corporate legal departments whose involvement in pro bono was now significant where, in the past, it was virtually nonexistent.[12] And over the next decades pro bono evolved from being litigation focused (death penalty and civil rights and liberties cases) to a greater mix that included immigration, bankruptcy, eviction defense, veterans' benefits, and nonprofit incorporation as well as family and poverty law.

PBI focused on finding pro bono models that worked well and were replicable. Through the Pro Bono Challenge, PBI became, in Lardent's words, something like a quasi-regulatory agency telling firms what counts as pro bono and what does not. At the same time, she tried to find ways to have participants think in strategic ways:

You could do 200 landlord-tenant cases for clients, and it would be important work, it makes a huge difference, those clients have benefited, but in terms of any kind of large impact, you might not succeed. What if you did 200 landlord-tenant cases but you did them where the landlord was the worst slumlord in the world and what you were basically trying to do was to do targeted litigation that held them to a particular standard and made it at a certain point economically unviable for them to have this horrible housing. A lot of people think we're talking about class actions versus individual matters. That's really not what it's about. It is about having an impact beyond simply the immediate benefit to the client.

Lardent, who died in 2016, said that she lucked out in being in the right place at the right time when she started what became the work of PBI. She began talking to law firm partners during the time of big firm growth—the go-go years. But in 2012 Lardent acknowledged not having a completely clear picture of the future: "I don't know where it's all going to go. I really don't, and I think there are some clouds looming on the horizon for both law firm and legal departments that worry me a lot, that could undermine the potential, but I still think the potential is enormous."

Conclusion

Nothing short of a seismic shift has occurred at educational institutions since Ruth Bader Ginsburg was hired in the 1960s by Rutgers Law School. In the twentieth-first century, women faculty members are numerous, as are women students. "You are taking the place of a man" is a taunt of the past. Still, there has been a long struggle to achieve salaries equal to those of male colleagues, fairness in granting tenure, and the hiring of women at top-ranked schools.

Women have also joined Barbara Black in being named law school deans. Over the past several decades several dozen women have been tapped to head law schools, including Kristen Booth Glen at City University of New York Law School, Herma Hill Kay at the University of California–Berkeley, Veryl Miles at Columbus School of Law of Catholic University, Jennifer Rosato Perea at DePaul, Martha Minow at Harvard, and, in 2017, Heather Gerken at Yale.

Public interest law careers also presented a powerful professional alternative for a number of Trailblazers. Some committed entire working lives to these organizations. Other women varied their careers, moving in and out of public interest jobs for academic posts, government positions, and, occasionally, as in the case of Irma Herrera, private law firms.

Lessons learned in the 1950s civil rights movement, 1960s anti–Vietnam War activism, federal legislation, and the expansion of the women's rights movement in the 1970s created the climate, activist training, and inspiration needed for the growth of public interest law.

Trailblazers came to various public law organizations with their legal talent and idealism. In general, they did not encounter the barriers to hiring experienced by their sisters in the private law firm world, although such prejudice was not entirely absent. They joined existing groups and started their own. In Cleveland Lizabeth Moody was one of the founders of the Women's Law Fund. The Law Fund, like most of the start-up public interest law projects, benefited from foundations such as Carnegie, Ford, Revson, and others that had begun targeting the defeat of sex discrimination as central to their philanthropic missions.

Public interest litigation also benefited from the decisions and jurisprudence of the Warren Court, 1953 to 1969, and, to a lesser degree, the Burger Court, 1969 to 1986. At the federal as well as local levels, public interest lawyers litigated, filed amicus briefs, and lobbied. They teased critical decisions from courts and new legislation from Congress and state legislatures. In the process, over nearly fifty years, these Trailblazers have critically altered public policy in virtually every area, including education, health care and medical leave, immigrant rights, housing, consumer protection, employment discrimination, the tax code, family law, and violence against women. They laid down trails that have changed the landscape of law in the United States.

7

The New Face of Government

The federal tax code hardly figures as everyday chit-chat among women (or men, for that matter). The code has, however, specific issues of concern for women and their families. One example is the child and dependent care tax credit that became part of the federal tax code in 1976. The credit gives taxpayers the opportunity to reduce their tax bill for money spent on dependent care.

Soon after the credit went into effect, however, activists discovered that not that many taxpayers used it. There was no line on the IRS's short form for the credit and, as Marcia Greenberger points out, most middle- and lower-income people in the United States used the short form. And so in the early 1980s, at the beginning of the Reagan administration, Greenberger and her public interest organization colleagues set out to get the short form changed. They petitioned the IRS, where officials were sympathetic but said that the point was to keep the short form just that: short. The obvious message: Pressure would be needed if a line for deducting the costs of dependent care was to be added to the form. The women began a lobby campaign, quickly learning that behind the federal government's new faces, female faces, were legislative and executive branch officials ready to help. Antidiscrimination employment legislation and the changing attitudes of voters had combined to create a modest opening for women who sought high-level government positions. Greenberger describes how a legislative and executive branch coalition of women made the IRS's short form one line longer: "Elizabeth Dole was in charge of constituency outreach in the Reagan White House at the time. She thought this was a terrific issue. And we organized both Republican and Democratic women in the Congress to write letters to the IRS to put it on the short form, which they ultimately did. Millions of dollars of these tax credits and deductions began to be taken by people all over the country based on this policy."

Elected to Congress

One of the new faces was that of congresswoman Patricia Schroeder, a Harvard-trained lawyer. Before her election to the House of Representatives at the age of thirty-three, Schroeder had been living in Denver with her lawyer-husband and two small children. She and Jim Schroeder had been very involved in civil rights issues as well as the anti–Vietnam War movement. They had been plaintiffs in a school busing suit. Before coming to Washington, Schroeder had worked at a regional National Labor Relations Board (NLRB) office, taught law, and served as a state personnel hearing officer. In 1972, she made the decision to run for a seat in the U.S. House of Representatives: "Jim talked me into running. He said, 'You go around telling all your students they have to become involved; practice what you teach. Someone needs to give voice for the changing scene.'"

Schroeder later called her run a Don Quixotesque adventure. Her opponent in the Democratic primary was the state Senate minority leader. He had all the endorsements and all the money.

> I was so "non-professional" I drove the politicos nuts. The Democratic Congressional Campaign refused to meet with me after I won the primary. They said I had no idea what I was doing. It was just awful. Labor gave me 50 bucks. The AFL-CIO, I couldn't believe it. I knew more about labor than anyone running and they gave Democratic candidates in Salt Lake and in Iowa $50,000 each, which was a lot of money, in those days. Everybody who supposedly knew anything about politics said the race was totally hopeless. The best part was when I got elected I owed nothing to anyone. Imagine, our average campaign contribution was $7.50—when I left office (1997) it had risen to $34.

In the presidential race that year, incumbent Richard Nixon trounced his Democratic Party opponent, George McGovern. The Democrats, however, maintained their majority in the House of Representatives, with Schroeder defeating her Republican opponent, incumbent Mike McKevitt, by four percentage points. In a swirl of last-minute professional obligations and family issues, she arrived in Washington, D.C.: "And it was in the middle of the Vietnam War. The Cambodian Bombing was happening. So all of Washington smelled like tear gas. Protests were everywhere. National Guardsmen were sleeping in the congressional tunnels. I had one day to move us into a new house I'd never seen. Jim bought it on a one day trip to Washington."

Her husband and children came with her, each with particular concerns: "When the election was over and Jim started to think what to do with the rest of his life, I remember saying to him you've been awful relaxed about all this change. This is really amazing to me. He said you know it's wonderful because very rarely do men get to sit down and think about career changes. You get on the track, you stay on the track."

And, her daughter said, "Please don't have reporters keep calling me, I feel like a science project."

The new representative from Colorado's first district joined thirteen other female House members, including Hawaii's Patsy Mink, New York's Shirley Chisholm and Bella Abzug, and Connecticut's Ella Grasso:

Everybody was surprised I won and treated me like I was just the fluke. "Well, she surely won't be here two years from now." At my swearing in it was funny because the Speaker kept trying to get Jim to raise his hand, and he kept saying "no it's her." The media found me a great novelty. Here's this woman with this baby . . . and I had a six year old. . . . One of my memories was Bella Abzug telling me, "I don't think you can do this." I kept wondering "Oh my God. What am I doing?"

Camaraderie marked her experience with Mink, Abzug, Barbara Jordan, Yvonne Burke, and Elizabeth Holtzman. But, she also had the starchy experience of being told by Missouri's Leonore Sullivan, dean of the congresswomen, to call her by her husband's name, Mrs. John Sullivan.

Schroeder, the "great novelty," won reelection eleven times, serving a total of twenty-four years. In her first term she was appointed as the first woman member on the prestigious House Armed Services Committee, and was there a story in that!

[As a new member] I didn't know much about the process or anything else. I did go see Chairman Wilbur Mills who was in charge of my region and I tell him what committees I wanted to be on. I wanted Armed Services, and Post Office and Civil Service. He got me on both and I thought I got on because I was qualified, confident, had a pilot's license and Congress thought it would be nice to have a woman. Six months later we learned about Fannie Fox. Then I put it all together. Congressman Mills had been messing around with Fannie Fox during the whole campaign while his wife had been out campaigning for him. His wife had gotten very interested in my campaign, unbeknownst to me . . . [S]he apparently said to Congressman Mills, "well you do whatever you can for that young woman." She was an amazing feminist in her own right, married to this guy. . . . [H]is guilt is really how I got on those choice committees, I think. And you know the story about the Armed Services Committee chairman [Mr. Hebert] being very upset. No way he wanted a woman. An African American was also put on the committee. He made us share a chair, saying we were each worth only half his other members. . . . Then the Watergate class was voted in . . . and decided Congress should start electing the chairman rather [than] let them be there for life.

In concert with several other women subcommittee chairs, Schroeder used her position on the Post Office and Civil Service Committee to make the federal civil service a model employer with flextime, job sharing, pay equity, and daycare. The Reagan years reversed the committee's efforts, but the template remained.

Schroeder was also acknowledged as a major force behind the Family and Medical Leave Act of 1993, work that did not go quickly:

It took nine years to get that damn thing through. We got it passed when Clinton came to power and he signed it at his first signing ceremony. The chairman of the committee that had jurisdiction told the Clinton people that "we can't have her on this stage at the signing because it's now my bill." Okay, thank you guys. The "boys" hadn't sponsored it till the last year, but no difference; it was not theirs! . . . [W]ho cares, it got passed. [But] the bill was just a mere shadow of the bill I introduced. This was such a lesson in how hard this stuff is.

While in Congress, Schroeder developed a reputation as a wit—recall her line, "Reagan, the Teflon president"—and had political ambitions that extended beyond the House of Representatives. Beginning in the late 1980s, she put out feelers concerning a presidential bid but never succeeded in winning sufficient support to claim the Democratic Party's nomination—although supporters circulated thousands of "Pat Schroeder President 1988" buttons. The political culture had changed but was still not so different from the year Schroeder entered Congress, when women could not use the congressional gym, there were no mentors, and, Schroeder reflected, "[Y]ou [were] not really welcome anywhere."

In dealing with this political patriarchy, Schroeder said that she benefited from her Harvard Law School years: "[My experience at Harvard fortified me.] It was a wonderful experience for getting ready for Congress. It's like I've been there, and this is déjà vu. Neither Congress nor Harvard was out with welcoming signs for women. When a young man was elected, the older members want to mentor him. . . . The gym was for men only and more bonding. . . . For the women, you're not really welcome anywhere. . . . It's certainly better now [2008] . . . but we still have only fifty some odd women in Congress."

Serving State Government

Elizabeth Lacey's path into state government service was altogether different from Schroeder's road to Congress. In 1969, a recent graduate of the University of Texas Law School, Lacey began her career at the Texas Legislative Council (a staffing unit of the legislature, a job she called "fabulous"), where she was responsible for drafting legislation. From the vantage point of the council, she watched and worked with an extraordinary generation of Texas women leaders:

> At that time Barbara Jordan was a State Senator [later, a member of the U.S. House of Representatives, 1973–79]. A woman named Sissy Farenthold was in the legislature—she ran a very serious race for Governor. . . . She was the Democratic candidate and came close to winning. Sarah Weddington was just beginning to argue *Roe. v. Wade.* . . . There was a bunch of women that were all good friends and kept together. Anne Richards [later, state treasurer and governor] was in town. . . . We also had the woman Senator—Kay Bailey Hutchison [who served in the Texas House and then the U.S. Senate]. . . . There were lots of women around

and Texas was really great about—the gender discrimination was minimal at that point. You just saw women doing things everywhere. . . . [T]hey were not [so active] in law fields but, they were very active in the political arena at that time. . . . I never really planned on being a judge [but] the practical training that I got at legislative drafting, and of course, the legislative process—was just invaluable. . . . I mean, so much of our law now is statutory law.

In 1973 John Hill, the new state attorney general, asked Lacy to join his antitrust and consumer protection division. The new position permitted her to litigate cases as well as to work on the adoption of a new consumer protection bill. In her next position as special assistant to Hill, she reviewed all appellate briefs, and took an original jurisdiction (a Texas-Louisiana boundary dispute) case and a redistricting appeal case to the U.S. Supreme Court. Success as Hill's special assistant led to her appointment as the head of the State and County Division of the attorney general's office and as the first woman deputy attorney general in Texas.

Lacy's reflections on her success rely heavily on her view that John Hill was committed to creating career opportunities for women, and on the openness of Texans' attitude toward women in government service:

John Hill was very good. We had a number of different women who were very capable and worked for him. He recruited and he put women in positions of senior responsibility over the years. . . . I knew a lot of the politicians and worked a lot with them. But again, and I can't emphasize this enough, in Texas at that time, there were a lot of very active women, politically and in the legal field. It was just not unusual to have women lobbyists and women legislators and women lawyers. There were not many women judges—I will say that . . . but some of that was because there hadn't been many women going to law school at that point.

And then Lacy met and married a lawyer with two children who worked in the Virginia attorney general's office. She moved to Richmond, gave birth to two children, and worked from home for six years doing contract work for the legislature and writing briefs. And she discovered that the nature of Virginia's political culture in the 1970s was quite different from that of Texas: "I always thought I would go back to work. I did find it much more difficult here in Richmond or in Virginia in terms of the fact that I was a woman and a lawyer. That just didn't fit people's, well it was very different, very different. And people were nice enough, but the idea of working outside the home and all that was not—more women did not work than did. Let's put it that way."

When asked if she had been surprised at the difference between Richmond and Austin, Lacy replied,

> Surprised is a word one might use. . . . Dismayed. In some ways, kind of disbelieving. At that time, 1976, in Richmond and probably the State, Austin was much more open and freewheeling. You could do anything that you felt you were big enough to do. It didn't make any difference who your parents were or where you went to school, you know, it was much more a frontier. Richmond had been around for much longer and had many of its ways of doing things and very established. It was certainly a center of finance and so forth, but it didn't have the influence or influx of non-Virginia people . . . the way it certainly has now.

In 1982 a long-time colleague, Jerry Baliles, was elected state's attorney general and offered Lacy a position as deputy, the same level position that she had left five years before in Texas. Lacy had a two-year-old at home, but she also had the confidence of a seasoned careerist:

> [I said to Baliles] I need to have a salary that will allow me to have good child care. I need to have a parking place. And I need to have it well understood that I've worked in Attorney General's Offices before and crises don't start at 5:00 at night. And if they do, call me on the phone, because I will have to leave when it's time to leave and—I'll be here, you'll get my work, but I know you guys and you tend to all of a sudden start talking about the problem at 4:00 in the afternoon. . . . He was very good, kept all of his promises, and there were times when I got up and walked out of a meeting at 5:00 and said, "See you later."

Lacy also pointed out the advantages of practicing in the 1970s and 1980s before the "reach-out-and-touch-me" moment changed the practice of law: "We didn't have Blackberries. We didn't have e-mail. We didn't have personal computers, and we didn't have cell phones. . . . [I]t was very different in terms of instant demand of other people."

In her new position, Elizabeth Lacy took part in many high-profile cases and thought about running for state attorney general: "Politics is such a matter of timing," she said, "and the timing for that certainly never was right." In 1985 she accepted appointment from Governor Charles Robb as judge of the State Corporation Commission (a tribunal with the powers of a court of record; an administrative body as well as a quasi-judicial body). Four years later the governor named her to the Virginia Supreme Court, where she served until 2007.

The Department of Justice

On March 12, 1993, President Bill Clinton administered the oath of office to Janet Reno, who became the first woman attorney general of the United States. An enthusiastic audience of government officials, friends, and family witnessed the event. The federal government had come a long way from the first half of the twentieth century when Annette Adams, Mabel Walker Willebrandt, and Beatrice Rosenberg were among the very few high-ranking women lawyers in the Department of Justice (DOJ). The number of women lawyers at Justice had most definitely increased in the second half of the century. However, Trailblazer Ruth Burg has argued that, in part, this was the case because "they are willing to work for less money," and were not tapped as quickly as male DOJ attorneys for private-sector jobs.[1] Salaries aside, numerous Trailblazers were brought into the Justice Department in the 1970s and 1980s.

Florence Roisman, Harvard Law class of 1963, wanted to work in the Antitrust Division at the Justice Department. When she graduated from Harvard, the division had no women and would not interview her, mirroring her experience that year with private firms. She took a job at the Federal Trade Commission, where she had interned during law school. A year later, perhaps because Attorney General Robert Kennedy had focused on diversity in hiring, she was taken on by the Justice Department to work in the appellate section of the Civil Division. She stayed three years and loved the experience but left when she was not given the raise that her young male colleagues received. Roisman made it clear to her boss that she was not willing to work for less money than the guys.

And then there is Ilana Rovner's DOJ story. The ninety-three U.S. attorneys' offices are part of the Department of Justice. The U.S. attorneys and staff prosecute federal crimes and represent the United States in civil actions in which the federal government has a concern. Their offices are spread across the United States, Puerto Rico, the Virgin Islands, Guam, and the Northern Mariana Islands. As a result, U.S. attorneys' offices often develop unique legal and social cultures. For many years before the 1970s, in offices headed by conservative U.S. attorneys, women lawyers stood no chance of being hired. Elsewhere, Trailblazers reported the need to be persistent. In Ilana Rovner's case, luck and a sympathetic secretary set her on the road to an assistant U.S. attorney's position. It was Chicago, in the early 1970s:

> My story is amazing. I went to a dinner party and I was seated next to Judge James. B. Parsons [Northern District of Illinois]. And he was complaining about having to start the search for a new law clerk on Monday. And I said to him, "I'll be your law clerk. . . ." And he said, "Really?" He said, "Well, bring me your resume and come in on Monday morning." I later learned that he went to work that Monday and said to his secretary, "I can't believe what I did. I sat next to this young woman and I told her to come in for an interview and I can't possibly have a woman law clerk because a woman will cry if I don't like her work. I won't be able to roll my sleeves up. I will have to wear a jacket at all times. . . . So when she arrives, tell her that I've chosen a law clerk." And his secretary who wanted to be a lawyer, but it was the Depression and she could not afford to go to law school, said to him, "You should be ashamed of yourself. You, the first Afr—," well in those days, they didn't use the word "African-American," "the first negro judge, not willing to give a woman a chance, that's just wrong. You cannot send her away. At least interview her." He interviewed me and gave me the job. She helped me immeasurably. And I will say this, I worked my heart out for him.
>
> And then I got my next job the same way. Jim Thompson, who was the U.S. Attorney, was in Judge Parsons' chambers on a case. And he came in and sat down in my office. And he said to me, "Do you have any interest in coming to the U.S. Attorney's office?"

Rovner had expected to go to work for a private firm, but Thompson said, "Send a formal application."

So I got a scroll. Put my resume on this scroll and attached a picture of my husband and me in formal clothing. Can you believe it? I still have it. It was a button of me in a gown and Dick in a tuxedo. "Here is my formal application." But it was 1973. They were looking for women. And I was, I believe I was the fifth woman in his office, which was considered very forward looking. I mean, they did articles in the newspaper about us. That was considered amazing to have that many women. We were all friends, but we were unbelievably busy because we were all trying to prove that we belonged there. When I became the first woman supervisor in the history of that office, there was one man that just would not work with me—wouldn't work under me. I mean . . . the young women today can't possibly . . . they can't possibly understand the pressures of being first. [At a Chicago Bar Association panel] I was asked what can we do about, you know, these men that are so mean? And I said, "The only thing we can do is outlive them. . . ." Because some of them were not welcoming in any sense of the word no matter what we did. Nothing was good enough. [The women were really good but] men that were hundreds of places below us in class were getting great jobs and there were no jobs for us.

Rovner said that when she encountered a hostile environment, she kept her esteem and confidence in the only way she knew how: "The raw desire to succeed. The desire to succeed was greater than any obstacles placed in my way. . . . But this I will say. There also were men who wanted us to succeed. Who greatly wanted us to succeed. They didn't want us to take the jobs that they wanted but they were happy to see us do well. They mentored the women, it was the only way then."

Opening the President's Cabinet to Women

Carla Hills was born in 1934 in Los Angeles. She returned there in 1958, after graduating from Yale Law School, and also joined the U.S. attorney's office, handling civil and criminal litigation. Hills recalls no gender discrimination at the office but encountered judges "who would remark on the fact that they would rather not have a woman in the courtroom." She remained an assistant U.S. attorney for three years before cofounding and becoming a partner of the Los Angeles law firm Munger, Tolles, and Hills, litigating and concentrating on antitrust practice.

By the time Richard Nixon won reelection in 1972, Hills was an established attorney and, with little effort, moved back into public service: "[In the spring of 1973] Elliot Richardson, who was the Attorney General, came to Los Angeles. I think he had hoped to bring a woman into the Administration. In any event, he contacted me, and asked whether I would come back and talk to him about being Assistant Attorney General in charge of the Civil Division. And I thought, how strange! Doesn't he know that I'm an antitrust lawyer?"

Hills thought about the offer long and hard, talking seriously to Rod, her husband:

> I think as a general proposition re-potting is good; it's good for plants, it's good for people. . . . I thoroughly enjoyed the meeting with Elliot Richardson; he was a wonderful man and we subsequently became good friends. His deputy was Bill Ruckelshaus, who also is a fantastic person, and their Solicitor General was Bob Bork, who is very, very bright. I kept postponing coming . . . and about September I received a call from Elliot, who said, "You know, I'm under considerable pressure; I need to have you come back. . . ." These were tumultuous times. Recall that Vice President Agnew resigned October 9 in the face of allegations of taking bribes. On October 15, President Nixon named Congressman Gerald Ford to be Vice President.

Hills flew to Washington, ready to bring her four children east from Los Angeles. She put a deposit on a house and prepared to join the Justice Department. A day later Attorney General Richardson and Ruckelshaus, his deputy AG, quit over President Nixon's insistence that they fire Archibald Cox, a former solicitor general and Harvard Law School professor. Richardson had appointed Cox as the independent special prosecutor to investigate whether the Nixon White House had been involved in a cover-up of its involvement concerning the June 1972 break-in at the Democratic National Committee headquarters in the Watergate office complex. The famously named "Saturday Night Massacre" weekend ensued. Hills decided that, having been recruited by Richardson, and now uncertain who would replace him, she would refuse the position. In the months following, the White House personnel office called her, as did people at Justice, including Bork, now acting attorney general:

In January [1974] I came back to meet the new Attorney General, who was Senator Bill Saxby. . . . These were very rocky times with Watergate and growing tension between the White House which had refused to release the tapes and Congress, the Viet Nam War, which caused much public dissatisfaction, and the souring economy. . . . I was worried . . . that there would be political interference with my running of the Civil Division. In my meeting with Attorney General Saxby I asked all kind of questions like will I have freedom to hire and fire, how will the Attorney General exercise his discretion on cases we take to the Supreme Court, will the Assistant Attorney General be permitted to work directly with the Solicitor General on these sorts of issues. And after about ten minutes of this, Senator Saxby said to me, "Carla, are you only going to hire women?" I was so astounded by his question and felt that I was not getting through. So I said, "Do you know who your deputy is going to be?"

Larry Silverman was hired as Saxby's deputy. Hills found him impressive and, in February 1974, took up her position: "Tom Kauper was then head of the Antitrust Division. He knew of my interest in antitrust and this was during the period when the government was bringing the AT&T cases. . . . And we worked together on that and a lot of other cases. . . . In addition in the Civil Division we handled the Mayday Riot cases, the Nixon Tapes cases, the Chicago redlining cases—we had so much litigation, involving both constitutional and statutory issues. It was extremely interesting."

One Saturday, a year later, Hills received a call from Donald Rumsfeld, President Gerald Ford's chief of staff. The president wished to see her. He wanted her to leave Justice and become head of the Department of Housing and Urban Development (HUD):

Then I went to see the President, who was just fabulous. As I found out, he was so right. The first piece of legislation that President Ford signed after taking office in August of 1974 was the Housing and Community Development Act of 1974. . . . President Ford was so knowledgeable about government. He knew everything about the HUD, what its mission was; what its budget was, because he'd served on the House Appropriations Committee for 26 years. He said, "I need a manager at HUD." As I found out, he was so right. . . . I arrived at HUD in March 1975. . . . I knew that

I would have to testify on the budget roughly ten days later. . . . [And I discovered] the regulations to implement the legislation had not been drafted, notwithstanding the legislation was signed August 9th 1974, seven months earlier. Something went wrong; nobody was managing the store. . . . I got a real beating-up when I told them that when I went up to testify on the HUD budget.

Hills served at HUD until 1977, the only woman in the Ford cabinet. She returned to private law practice, and was the first woman on the Chevron board (which could no longer hold its board luncheons at the Pacific Union Club because women were not permitted at lunchtime). In 1989, Hills accepted President George H. W. Bush's request that she take on the position of U.S. trade representative. In that position she followed her philosophy that markets should be kept open, and started the NAFTA negotiations for the Bush administration.

Hills's confirmation as a member of Ford's cabinet made her the third woman in the history of the United States to hold a cabinet position. Reformer Frances Perkins was the first, nominated by President Franklin D. Roosevelt in 1933 to head the Department of Labor. Twenty years later, President Dwight D. Eisenhower named Oveta Culp Hobby, previously director of the Women's Army Auxiliary Corps, to head the newly created Department of Health, Education, and Welfare.

Times changed after Hills's service. Reno's 1993 appointment to head the Justice Department occurred in the same year that Donna Shalala (Health and Human Services) and Hazel O'Leary (Energy) joined President Bill Clinton's cabinet. Clinton came into office, after his November 1992 election, committed to nominating a woman to head the Justice Department. According to the *New York Times*, his short list for the position of attorney general included the names of Judge Patricia Wald, Judge Amalya Kearse, Judge Judith Kaye, and Washington attorney Brooksley Born.[2] The White House was also vetting Reno; Zoë Baird, general counsel of Aetna Life and Casualty Company, who had worked previously at DOJ and the White House; and Judge Kimba Wood. When Clinton settled upon Reno he gained a nominee with experience as a litigator who had served five terms as state attorney for Dade County, Florida. She had been active in the American Bar Association where Pat Wald, among others, had mentored her. As state attorney, Reno had gained respect for a number of policies, including the use of her office to collect child support and her commitment to the creation of the nation's first Drug Court. She did this while handling several very difficult prosecutions as well as the aftermath of the 125,000 Cubans—some criminals and mentally ill—who landed in Florida in the 1980 Mariel boatlift. Still, as Reno was quick to point out, her resume contained no federal government position although she also emphasized her longstanding experience working in partnership with federal law enforcement and immigration agencies.

Reno's first months as United States attorney general may only be described as trial by fire. She took office two weeks after terrorists detonated a truck bomb in the garage area of the World Trade Center's North Tower. Two days later, after a failed attempt by agents of the Bureau of Alcohol, Tobacco, Firearms, and Explosives to search for weapons at a compound near Waco, Texas, owned by the Branch Dravidians, a religious group, the FBI initiated a siege that lasted fifty-one days and ultimately left as many as eighty people dead.

The attorney general described her first days:

> I [met] with Stuart Gersten, who was the acting Attorney General. . . . We met at one point at Blair House [the President's guest house] over issues with respect to Waco and the World Trade Center One bombing. My first attention was given to the World Trade Center. . . . The U.S. Attorney for the Southern District of New York has traditionally had hands-on say as to what course should be taken with respect to investigations in New York. They are very independent and its [sic] been referred to as the "Sovereign District of New York." They put together their team [and briefed me]. Then what I tried to do was have meetings as soon as possible with the Department heads asking them what the major issues were that they faced and to prioritize them. . . . [Also] I was briefed on the issues of encryption with respect to computers and the internet and what we could do. . . . and the concern that applications for electronic intercept surveillance were not being done in a timely fashion. . . . We developed a new, revised process.

In these early days, Reno also experienced the sensitive nature of political transitions. She had agreed with Clinton aide Bernie Nussbaum that the president would make nominations for positions at Justice with Reno retaining veto power, as well as the power to make suggestions. Reno observed that "it took a long time to get people confirmed and the Administration did not foresee some of the difficulties that would be involved." She named Professor Lani Guinier's nomination to be assistant attorney general for civil rights as one "of the big problems we had to face." In April 1993, Clinton nominated Guinier, a University of Pennsylvania professor. A firestorm of opposition ensued when journalists and Republican senators attacked her writings on minority groups' lack of voting power. In June Clinton withdrew the nomination.

When New York authorities were ready to arrest the "blind sheik" in the World Trade Center case, Reno demonstrated her trademark management style:

> Before I gave my approval for his arrest, I called all the relevant people into my conference room and asked everyone to express their thoughts about the prosecution. . . . This was the first time on many occasions when I used the conference room as a briefing place and requested that all the people involved come and brief me. I made a practice of trying to bring together agencies, lawyers, people with different ideas to give me their views and it became a standard practice for the Department. We had a lot of concern with building a good structure to deal with these FISA issues [Foreign Intelligence Surveillance Act].

Reno served as Clinton's attorney general for eight years. In her oral history, she elected not to speak about Waco. However, she was specific about feeling constrained by a report on the FBI accepted by her predecessor:

> I was hampered by the fact that the prior Attorney General had received a report recommending the resignation of the FBI Director and that was a real problem because I had not commissioned the report, the report left something to be desired but it was there and could not be ignored. Much of the focus of what I wanted to do involved the FBI and they were preoccupied by Waco. There were questions that had been raised about leadership at the FBI at the time. I tried to prioritize in terms of danger and risk and focused as much as possible to do everything necessary to

address the issue of the FBI leadership. We began to see the need for the FBI to have a leadership change. From one agent to another and from one office to another.

Reno led the DOJ through the final assault on the Branch Dravidians, the aftermath of the 1995 bombing of the Federal Building in Oklahoma City, the armed seizure of the young Elián González, whose relatives were seeking to keep him from living with his father in Cuba, and the decision to bring a lawsuit against Microsoft. She continued her predecessor's investigation into bias in mortgage lending. Cyber issues also loomed large as a critical issue for DOJ:

> Scott Charney [in the Criminal Division's cyber unit] had the vision, he knew what was necessary if we were going to make cyber resources work for America and he educated me. . . . [H]is unit spent hours educating me as to what was necessary when I went to a foreign country to talk about the need for 24 hour response around the world with all of us working together and taking steps to make sure that we identified the person who is sitting in his kitchen in Russia packing away banks' resources and it was really fascinating to see people try to learn to speak the same language, to try to understand the tools of cyber technology and what an opportunity they present for us.

As attorney general, Reno served an administration marked by controversies and crises, several of which involved the Justice Department. The issue of independent counsels appointed during her tenure was perhaps the most difficult for Reno. The Independent Counsel Act (ICA) established the template of the AG's powers and responsibilities. Reno said that "the Independent Counsel Act was one of the most confusing pieces of legislation that I have seen and I don't think we need it."

Reno's need to deal with the independent counsel issue emerged as the so-called Whitewater investigation unfolded (involving real estate investments made years earlier by Bill and Hillary Clinton and Arkansas associates):

> The pressures were building on President and Mrs. Clinton. [Webb] Hubbell talked with the President [who told] me to go ahead and to

get a Special Counsel so that we could put it behind us. We got the Special Counsel [January 1994]. And I told the President, I said "it's just going to be a problem." We asked Bob Fiske [partner at Davis Polk] to be Special Counsel. That means he reported to me, but he was outside my regular authority. He got into it, handled it with dispatch, resolved many of the Whitewater cases. We were moving ahead when the special division of the court [established by new ICA legislation] came back with a "we will appoint a Special Counsel, but it will be somebody of our own choosing so as not to have a conflict." And we got Ken Starr [former federal judge and former solicitor general]. Ken Starr took on a very broad coverage of the Independent Counsel Act and we've seen what ultimately arose.

Under the new act, while Starr was conducting his investigations, spending millions of dollars, subpoenaing hundreds of thousands of documents, Reno only had the power to remove him, according to her, if Starr "did anything wrong," committed malfeasance of some sort:

> I very seriously considered asking him to resign. One of the problems is that you cannot tell what act was specifically the act that would trigger his resignation. I finally asked for something that would take what Ken Starr had done, match it with what somebody has done in the Criminal Division over time. . . . and tell me what would happen to him. . . . Bill Clinton says in his memoirs that I think he—the way he put it to me—that was one of the things I most regret, asking you to [appoint a Special Counsel].

Independent Financial Agencies

By the Obama years, the monopoly of male power in the federal government had been eroded. One measure of this power shift was the presence of women like Reno, Hills, Brooksley Born, and Hufstedler, who had held cabinet positions, or headed independent agencies. The departments of Defense, Veterans Affairs, and Treasury had yet to be led by a woman, but Trailblazers had made headway at three federal financial agencies other than the Treasury Department—the Commodity Futures Trading Commission, the Federal Deposit Insurance Corporation (FDIC), and the Securities and Exchange Commission (SEC).

In 2006 President George W. Bush appointed Republican Sheila Bair to the Federal Deposit Insurance Corporation. She continued to serve under Barack Obama until her five-year term expired in 2011. Bair was born, raised, and educated in Kansas. After graduating from the University of Kansas Law School, and holding a teaching fellowship for a year, in 1979 Bair, politically ambitious, set out to establish her career:

My first job was with the old Health Education and Welfare counsel's office working for a woman supervisor. For job opportunities for women lawyers, government was the most receptive place. I interviewed at a couple of [Kansas] law firms too, but they didn't seem very interested or supportive of cultivating women attorneys. The HEW general counsel, it was in the regional attorney's office in Kansas City. I worked there for a about a year and a half. I got promoted to Washington. . . . That was a nice job. We enforced Title VI and Title IX and Section 504. We were attached to the Office of Civil Rights.

In 1979, when HEW was split into two cabinet agencies, Bair found herself at the newly created Department of Education doing work that did not interest her. Republicans had just regained control of the Senate. This is when Bair heard from her Kansas family's Republican connections that Senator Bob Dole, now the chair of two important committees, had a vacancy on the Senate Judiciary Committee for a person who had worked on civil rights issues: "This was a real watershed moment in my shift of career paths. I just learned a lot from Dole, and I got the opportunity to work on a lot of high profile issues and meet important people. And it really opened a lot of doors later on. . . . And most importantly it was very rewarding work because we did get the Voting Rights Act extended."

She stayed six years and then moved on, becoming research director for Senator Dole's 1988 presidential campaign and, later still, working at the New York Stock Exchange, "where I learned about capital markets, equity markets." Then, in 1990, at Dole's suggestion, Bair ran for the House of Representatives in a rural Kansas district, the only pro-choice candidate. She lost but was approached in 1990 by President George H. W. Bush to become a member of the Commodity Futures Trading Commission, the government's derivatives regulatory agency. The commission tangled with the giant Enron Corporation, which was lobbying for antifraud exemptions:

In the Clinton Administration it got worse. Mary Shapiro didn't stay long. And then Brooksley [Born] came in, of course, and tried to put some muscle into derivatives oversight and got [over]ruled by Rueben and then Greenspan and Larry Summers. And so the residual authority we kept at least for anti-fraud and anti-manipulation was just completely taken away with that Bill [the Commodity Futures Modernization Act]. . . . And she [Born] was right and they were wrong. . . . We didn't know a damned thing about these derivatives markets. . . . And nobody was watching. And we had bank regulators regulating the dealers but those are the big banks. . . . So it was bad. I stayed about four and a half years. Then I went back to the Stock Exchange [to head the government relations and public affairs department].

Bair came back into the government in 2001 as assistant secretary for financial institutions at the Treasury Department. It was, she said, her segue into financial services, "economic empowerment and access to mainstream financial services . . . and banking services . . . for lower-income folks and traditionally excluded folks." At Treasury, as a member of the Bush administration, she had a say in banking policy but was unsuccessful in reforming mortgage lending standards. And then, in 2006, when the Senate Banking Committee blocked Diana Taylor's nomination to become chair of the FDIC, Bair was approached by the White House, hoping that she would accept the position. Bair assumed office in June 2006, only months before the full-blown subprime mortgage crisis and recession of 2007: "The FDIC had had two women chairs before me. So the agency was used to that, or had experience with that in the past. But the banking sector is still a heavily male sector and the bank regulators and the agencies that oversee banks are still predominantly male. It is a male-dominated environment, still is. And there had been some progress within the executive staff ranks to bring women up. But there, it was still primarily a male-power structure. . . . [T]here was some resistance at the beginning."

Bair asked for a briefing on mortgage lending standards:

When we saw how out of control things were getting, I started pushing for tougher lending standards for banks. . . . [W]e started pushing for mortgage lending standards for subprime mortgages and a whole slew of mortgage bankers came in to see me and tell me how awful that was going to be in early 2007 and that was going to constrict credit and yes, delinquencies and fall rates were going up but that was just because people didn't care about paying their mortgages any more. . . . [W]e focused on the real estate market turning very early on. How it was going to impact banks, how was that going to change risk to the FDIC. . . . Well, I knew we were going to have serious problems. I never thought they would spin out of control as badly as they did. . . . [As I argued for certain regulation] I think it helped being a Republican. It's kind of like Nixon going to China.

Bair loved doing intra-agency FDIC business. She found agency staff very motivated to protect depositors, "main street users of banks." But the interagency process was, she said, "miserable." She believed that the Office of the Comptroller of the Currency (OCC) and the Office of Thrift Supervision at the Treasury Department, and to some extent the Federal Reserve, "tend to view the world through the eyes of the institutions they regulate and not through the eyes of the people who use those institutions and rely on those institutions for credit." She was thrown together with influential economists and public officials, including Ben Bernanke, Larry Summers, Henry Paulson, John Dugan at OCC, and Timothy Geithner, often experiencing pitched battles over "loan restructuring policy and whether to contain subprime lending." Bair argues that she "built up credibility with Hank [Paulson] and Ben [Bernanke] and I think with John Dugan and Tim Geithner, it was just more ideological warfare. It wasn't so much credibility as it was just profoundly different world views. They just didn't agree with my worldview [viewing her as the enemy of the big banks]. They viewed the issues through the prism of big national banks. Big New York banks mainly. And I think Ben and Hank had a broader perspective."

Much of the time Bair had to stand up and fight on her own in these interagency debates. Some observers attributed this to gender. Bair did not deny this may have been one of several factors:

I was the only woman among the major agency heads. I think there was some sense that the FDIC was about small banks and only understood small banks and we should leave the regulation of capital rules for the big banks to the Fed and the OCC. So I think that was part of the reason why our views were discounted as well. . . . But I think we fought our corner pretty well. We always made a difference. Did we always win? No, we almost always ended up with a negotiated compromise but we always made a difference. And I take some pride in that. . . . And the thing about excluding people or discounting views whether it's because of their gender or their background, it's bad. I went to public universities, maybe some people discounted me because I didn't go to an Ivy League school. Or because I ran an agency that's viewed as knowing small banks better than larger banks. Discounting views leads to bad decision-making. You just start to reinforce your own biases.

* * *

Roberta Karmel graduated from NYU Law School, and in 1962 went to work for the Securities and Exchange Commission (SEC) in New York. She had to work her way through the male culture of the SEC but found that regional offices, such as the one in New York where she served, also had particular cultures:

> The government was not especially hiring women. This was before the Civil Rights Act [of 1964]. So nobody had to pretend to be welcoming to women. The SEC was not generally hiring women. But there was some kind of honors program I applied to in New York. And a man who was a deputy to the regional administrator had a mother who was a lawyer, and he decided that the office should hire a few women. So I was admitted into the honors program . . . and when I got there, much to my pleasant surprise, my boss who was a branch chief was a woman. And there were a few of us in the New York regional office. There were not very many anywhere else at the SEC at that time.

By the age of twenty-nine, Karmel was branch chief and had fifty people working for her. She stayed at the SEC for several years, during which time she had three children. Around the office she was called "the pregnant enforcer."

Karmel's hiring experience reflects an oft-told story among her sister-lawyers: the importance, particularly before passage of the 1960s and

1970s civil rights legislation, of interviewing with a man who was attuned to the value of women professionals and, therefore, willing to hire them. Senator Dole provided advice and opportunities for Sheila Bair, as did Texas attorney general John Hill for Elizabeth Lacy, and Jim Thompson for Ilana Rovner. Yet Bair acknowledges that in these earlier days, gender bias often resulted in an "only one girl spot" on government commissions and agencies, leading to the temptation for all the women to compete for that one slot.

Conclusion

A number of Trailblazers consciously set out to establish careers in government. Others hit the hard wall of private firm discrimination and turned to government employment as an early career alternative. Schroeder, fresh out of law school, interviewed with private firms, where it was made clear that there was no interest in hiring women. She was constantly asked if she could type. Schroeder found a welcome at a regional National Labor Relations Board (NLRB) office. The NLRB had a reputation both as one of the best agencies in Washington and as an agency that would hire women. Trailblazer Betty Murphy received friendly advice from a Washington law firm partner to go to the NLRB: "They have the best supervisors in town. . . . Labor law is not the reason. You don't care about labor law but go to the NLRB and you'll learn how to write a brief and you'll learn about government. Both are very important no matter where you live."

Murphy found the NLRB experience was "terrific." Four months after being hired she was arguing her first case at the U.S. court of appeals.

The NLRB of the late 1950s and 1960s hired women lawyers, often forty or fifty a year, but there was discrimination in pay grade and in promotions, with few women getting to be supervisors. Until 1975 no woman had risen above GS-15 status (GS-18 was the highest).

Washington is a political town and, according to Murphy, new hiring usually sorted out at half Democratic and half Republican lawyers. Murphy, a Republican, stayed at the NLRB for eighteen months and then went into private practice. When she returned as NLRB chair in 1975, fifteen years after leaving, she was surprised to find that among her earlier "class" of hires, 90 percent of the Democrats were still there. "They made government a career and the Republicans did not. There was only one Republican . . . who remained." Her young Democratic friends liked the idea of a good pension, and were perhaps, she thought, more idealistic while Republicans were more entrepreneurial.

New agencies also provided an early workplace for Trailblazers. The Equal Employment Opportunity Commission (EEOC), created by the 1964 Civil Rights Act, became operational by 1965. Sonia Pressman Fuentes, a cofounder of the National Organization for Women, fresh from positions at the Labor Department and DOJ, joined the EEOC in its earliest months. In her eight years there, Fuentes educated male superiors about the unfolding issue of sex discrimination at a time when most of them were at the EEOC to fight for the rights of African Americans. She pushed them to commit commission resources to challenge employment practices that were illegal after 1964, such as airlines hiring women only for stewardess positions, and then firing these employees when they reached a certain age. She later wrote the EEOC's lead opinion in the airline stewardesses' case.

In 1969 Patricia King also started her legal career at the EEOC. She had been asked by William Brown, chair of the commission, to be his special assistant. She stayed two years. She attended EEOC industry hearings in New York, where she heard powerful testimony from African American women speaking about racial and sex discrimination at various telephone companies. This experience reinforced the belief of King, an African American woman, "that a black woman needed to be interested in feminism as well as race." During her time at the EEOC, King watched as the first Title VII sex discrimination case, *Phillips v. Martin Marietta Corporation*, reached the Supreme Court. (The company had a policy that mothers with pre–school-aged children could not be hired.) She also viewed the process by which the new agency, in part influenced by Fuentes, began to draft the sex discrimination guidelines that would guide the EEOC's subsequent work. In 1971 the director of the Office of Civil Rights (OCR) at the Department of Health, Education, and Welfare recruited King to the position of deputy director at the OCR.

In her oral history Sonia Fuentes argued the critical importance of congressional legislation in creating greater opportunity for women wanting to work in government positions—the 1963 Equal Pay Act, the

1964 Civil Rights Act, and the Equal Employment Opportunity Act of 1972. Certainly, before the enactment, and enforcement, of these laws women lawyers found few opportunities in government. As antidiscrimination legislation began to have an impact, as more women used the legislation to break down law school quotas, as the public came to see the placement of women in senior positions as acceptable, and desirable, as the background and norms of the men responsible for hiring became less patriarchal, the meaningful presence of women in government became a reality. And in this period, in 1976, James Earl Carter was elected president. In the four years of his presidency, Carter brought several hundred high-ranking woman lawyers into the executive and judicial branches of the U.S. government. In particular, he changed the face of the federal judiciary.

8

"Judge Cookie to You"

Women Lawyers Join the Judiciary

"I hear Carter is looking for women."

After Roberta Karmel heard the rumor at an American Bar Association meeting, she turned to her fellow committee members and said, "Tell him I'm available."

It started as a joke. "But, they asked, 'Are you serious? Would you do that [accept an appointment to the Securities and Exchange Commission]?' I said, 'of course I would do that.' In any event, that's how it all started. That's what put the idea into my head."

Jimmy Carter won the presidency in November 1976. He was, according to Barbara Babcock, very conscious of the political clout of the vastly expanded women's movement. During his campaign Carter promised a concerted effort to consider women and minorities for all governmental positions. Babcock recalls that after his election, in the transition period, Carter established a committee charged with identifying women who were qualified to fill some of the many executive and judicial branch positions at the new president's disposal.[1] Carter intended that merit rather than partisan politics would guide the search for candidates. Babcock later described the aura of these transition teams and how she came to the attention of the White House:

> It was just sort of real and sweet and naïve almost that we're going to find the best women in the country and give them the jobs that they've been denied all these years. Nobody said, "well, how do you define 'best'?" and "what are you talking about?" He set up these transition committees and these women that I didn't even know, but they knew my name and had used my book. . . . Some of them knew my students, so I kept getting recommended. It was like that. It wasn't knowing anybody important. It really was the women's movement and Carter, his sincerity.

Babcock was not a wealthy contributor to Carter's political party, and ten years before had participated in a protest march on the Pentagon. She did, however, have stellar credentials as a feminist educator concerned with social and criminal justice as well as an earlier reputation as one of Washington's best trial lawyers. And so she was called to Washington, and interviewed for "lofty legal positions, some of them never before held by women."[2] The administration selected her to become the assistant attorney general of the Civil Division in the Department of Justice, the division established in 1868 to handle claims against the government. In March 1977 she was sworn in to hold the position previously held by Carla Hills.

Babcock's selection, and that of Pat Wald as the DOJ's assistant attorney general for legislative affairs, reflected the new power of women. Babcock also became the agent of that power when Carter's attorney general, Griffin Bell, requested that she take responsibility at the DOJ for carrying out Carter's commitment to increasing the number of women on the federal bench:[3]

> Democrats had been out of office for years, and because the legal profession had until recently been overwhelmingly male, there was a long line of qualified men who had worked hard for the party, each of whose life's ambition was to be a federal judge. To elevate a woman, often younger and with less party service and professional experience, would mean thwarting one of these identifiable, faithful, and deserving men.
>
> Largely because of discrimination, women's resumes did not look like those of the men who typically were chosen. Persuasively setting out women candidates' experience to show that they were qualified was a big part of my role. I met with support groups and politicians and candidates, and had many conversations with Margaret McKenna who was in the White House counsel's office.[4]

Margaret McKenna was the first woman to hold the position of deputy White House counsel. She was thirty-two years old and had, according to political scientist Sally Kenney, made diversifying the judiciary one of the top priorities of her time at the White House.[5] She was supported in this work by her boss, White House counsel Robert Lipshutz. To back up Carter's commitment to a diversified judiciary, McKenna worked closely with a network of women's groups that, in turn, made effective use of the media. Together, they persuaded the newly created circuit nominating commissions, as well as U.S. senators forwarding names for federal district court nominations, to include women.

Many of the Trailblazers who joined the bench during the Carter administration spoke of the president as the patron saint of equal opportunity. When he took office five women out of nearly four hundred federal trial judges sat on the federal district court bench, while only one woman and ninety-seven men served on the federal courts of appeal. As the White House prepared to nominate a large number of women, McKenna and Lipshutz expected contention. They were not disappointed. Kenney, however, observed that "the combination of tenacious insiders linked to well-organized outsiders" fashioned a political climate necessary to successfully push Carter's policy.[6] This was aided by passage of the Omnibus Judgeship Act of 1978, which created an environment of abundance. The new law, which established an additional 117 district court and thirty-five circuit court judgeships, greatly helped the White House and the Senate Judiciary Committee in their horse trading. Women and minority nominees were balanced in the confirmation process by white male candidates.

Carter's plan to change the face of the federal judiciary also gained a firmer footing when the American Bar Association's Standing Committee on the Federal Judiciary adopted "new experience" criteria to use in its evaluation of judicial nominees.[7] Brooksley Born was the first woman member of this ABA committee. Born has written that both Carter and his attorney general, Griffin Bell, held meetings with members of the Standing Committee on the Federal Judiciary during which they stressed the importance of diversifying the federal bench by appointing women judges and judges of color. The ABA responded positively. Born has concluded that "after the committee adopted these changes, the committee played a constructive role in the diversification of the bench."[8]

The Selection Process

Stephanie Seymour graduated from Harvard Law School in 1965. She began her career at Goodwin, Proctor and Hoar, an old-line Boston firm. Harvard had prepared her, she said, to be "very comfortable spending my entire day with all males." For the next decade she worked at several firms, lived in Singapore, and in 1975 made partner at the Tulsa firm of Doerner, Stuart, Saunder, Daniel and Langenkamp. She was the first female law partner in the city of Tulsa; her practice, defense oriented, focused on federal law and federal courts.

The Omnibus Judgeship Act created a new position in the Tenth Circuit, designated for Oklahoma. Seymour had always loved writing and liked the legal issues in the cases that she handled. She thought that becoming a U.S. court of appeals judge for the Tenth Circuit would be interesting, although she admitted to not having "any idea about the quantity of workload or anything else for that matter. I knew I would, if I got the job, would be the only woman on the Court of eight judges." The court sits in six states, and the judges come from the various states in the circuit, which are Oklahoma, Colorado, Utah, Kansas, New Mexico, and Wyoming:

> One [other woman,] Alma Wilson, who was a state trial judge applied. So there were two of us and they [the nominating commission] had a total of thirty-five applications. And I heard this story afterwards. Apparently the chairman, Mr. Pense, I'll never forget him—he was a 70-year old trial lawyer from Wyoming and he came to my interview in his cowboy boots . . . changed the procedure for the Oklahoma position. At the first meeting he called, he said, "We have thirty-five applications and we need to reduce the number so let's go around the table and everybody throw out somebody who's obviously not qualified." And he started with me and threw my name out. Josie Heath, who was not a lawyer, a lay person from Denver, said subsequently that she was sitting halfway around the table and she was stunned. She said, "Why are you throwing her name out? She's pretty well qualified, it seems to me." And he said, "No, she's not. She's got four children and couldn't possibly handle the job." Then she was really stunned and didn't know what to say. So it was going around the table and it got to her. Fortunately, for me, she gathered her wits and threw out Pat Irwin, who was then a sitting justice on the Oklahoma Supreme Court, who turned out to be Mr. Pense's favorite candidate. Mr. Pense was horrified and said, "He's clearly qualified. Why are you throwing him out?" And she said, "Because he has five children and couldn't possibly handle the job." They

then had a discussion about whether the number of children should be a disqualifying factor, decided maybe it shouldn't be, threw both of our names back in the pot, and we were both on the list of four that they ultimately proposed.

Seymour's selection occurred only after political maneuvers on the part of all four candidates. As the sole woman on the short list, Seymour drew upon the influence of her work network as well as women in Washington, D.C.:

> There had only been two women ever in the history of the U.S. appointed to a federal court of appeals. FDR had appointed [Florence Allen] and Johnson had appointed Shirley Hufstedler. . . . So all the women's groups in Washington were lobbying for me to get it. Dobie Langenkamp, who was my partner at Doerner, Stuart had left and gone to work for the Carter administration in the Department of Energy, and he was in D.C. He was a friend and he had a contact in the Carter Administration. So Dobie did some work for me. And when I went back to D.C. to do my own lobbying, he hooked me up with a woman, who was a friend of some aide of Roselyn Carter. She worked at the White House and I got an interview with her [the aide]. . . . I got nominated, I'm sure, because the President was looking for more women. . . . I've heard that Roselyn was a big force in this whole process. . . . and women in the Justice Department. I [had a] call from one of the women, my contact in the Justice Department, who said that they had gotten a call from the ABA which was proposing to rate me unqualified for insufficient trial experience. And she said because the ABA had taken so long, the Justice Department had done their own background check, and the Attorney General thought I was exceptionally qualified, and they were not going to withdraw my name. They were going to ask the ABA to appoint somebody else . . . and to do a recheck. . . . My name was sent to the Senate.

In fact, the ABA did find her qualified, a status she took to her confirmation hearing. Seymour recalls that her confirmation hearing was not at all combative and that, in fact, deference was paid to each nominee. In her case, Senator Robert Dole asked some questions. He was married to Liddy Hanford Dole, who had been Seymour's law school classmate.

Mrs. Dole "sent him over to be nice to me, which he was." Seymour was sworn in on November 16, 1979, at the age of thirty-nine.

* * *

In 1986, ready for a career change, California trial lawyer Fern Smith drew upon the advice and connections of a male colleague and, later, women's groups, to make the move to the bench:

> There just really wasn't anything that excited me any longer. And so I went to talk to Dan Weinstein, before whom I had tried my last big case. . . . He said he thought I belonged on the Bench rather than in practice. And we talked about the fact that I had never thought of it before, in part because I really am a very apolitical person, and I had never been involved in politics. I had always assumed that is what it took to get on the Bench. I didn't think I had any connections, etc. So he said that he would make a few phone calls.

Weinstein knew then-governor George Deukmejian's appointments secretary, Marvin Baxter. Weinstein knew that downtown lawyers were getting "restless" with the governor's repeated appointment of prosecutors who, Smith said, while "often very bright, know tiddlywinks about discovery and other issues having to do with civil trials." This, along with her gender, gave Smith an opening. In 1986 she won appointment to the California Superior Court after receiving the support of the Queen's Bench Bar Association and the California Women Lawyers.

After less than two years on the superior court bench, Smith became a fast-track candidate, spoken about for a position on both a federal district court, and the California Courts of Appeal. Pete Wilson, the state's junior U.S. senator, came forward first. He was looking for women to nominate to the federal bench. His staff asked if Smith would send in an application. She did, again drawing upon the recommendations of the Queen's Bench, California Women Lawyers, and a number of "good friends who were Democrats." Wilson recommended her to President Reagan, who sent her name to the Senate. Once senior U.S. senator Alan Cranston agreed not to oppose her, Smith sailed through the Judiciary Committee hearing: "I was picking a jury for a criminal case, and the phone rang in the court room [which my courtroom deputy answered].

I wasn't paying much attention, and all of a sudden she turned around and looked at me, and she had turned just white. I said, 'What's the matter?' And she pointed to the phone and mouthed, 'It's the White House.' It was President Reagan . . . I thought it was very sweet that he called personally and really quite touching and thrilling."

Smith joined the federal bench in September 1988.

* * *

Law professor Rosalie Wahl joined the Minnesota Supreme Court in 1977. In many states, the women's movement was also having significant impact on the local selection of officials, making it nearly impossible for politicians to ignore the absence of women judges on state courts:

I think there wouldn't have been any women on the court if it hadn't been that the women here in Minnesota became very politically active. This was the end of the '60s and the beginning of the '70s—the women's movement was really gearing up. That's when the Women's Political Caucus was founded. That's when the DFL Feminist Caucus, a Democratic Farmer Labor, and the IR Republican Caucus and Feminist Caucus [started]. . . . I can remember being at the annual DFL Feminist Caucus meeting, in February, 1977, when Governor Rudy Perpich came to speak. . . . Governor Perpich said "when there's an opening on the Minnesota Supreme Court I will appoint a woman." Well, there he said it. This was in February, and this was the year that the U.S. Congress was going to create new federal judges, and Minnesota was going to get two. So we thought, this would be it. Walter Mondale was the Vice President and his old law partner Harry MacLaughlin was on the Minnesota Supreme Court. We knew he was going to get appointed to a federal district judgeship and when that happened there'd be an opening. . . . And there was the opening. Within three days, Gwen Jones, who was a reporter with the *Minneapolis Tribune* wrote up a story reminding Rudy of his promise. Nailing him to the wall. . . . [T]here were 18 candidates by the time we got down to the wire . . . and the women lawyers were very active in it. They had a process to interview people. . . . The women lawyers submitted a list. The DFL Feminist Caucus submitted a list of candidates that they felt were good. And the Women's Political Caucus submitted a list. And I was on each of those lists which didn't hurt.

In June 1977, Governor Perpich called Wahl to his office. He was interviewing short-list candidates. The governor asked Wahl two questions, her position on the death penalty and where she stood on *Roe v. Wade*. Then they conversed with counsel and advisers. The next evening Perpich announced Wahl as his nominee. She heard the news while attending a statewide meeting of several thousand women:

> The auditorium just went wild. . . . And then I got to make a little speech. [I said] there never would have been a woman appointed if it hadn't been that the DFL women were politically active. Anybody who thinks they get where they are by their own efforts alone is just wrong. . . . I was remembering some of our famous foremothers. I was remembering Sojourner Truth who said, "ain't I a woman." And I said, "Ain't we women? Ain't we women enough to make the equal rights amendment the law of the land." The women just fell out of their chairs. Even the pro-lifers who were there forgot and stood up. It was amazing. . . . On the third of October [1977] I was sworn in as a member of the Minnesota Supreme Court.

In 1977 Wahl succeeded. Three years earlier, in Alabama, law professor Janie Shore ran successfully for the state supreme court. Her victory came the old-fashioned way, without the full force of the women's movement.

Shore made the decision to run "believing I had as much of a chance as anybody, cause we hadn't had real elections for judges in forever." She was an Alabama native, had taught a generation of lawyers, and had lawyer buddies all over the state who had used her famous law school notes. Shore's desire to become a judge occurred several years before Carter and the women's movement influenced changes in judicial selection. Her campaign for the position was not unlike those run by generations of local male attorneys:

> My friend, Annette Dodd, [campaigned with me]. You know, we had no money at all, couldn't think of television ads, that's way too expensive. But we got all over the state's editorial boards of the newspapers, and we'd stop at every radio station, see the radio towers and we'd just go in and see them. [Laugh] It's amazing! They most always, you know, play records and talk to you and interview you and welcome you to town. . . . just

fun.... So, my campaign consisted largely of lawyer endorsements, editorial endorsements, and radio. Then I found that you could get people to cut tapes for you, and send the tapes to the radio station, and they'd play them for you.... So you get quite a lot of mileage off a long trip to a little town.... I spent $34,000 total. (People spend millions now.)

* * *

The women's movement–meets–Jimmy Carter–moment unquestionably created the previously absent opportunity for women lawyers to trade in two-piece suits for judicial robes. Ninth Circuit Court of Appeals judge Dorothy Nelson, previously the first woman dean at the University of Southern California Law School, described the development of her career:

Every U.S. President who came in who was looking for a woman to appoint to commissions.... I got appointed to all these Presidential commissions. [I also received] national exposure as Chairman of the Board of the American Judicature Society (AJS).... When President Carter ran for office against Ford, as Chairman of the American Judicature Society, I wrote them both and said, "If you are elected, will you adopt a merit system for selecting federal judges?" And some staff member wrote back, "Of course we will." But I was very, very amazed when Griffin Bell who was appointed Attorney General ... called me up, said, "Okay, Dorothy, bring back your team and we're going to set up a system of merit selection for federal Court of Appeals judges." And President Carter came in and said, "I want these commissions to seek out qualified women and minorities" ... and we [AJS] set up 12 commissions around the country.

Then I got a call [from the chairman of the commission in the West] who said, "We want to put you on the list." And I said, "No. I'm just about to retire as Dean. I think I want to do something else." I went home and my husband said, "You've been criticizing judges all your life, why don't you see what it is like to be one." So I let my name go on the list and ultimately got appointed. But that was because I had all these other national contacts.... I was neither Republican nor a Democrat. I've always been an Independent because as a Bahai, we don't belong to political parties. So that's sort-of how I got to be a judge. I would never get through today. I mean there wouldn't be a chance of The Teahouse in the August Moon of my getting through today.

For Nelson, becoming a federal judge in December of 1979 mirrored what had occurred when she was selected as USC's first woman dean: "I was in the right place at the right time." Jodi Bernstein echoed this conclusion, saying that she, Pat Wald, and others were "wonderfully positioned for the Carter Administration." Many other women judges of Nelson's generation, including Ruth Bader Ginsburg, have also said that they were "fortunate to be born at the right time, and to be at the right place."

So, there was agreement that it was time to bring women into high government positions. The choice of *which* woman often fell to a male elective official with input coming from various quarters. Several women said that it had taken quite a bit of politicking on their part to obtain a nomination. They also pointed to problems that sometimes arose for local women's groups when more than one woman was tapped for the same short list. In 1983, New York governor Mario Cuomo, making good on a campaign promise, announced that he would appoint the first woman to serve on the New York State Court of Appeals. He asked for names and received several, including those of state appellate division judge Betty Weinberg Ellerin and Olwine, Connelly partner and commercial litigator Judith Kaye. In a very public and contentious campaign for the position, women supporters were pitted against one another, with the New York Women's Bar Association, of which Ellerin had been a leader, judging Kaye "not qualified." Cuomo ultimately selected Kaye, who went on to serve with distinction, rising, in 1993, to become the first woman chief judge of the court.[9]

Settling In, Learning the Job

Being a newbie judge, state or federal, presented challenging early-days experiences. After Governor Jerry Brown appointed Trailblazer Joan Klein to the California Courts of Appeal, First Division, Klein experienced a bench that "was entrenched with three male judges who weren't very welcoming." Across the country, the nature of the welcome in local and federal courts varied, following no particular pattern. Some older, traditional male judges mentored new female colleagues while others provoked the women, doing their utmost to undermine their professional confidence. Everywhere, however, civil rights employment legislation, the women's movement, and the example of the Carter administration made their mark.

The lack of orientation sessions for a particular court, formal judicial education seminars, or methods of collegial coordination surfaced repeatedly as problems mentioned by these new women judges. In 1992 Catherine Kimball moved from her position as Louisiana district court judge to that of state supreme court judge. She had hoped for and expected support from her new appeals bench colleagues. It was an elective position, and she was the first woman to obtain it in the history of the court:

> I guess one of the first things that surprised me a bit and frustrated me a bit was when I asked a question, how do you do this, or how do you set up the office to do this, or whatever. Almost at every turn, I was told you do it however you want. . . . [T]here really was no plan for the way that you came into the process. You just did what you thought you needed to do and there was really no guidance. No training at all . . . I don't mean that the justices were not helpful because they were.

In 1979 Carolyn Dineen King, a Carter appointee, moved from her position as a corporate lawyer in Houston to a seat on the U.S. Court of Appeals for the Fifth Circuit. She provided an achingly honest appraisal of the journey:

> I knew that if I became a judge I would have to start all over again. I had no background for being a judge, and so why would I want to go from being a happy 40-year old, doing something I really knew how to do and do well, clients who loved me, to a place where I had no idea how to do it?
>
> It was quite a transition, very, very difficult. . . . So I decided that if you're just going to be starting from scratch in this job, you need a mentor—or two. I spent six months watching these judges, trying to figure out who there was in the crowd that was really good and who would be a good mentor, and I zeroed in on Judge [Alvin] Rubin. So I asked him to help me and the teacher in him just came to the fore. . . . But I think it's an uncommon experience for a judge to say "I need a mentor" like I needed when I started practicing law. . . . In the beginning, I really got far behind. It took me so long to do things because I didn't have any background in

most of the law that came before me. We had very little by way of a securities docket, so the one area of law that I knew something about we had
very little of. I had to get a good grasp of maritime law and all kinds—
constitutional law, which I hadn't had since I was in law school and which
in any event had made major turns since I was in law school. . . . I actually . . . went out to the University of Houston and sat in on a course on
federal jurisdiction for six months.

At the Oregon Court of Appeals, Betty Roberts depended on her law
clerk to teach her about procedures because there wasn't an orientation. When Peggy Quince left a position at the Florida attorney general's
office for the Second District Court of Appeal in 1994, she brought a
background as an appellate practitioner. It took her time to feel comfortable calling her fellow judges by their first names. She had argued
before them and now they were colleagues. Quince was, proudly, the
first African American woman on that court and found herself in good
relationships with the other members.

Bernice Donald left her federal bankruptcy judgeship in 1995 for a
seat on the U.S. District Court for the Western District of Tennessee:

> When I came to the District Court, I was basically left to fend for my-
> self. . . . [T]he Chief Judge was not as embracing. . . . She was nice,
> friendly, but not very helpful. . . . [M]aybe it's because I had already been
> a criminal court judge. But, I mean, my first week on the federal court, I
> was actually sentencing people. And, remember, I had been on the Bank-
> ruptcy court seven and a half years so I hadn't sentenced anybody in a
> very long time, but even when I had, I was not using guidelines. I got
> all these tapes from the Federal Judicial [Center] on sentencing. . . . I
> would sit home at night and put those tapes in [the VCR] and that's how
> I learned to do the sentencing.

And then there was the experience of a new type of workload.

Despite grueling hours in previous jobs, many women raised the
issue of workload as well as the lack of orientation. Catherine Kimball
said, "Oh my God, the volume. I remember there were probably 2500 to
3500 pages per week that I was expected to read. . . . My husband wasn't
totally overjoyed by any stretch of the imagination that every time I was

home, I was still working. But it truly is a seven day a week job because of the volume of work that exists at that court."

Elizabeth Lacy had a parallel experience starting out on the Virginia Supreme Court:

> You start off with 30 cases on the writ panels, and 45 cases on oral argument, five opinions [to write in a session—seven weeks], and over 60 cases with staff attorneys that we do just in a non-oral thing, and you do all that in seven weeks. As a new judge there were so many unwritten rules that I didn't know. And while I had a broad experience, I hadn't done a personal injury case for years, or issues of sovereign immunity. I mean, it's the last of the general practices, and I had to really, really spend time catching up on where the Court was on so many issues—such as worker's compensation. It was very, very challenging. I didn't know things. The first time I wrote an opinion, I had been assigned to write the opinion, but I really was in the minority, I didn't know you could trade off your opinions, so I wrote the majority opinion, and then wrote my dissent. When we got back together for conference, I said, "Somebody is going to have to sign this." And they all said, "Didn't you know, you just trade?" I'm like, nobody told me! And it wasn't like they didn't want to tell me. It's that there were things they just didn't think of, or would think I would know. I didn't know, for example, that it just took one Justice to grant the petition for appeal.

Fern Smith was asked what aspects of beginning her job as a federal district court judge surprised her: "It's hard work to be, I think to try to be a good judge. I was surprised really at how much power a judge has. I mean, you know it theoretically, but when you are the one that's got it, it's a surprise. I was surprised at how much, at least the appearance of respect you get from the lawyers. Whether they really mean it or not is of course a whole other story. I was surprised at how terrible some lawyers really are."

Trial versus Appellate

Are there two jobs more different than those of the trial versus the appellate judge? That was a question that confronted and, in some instances, confounded Trailblazers, as judicial career opportunities presented themselves. It was, in Shakespearean terms, a "to be, or not to be" dilemma: to be in the thick of matters in a courtroom, or to be isolated, alone with a pen in chambers. Or so it appeared to many women when career advancement decisions had to be made.

Corporate lawyer Carolyn Dineen King had her U.S. court of appeals investiture ceremony and then,

> You take your place in your chambers, and it's as silent as a tomb. The phone never rings, nobody ever comes to see you, and it's the exact opposite—180 degrees—from the kind of practice that I had had, which was filled with people and problems and opportunities and all kinds of human interaction. An appellate judge lives essentially in a very cloistered environment, and I found that excruciating. I remember one day coming into this office [in my first days here] and about 2:00 in the afternoon the phone hadn't rung all day, and I just burst into tears, just miserable. But, here I was and I had to learn how to do it.

Judge Betty Ellerin, a self-described "people person," moved from a New York trial court to the appellate division. She had not applied to make the move before being approached by the state's chief judge, because she had thought that "it would be very monastic, very isolating":

> Absolutely not true. I loved every minute of it. Part of it being, we sit in benches of five. That means I have to convince at least two other people I'm right on a case in order for my position to prevail and that is in and of itself, in a sense, an art and a constant struggle. When I first came on, there were several I was able to convince frequently on women's issues. . . . I have always felt, as the only woman here for a long time and the first, I had an obligation to sensitize them to some of the realities of what it is to be a woman in the work force.

Betty Fletcher said that before joining the Ninth Circuit appeals court, she had "this naïve notion it was going to be a job which would be quite contemplative, time to think about policies, a lot of time to kind of take a step back and take a look at the law. Of course, it turned out that wasn't the case at all."

Appeals court judges enjoy thinking through and writing opinions. And many women appeals court judges, like Ellerin, loved the job of persuading bench colleagues to vote with them.

Ann Covington, who sat on the Missouri Court of Appeals and then the Missouri Supreme Court, considered personality to be an important variable, distinguishing those who like trial work from those who thrive in the appeals setting, where confidentiality is required and writing is a largely solitary activity:

> [Appeals] is very isolating. Fortunately, however, it sort of fits my personality. The persons for whom I hurt a little are those who love the rough and tumble and who are nourished by lots of daily interaction with other people. I'm more of an introvert and love reading, thinking, and writing and would be delighted, as I laughingly say, to sit in a corner. . . . [I]t is isolating, and most of all because one has to be much more careful with one's friends who are lawyers. . . . How often can we go to lunch without looking inappropriate. Obviously, one can't discuss work with anybody. Even my husband Joe, as we talked . . . [was] a bit affronted that I would not go into great detail when he knew of cases from reading of them in the paper.

District court judge Fern Smith knew herself to be one of those nourished by daily interaction with people:

> I liked the give and take of the lawyers and the Court and I liked dealing with juries and I liked looking the parties in the eye and I loved sitting in the court room and watching all of this. I love the theatre and I love movies. And the court room to me frankly has always seemed like a magnificent human drama most of the time, not always a patent case, but you know, especially in the two court rooms I was in [early in my career], in the Juvenile Court and the Hall of Justice. I mean, it was like watching "Law and Order" eight hours a day.

Courtroom Persona

No doubt about it, humor helped these women. In 1972 Ruth Burg became the first woman judge to serve on the Armed Services Board of Contract Appeals. At the beginning of each case she was in the habit of giving "a little spiel." One day, early in her tenure on the board, Burg arrived, started her talk, and, quite suddenly, went off the record:

> I heard this voice asking "who's that dame sitting up there?" From the expressions on the faces of everyone in the room, especially of the attorney, I could tell it was the contractor who was appearing before me who asked this. The expression on his attorney's face was a sight to behold. Nobody knew how I was going to react because, of course, I was an unknown. I couldn't help it but I broke up laughing and I said "that dame is the one who is going to decide your case for you." Whereupon everyone decided to laugh. The tension was broken and we went on from there.

As an attorney in Oregon, Trailblazer Katherine O'Neil drew upon the "sage and humorous advice" offered by Judge Kim Frankel, who counseled local women lawyers about how to deal with sexist remarks. Frankel encouraged the women to consider whether responding would make any difference and to carefully evaluate the power equation represented by the situation. Frankel favored sober reflection, but she, like Ruth Burg, appreciated the balancing power of humor. O'Neil once heard Judge Frankel relate a story about the sentencing of a male defendant: When the judge finished pronouncing sentence, this defendant turned to her and said, "Okay, cookie, but I'll be out." And the woman responded, "That's Judge Cookie to you."

Sisterhood

These judges did not flinch in applying humor where it could serve the purposes of justice and courtroom dignity. It is difficult to imagine juggling gender discrimination, steep on-the-job learning curves, professional and community activities, domestic obligations, along with day-to-day courtroom demands without more than a little laughter, and, for many, sisterhood.

Norma Shapiro was a "Carter" judge, the first woman to serve in the Third Circuit. She joined the trial court in 1978. As the sole woman she found herself "lonely." Her male colleagues were courteous, but she was an unknown quantity, and while one or two of the judges reached out to help her, by and large she was left on her own:

> It was like throwing a child into a swimming pool and saying, "Learn to swim, or you'll drown." . . . That was why a year after I became a judge I participated in the founding of the National Association of Women Judges. . . . [in] '79, I guess . . . [with] Sandra Day O'Connor and Joan Dempsy Kline and others. . . . The first year I felt a little too unsure of myself. By the second year, I was really ready. They had an organization, and I spoke to the other judges on my court, and I said, "I'm all alone here, and it's lonely, and you're very nice, but I'd like to talk to other women about problems we have in common." And they were very understanding. They said, "It would be nice if you didn't need it, but it's like the NAACP." And so I've become very active in the NAWJ. . . . We started the first study of gender bias in the courtroom; not just against women judges, but women witnesses and parties. We got some academics to do research on verdicts against women. . . . In recent years the meetings had much more of an educational component than this kind of advocacy. . . . And we've had a genome project, we've had a project on how to address drug sentencing, how to address female sentencing.

Shapiro was also one of several judges who described how changes in law, politics, and culture affected her docket and her courtroom:

> When I first became a judge, we had a tremendous number of FELA [Federal Employers Liability Act] cases. . . . There were also many more admiralty cases than there are now. And when I became a judge, I hadn't had admiralty in law school; I barely knew a ship from a boat, and the first time I was asked to arrest a ship, I went running to one of the other judges and asked, "How do you arrest a ship!?" [You sign the papers.] . . . Now, in the criminal cases, so many are drug cases, so that's changed. Most of the cases are guilty pleas, except certain white collar crimes. White collar criminals never can admit they did anything wrong. And they're the ones that you get to try. . . . The constitutional law cases are always more fun, and we're seeing them a lot more. . . . Section 1983 cases [a federal statute enabling individuals to file a writ concerning rights] and

Title VII cases. I just tried two cases under the Family Medical Leave Act, and age discrimination in employment. So we're getting discrimination cases based on age, gender, some race, but not much. People seemed to have learned that's a no-no. But the gender cases are troubling, because defendants don't take them seriously; they think it's sort of funny that a woman claims discrimination, or that she should accept a certain rough-housing in her employment as a matter of course.

The lawyers that appear before us are, in general, very good. Particularly the lawyers who get pro bono assignments. I'm always amazed by how they put their heart and soul into that representation.

Judging in State and Federal Court: A Profile

In Florida, former Catholic nun and teacher Rosemary Barkett looked at the law through the lens of serving as a state and, later, federal judge. In 1979 Florida governor Bob Graham appointed her to the West Palm Beach Fifteenth Judicial Circuit. As a circuit court judge, she heard everything—felony criminal cases, civil matters in controversies over (then) five thousand dollars, divorces, custody disputes, probate, and contested wills. She "totally loved it."

> I loved actually thinking about the law. I loved the ability to apply the law—to decide. But ultimately, I loved seeing the system from the inside. I mean, for an immigrant to see that police officers actually did have to ask permission before they could forcibly enter someone's home and be required to justify asking. It was terrific. I mean, it made everything real. All of the altruistic things that you used to think about this country and freedom and due process were real and you could see those protections being actually employed. I mean, if you were the duty judge, state attorneys would call you at 3:00 in the morning to apply for an emergency warrant. It had to be justified. . . . [I]t was just remarkable that there was a country where really and truly the government had to justify themselves to somebody and you were part of that system and helped to make it work.
>
> Things seem a lot different now [2006]. Partly because of the Patriot Act, but it's more than just one piece of legislation. It's the erosion of the

Fourth Amendment [search and seizure], everybody accommodating. People don't see the long term consequences of eroding those kinds of principles. If people saw them I think they would be more cautious. . . . [T]he beginning of a shift was occurring before [the attacks on 9/11]. . . . [M]any difficult choices will have to be made to balance civil liberties with security concerns.

Barkett went from the trial court to the state district courts of appeal, which she also loved:

I loved being able to have time to reflect on the law—to trace precedent—to decide which direction a strand of law should go next. It was terrific. On a personal level, I felt like it was a vacation because you have control of your life and you know for a lawyer that's so huge. . . . Although I think I worked harder, you could work on your own schedule half the time. Other than oral argument, you could work at night or at five in the morning, which would give you the middle of the day if you needed to go running at lunch or whatever.

An opening on the state supreme court prompted another move for Barkett, and the opportunity to write the opinion, in 1990, for the court in "*In Re Browning*: [The decision] assured an individual's right to control their own destiny when it comes to deciding whether to terminate life support systems, if it is clear that there is no chance that they are going to survive with any kind of quality of life. We held that people have the right to make these decisions ahead of time, and convey those decisions for others to implement that will assure that their wishes will be carried out. I thought that was a very important decision."

In 1993 President Bill Clinton nominated Barkett for the Eleventh Circuit Court of Appeals. She was confirmed in the spring of 1994 despite a heated challenge in the Senate from conservatives. The nominating process "opened" her eyes, and she realized it had nothing to do with ascertaining whether or not the nominee is competent and able to perform the job of a circuit judge. Rather, she felt it had become a political opportunity to "get" the president who nominated the candidate.

Federal Court: A Profile

In 1978 Senator Edward Kennedy appointed a nominating committee through which Rya Zobel, a partner at Goodwin Proctor, found her way to the federal district court. Unlike Barkett, fifteen years later, Zobel did not experience a contentious selection process. Kennedy had made it clear at the start of the search that he favored at least two women for the four vacancies. Ruth Abrams, a long-time and much-respected state judge, had taken herself out of the running. In addition, Zobel believed that "there were not that many women who were in the running, really in the running, because there were so few of my generation, you know, it couldn't be a 20 year old." She was quickly confirmed after President Carter sent her name to the Senate Judiciary Committee, which Kennedy chaired. It was, Zobel said, "A very short process. . . . In those days [the process] had not yet become politicized, fortunately for us."

Zobel brought a "fairly brisk and decisive" style to her courtroom. She, too, was not opposed to employing humor in order to run a good trial. She once used a three-foot-long gavel, placed strategically before her, to corral warring patent attorneys who were trying the patience of the jury. And she voiced strong ideas on the qualities of a *good* litigator. She offered Boston lawyer Bill Lee as a model:

> [He] would come into the first conference in a case and he knows more about the plaintiff's case, usually he's on the defense, than the plaintiff does. He is able to provide a roadmap for the judge as to how we should deal with the case. He gains unbelievable advantage doing that, of course. But it's very helpful to me and he is able to cut options. One of the things that is so difficult is that plaintiffs come in with 20 causes of action, particularly in Civil Rights Act cases. You know, you get the state claims, the statutory claims, the Federal claims, and they don't want to get rid of any of it. Well, then you do the discovery first, but even then it's hard for them to give up any claim. And yet, as I try to explain to them, "How are you going to explain this to the jury? How do you expect me to explain to the jury the fine nuances between all of these different claims?" They never thought about that. They come in with huge amounts of dollars in their mind and then when you really talk to them about what really happened, it's a $10,000 case. But they are talking about taking five depositions. I

said, "How can you afford to do that?" So it's that kind of not thinking through that makes a not very good lawyer. Somebody who can't see the other side is not a particularly good lawyer. . . . And in the context of a trial or a motion, I think economy is terrific, and knowing, and being focused and getting there without meandering off into too many side issues, and presenting your case in a chop-chop way so that the jury, and persuasively all the time, so that the jury can really follow along with you. You have to be a teacher. You have to get good experts who are also good teachers and are not arrogant. Those are all qualities that a good lawyer will bring to the case. . . . It's a very difficult job, I think.

Gender Bias in the Courts: Educating Judges, Prosecutors, and Staff

Throughout these narratives the judges' concern over preparation for the job and the presence of gender discrimination in the courthouse emerged as issues. Over a period of decades, different aspects of these problems have been taken up by organizations including the Federal Judicial Center, the National Judicial College, the National Center for State Courts, and the State Justice Institute. But in the early 1970s, the question of gender bias *in the courts* did not command institutional attention. Most male judges and prosecutors did not make the connection between the ideas (and charges) of the women's movement, and the culture of the courtroom. The specific discussion of gender bias on the part of judges, prosecutors, and justice system professionals did not take form until the late 1970s when a new, unique project—the National Judicial Education Program to Promote Equality for Women and Men in the Courts (NJEP)—took shape. Trailblazer Lynn Schafran belonged to the group of women, including members of the National Association of Women Judges, who gave definition to NJEP (later a project of the organization Legal Momentum). Since the project's inception Schafran has worn two hats, slicing away at gender bias through NJEP education, and briefing and arguing sex discrimination cases as a Legal Momentum senior staff attorney. She describes the birth of the project: "NJEP was born at the same time that NOW Legal Defense and Education Fund was born. The lawyers on the original board were trying the very first Title VII cases that related to sex discrimination, and they were finding that the judges either didn't understand certain behaviors to be discriminatory, or else thought that they were not only not discriminatory but actually favored women."

Schafran relates how, in handling a particular Title VII employment discrimination case, NOW lawyer Sylvia Roberts realized "that there was no point in having Title VII if it was going to be a situation where every time a judge had to make a decision, he (and in those days they were almost all 'he's') would be mired in his own preconceptions about what women can and cannot, should and should not do, and the whole judicial legislative effort would have been for naught."

Schafran joined NJEP's staff as director in 1981, working with Norma Wikler, a University of California gender issues expert. Wikler urged the organization of a program in which the first step was the collection of information: "You could not go to a state and talk about this problem [gender bias] unless you had local information." The inquiry was wide open: Did gender make a difference in how women were treated as witnesses, victims, parties, or lawyers? How did gender affect judges' view of the economic consequences of divorce, or the death of an unpaid homemaker? How did judges understand and implement the rape shield laws? What did judges, lawyers, and courtroom employees consider acceptable humor? How did local bar associations treat women lawyers? What did lawyers and judges know about domestic violence?

Over the course of several decades, Schafran established an agenda of educational programs in a variety of venues, including the annual meetings of judges, publications (manuals and curriculum), and support for the more than forty state task forces on gender bias in the courts. New York Judge Betty Ellerin has called Schafran and Norma Wikler "truly the godmothers of this movement."

Schafran said that any social movement has a natural life, and that some states are still hard at work on the issue of gender fairness in the courts while others are tapering off. She has also seen differences in the response to the issue in the federal courts: "[T]he circuits went forward in different ways, depending upon the interests of their chief, depending on what kind of funding they could scare up. Some of them did nothing. Some of them did a substantial amount. Some of them closely limited their inquiry to the status of women court employees, and I would say that their implementation efforts were nothing like those in the states."

The "aha moments" of certain judges delighted Schafran:

I think my favorite response ever was the judge who wrote an evaluation: "I didn't know what I didn't know." And certainly in the area of the economic consequences of divorce, the judges who realized that they didn't know what a quart of milk cost, they were just making these ad hoc rulings about what should be paid in child support or they were making assumptions. I remember having a dialogue with a judge about how do you set child support and he said, "Well I ask the man what he's going to need and I make the assumption even before I do that, that he probably needs a car to get to work and he has to buy lunch, and he has to buy dinner." And I said "Well, excuse me, what do you mean he has to buy dinner?" And he said "Well he's got to go buy dinner." I said "Do you assume that the wife has to buy dinner?" "Well, no. Oh I see what you mean, he could cook, too." And it was like a light bulb.

Program participants also educated NJEP staff: "The judges said, now we know what we're supposed to be doing, but you need to do this for prosecutors. For example, they said, we understand that if a prosecutor wants to call an expert witness to explain why a victim delayed reporting [in a sexual violence case], we should let them do that. But we don't have the power to call an expert witness, and if the prosecutor doesn't know that they ought to call an expert witness, it's not going to happen. So the next thing we did was that we created a four-day curriculum for prosecutors."

Still later, after Schafran had written a curriculum concerning the adjudication of child sexual abuse allegations in custody disputes, her evaluating team heard from one judge who had participated in the course: "'I'm no longer so punitive toward the protective parents.' That's quite a statement," said Schafran. "Here was this judge just assuming that the protective parent was a liar and [taking a] punitive attitude toward that person."

Conclusion

In a public interview a year after Sonia Sotomayor became the third woman to serve on the U.S. Supreme Court, her colleague Justice Ruth Bader Ginsburg said,

When I was a new justice on this court, for the twelve years that I sat together with Justice Sandra Day O'Connor, invariably one lawyer or another would call me Justice O'Connor. They had become accustomed to a woman on the Court, and Justice O'Connor was THE woman, so if they heard a woman's voice, well, that must be the lady justice, even though we don't look alike, we don't sound alike. But last year no one called Justice Sotomayor "Justice Ginsburg" or me "Justice Sotomayor," and I am certain that lawyers will perceive the difference among the three of us, and we will each have our individual identities.[10]

The American judiciary, state and federal, underwent a profound and long-anticipated change in the last quarter of the twentieth century. The more than forty women brought onto the federal bench during the Carter administration transformed the judiciary, at long last creating more equal career opportunities for female lawyers. Justice Ginsburg was once asked if she had always wanted to be a judge. She replied, "It just wasn't in the realm of the possible until Jimmy Carter became president and was determined to draw on the talent of all of the people, not just some of them."[11] Influenced by the example of the federal government and changing legal and cultural norms, women lawyers also found that "the realm of the possible" had altered at the state and local level.

Christine Durham surveyed this landscape of change both as an active member of the National Association of Women Judges and as a judge, appointed in 1982, on the Utah Supreme Court:

When the National Association of Women Judges was organized [1979], there were about 125 women judges from all over the country who met in Los Angeles at the instigation of two trial judges from California who decided it was time. It was a very heady experience to be there. I had never seen more than two women judges together in Utah and to see 125 was staggering. I came home and I was having lunch with a friend—a lawyer—and I said to him, "You know, I'd been feeling that there has been so much attention paid to my appointment. I have been feeling so good that I broke this barrier, but I now realize that it's a drop in the bucket and, we will not have made any progress in terms of integrating the bench until half of the bench is female." And he said, "I hadn't thought about anything quite as drastic as that!" He came around, though. It was interesting how conditioned we all were by the nature of the world that we had experienced. I think that was especially true for women like me who were just on the edge of the changes. The women just behind us—even two years behind me in law school—were much more militant, no nonsense, get it done.

There is no question that social change demands a constantly altered learning curve, for men as well as for women. Tenth Circuit judge Stephanie Seymour seemed to be chuckling as she gave this account of an evening spent at the U.S. Supreme Court shortly after she joined the federal bench in 1979:

> There was a black tie dinner in the Supreme Court for all of [us] new appointees, who were there at the new judges' school, and Warren Burger was the Chief at the time. We had cocktails . . . dinner . . . toasts. Finally, Justice Burger clinked on his glass and announced that Justice Blackmun would give a tour of his chambers to all the attendees and their spouses except for the women judges, and they would meet Justice Burger at a different location. So . . . he gives us a tour of his chamber. . . . a separate tour. . . . and he says, "Oh ladies, come here and let me show you—you'll be particularly interested in this." And he showed us his kitchen. Whereupon I thought Mary Schroeder [Ninth Circuit] was going to come unglued and punch him out, but she was doing all of this behind his back.

The legal learning curve was also substantial. The oral histories are replete with accounts of issues of law that were new to these judges, or particularly demanding: mandatory sentencing guidelines, administrative law and Freedom of Information Act cases, Indian law, environmental cases with their extensive administrative records, the complex and much-amended Medicare legislation. Several judges discussed the "federalizing of drugs and guns," and the ways that legislating additional federal crimes had vastly increased the workload of the federal bench. Cornelia Kennedy, on the bench in Michigan's Eastern District, never liked trade secrets cases. Peggy Quince adamantly disliked termination of parental rights actions: "I just saw them as so heartbreaking." State judges were challenged to learn more about drugs and drug addiction.

Catherine Kimball worked from the "higher level" of the Louisiana Supreme Court in implementing drug court programs, innovated earlier by Janet Reno in Florida, "that help children and adults extricate themselves from drugs and alcohol." Kimball lobbied for these programs by instituting a "ride along" program in which legislators spent a day in a drug court with a judge.

Death penalty cases were repeatedly described as demanding. When possible, often after taking senior status, several judges stopped taking these cases. As a senior judge Zita Weinshienk decided that she would only hear civil cases, and not be in the criminal draw—although years earlier she had fought her chief judge's opinion that women should not be dealing with criminal cases:

> And the reason I did was because of one case that just got to me emotionally. I was hearing a lot of crack cocaine cases in the criminal division, and there was a case in which the defendant was being sentenced for distributing crack cocaine, and his fiancée was delivering crack for him at his urging. Now this was a young woman who was an A and B student at one of the high schools who'd had scholarship offers for several sports. She had a small child by this man and instead of taking a deal which was offered to her . . . she agreed with him that she would go to trial. . . . They were both convicted and I was looking at sentencing her to a minimum of 12 years, and here was this baby. . . . I finally figured out a way and worked with the U.S. Attorney to give her 10 years instead of 12, which was still too much time. It was after that very difficult decision that I decided that I didn't want to sentence any more young people to these very long sentences because they were delivering cocaine for a boyfriend. . . . I think it was the mandatory sentences that just got to me.

As a matter of individual opportunity, as well as the validation of American ideals of fairness, the "Carter" revolution unquestionably mattered. But what of the often-asked question, "Does it make a difference having *women* on the bench?" The oral histories yield no consensus. Judge Shirley Hufstedler suggested that the answer is shaped by time and culture: "I think it makes a difference, because women have a different perspective, at least they have for many years, because life expectancies and opportunities for women have been vastly different. . . .

Whether they should or not, men and women have been trained to think differently about all sorts of topics."

Other women felt male judges did not always understand sexual harassment cases with the same clarity as their female colleagues. Several judges spoke of their female colleagues as better listeners and as more empathetic.

In her oral history, Rya Zobel addressed the question of jurisprudence, of whether the presence of women judges had made a difference in how the law developed:

> I have no idea. I think it has made a difference in the perception of justice, certainly by women. . . . And I think, in some ways, it makes a difference substantively too. Sandy Lynch wrote that famous dissent in an opinion that held that rape was not a physical injury for purposes of enhanced sentence. . . . [It] made a big impression and I think changed the law . . . I mean, I can't imagine how men can say rape is not a physical injury. And that dissent would not have been written if she hadn't been there.

Justice Elizabeth Lacy summed up the case for women's presence, arguing that, as "keepers of the flame" for the concept of rule of law, "people in our society must have respect for those who are intimately involved" in running that branch of government:

> The more the population can identify with those who are making those decisions as having something in common, the more respect I think they have for the administration of the law. I really do think it's true that you often feel comfortable with somebody with whom you feel you have something in common. That can be age; it can be gender; it can be ethnicity; it can be knowing you came from the same neighborhood. . . . [W]ith women on the bench, you've broadened the life experience which is brought to the bench, which is very important . . . [T]he law should be reflective of the people to whom it applies and who should be part of the group. . . . Women are part of our population and that needs to be part of the discussion.

ENTR'ACTE

Home, Hearth, and the Pursuit of a Career

Today, parents call it the question of work-family balance. Although decades ago that phrase had yet to be coined, in their interviews many of the Trailblazers spoke about the issues of marriage, children, and elder care, as they intertwined with building careers.

Ninety percent of Trailblazers married. Most followed family and society's expectations that they marry soon after college. Several women married while still undergraduates. Slightly more than one-third of these married women later divorced, several of them twice. Some observers have argued that the changing social conditions and opportunities of the 1970s and 1980s played a role in the higher divorce rates of those decades. Increased rates of higher education, feminism, careers, and salaries gave women a greater push toward independence. The rise of no-fault laws also eased the process of divorce.[1]

Trailblazers spoke of themselves as caretakers. Women and their male and female partners raised children, generally two or three, but there were also families with a single child and others with four and five children. Some Trailblazers cared for stepchildren, nieces, and nephews, while others sheltered elderly parents.

Marriage

Jodie Bernstein laid out the expectations and dilemmas shaping the postcollege decisions of many Trailblazers:

> I always felt that really in order to really be successful as a person or as a professional, one needed to be successful in both, marriage and the career. I found that difficult. I found it difficult to even sort of conceive of. . . . I don't mean that I got married because I needed to conform; I

don't mean that. I was, I think, ready to get married. I was not real young when I got married. . . . I had some reluctance to marriage for quite a long time because I couldn't figure out how I was going to try to work these two things that I thought were important to me together. . . . [My husband] was always, and always has been, very supportive of me, was never threatened by it [professional life after having children], I think that was probably the key to my marrying in the first place. He's very secure in his own abilities [as a physician] and is very, very capable.

Other women also cited the importance of a supportive husband who was not threatened by a career wife. Those who married a man with that view of women experienced long marriages; those who did not often divorced. Ruth Bader Ginsburg gave eloquent expression to the importance of her marriage to Martin Ginsburg, her husband and biggest supporter:

It's the best, most fortunate decision I ever made. It was extraordinary in those days for a man to be supportive of his wife as a peer. In my first year at Harvard, his second year, he told everyone that his wife was going to make the Law Review. . . . He always made me feel I was better than I thought I was, that I could accomplish whatever I sought. He had enormous confidence in my ability, more than I had in myself. . . . Part of it is, he's so secure about himself, he never regarded me as any kind of threat to his ego. On the contrary, he took great pride in being married to someone he considered very able.

Betty Murphy's husband, Cornelius, a radiologist, shared Martin Ginsburg's values: "He never had any idea that something was 'woman's work or men's work.' . . . He was happy to shovel snow and set the table, cook, wash or iron. He would say that, 'if a man is sure of his own masculinity, there isn't any such thing as woman's work and men's work.'"

Sheila Birnbaum, born in 1940, felt the pressure to conform to contemporary mores about marriage. She was one of a handful of Trailblazers who did not pursue law school immediately after college:

I taught fourth grade in the southeast Bronx, soon after I graduated from college. I think there was still a real pull as to what other people expected me to do and what I wanted to do. And so in my last year of college I got married and my husband then was going to law school. And so I just felt that I had to go out and work, and put my desires on hold because that's what was expected.

And after a year or two of that I clearly knew that I needed to go to law school because there was no intellectual piece to my life teaching fourth grade. . . . [My husband] was very supportive. I remember when I told my parents that I was going to go to law school, I didn't get any encouragement from them to do that. They thought that it would have a deleterious effect on my marriage because I would get too smart, he would be left behind and it would affect my marriage negatively.

Tamar Frankel also spoke about the impact of local values concerning marriage and careers, in her case in Israel: "I wanted to love and be loved. I was a romantic, and I think I stayed a romantic to this very day. But I did not do what is being done here [the United States] now by young people and older people. And that is, 'What is my career? What do I want?' These questions did not arise. . . . I never asked that question."

Frankel never thought about how marriage or having children would affect her career. When interviewed, she said that in Israel, in her time, there was a totally different culture around these issues than in the United States: "When I came here I found out that some women thought that if they were professionals, they would not have a husband and never have children. This never occurred to me. This was life. My Prime Minister [Golda Meir] at the time . . . was a woman. And she had a husband, and she had a lover if you don't mind, and she lived, and she cooked. And she had sometimes a cabinet meeting in her kitchen, and she was like you wouldn't believe. She was strong, she was smart, and everybody followed her."

Divorce

In giving their oral histories, most Trailblazers who divorced acknowledged the end of their marriage but spoke very little about the cause. Some said they married at too young an age. A husband with a problem he could not, or would not, address was another cause of divorce. As one

Trailblazer said, "His problems affected me but at the same time, I had no way to control his problems. So I felt relieved insofar as pressure is concerned when we were divorced."

Dual careers and career competition also led to divorce for some women. Rya Zobel described how this occurred in her two marriages, one to another judge:

> [——] used to tell me how his job was more important than mine. I also always earned more than either of my husbands. And I think those were difficult things for these two men. And for [——] it was difficult that I was on this Bench with all the prerogatives of a Federal judge that he didn't have. I had a secretary, I had law clerks, I had an office, I had parking, none of these things he really had. . . . [H]e used to refer to me as the Real Judge Zobel and I just sort of pooh-pooh'd it but it turned out that he was really very unhappy about that. He said that part of the problem for him in the relationship was that he envied what he regarded as my success compared to his. I am sorry about that. I didn't recognize it at the time. . . . I offered to help him with this and that, that I was able to do because I was here and he was there. Be he regarded it as controlling or I don't know what. . . . I think it's not a surprise that at least in my generation, the successful women either never married or had failed marriages.

Motherhood and Caregiving

Not surprisingly, the women who joined the legal profession after 1963, when the birth control pill first became available, spoke of its importance to their ability to determine when they had children. With this more reliable and convenient form of family planning, the "my career" versus "having children" question was reshaped. Women could make decisions based upon their judgment of what was best for their health, marriage, and career. Carol Dinkins said it all in a very few words: "I cannot stress how important the availability of dependable birth control was to being able to have done what I did when I did it."

Barbara Babcock recalled women in the feminist movement saying that they would not have children because they wanted to dedicate themselves to the cause. That struck her as upsetting: "It sends chills through people. I would never say it because it was really considered unnatural, and probably still is for a woman to say she doesn't want to have children."

Most of the women who divorced settled into second marriages and many then took on the responsibility of stepchildren. Families were "blended"; one Trailblazer mothered several stepchildren and did not have any biological children because she felt her stepchildren were not ready for new siblings. Still other women cared for an elderly parent.

Here are the voices of Trailblazers on the subject of caregiving:

CAROL DINKINS: I worked hard to make sure that I would carpool in the morning before I went to work, and that other mothers would bring them home at lunch time. So I did a lot of balancing. And I tell young women now that they shouldn't try to do everything, that when I was an associate here at the firm, all I did was practice law and deal with my children and husband. . . . All you can do is what you can do. You have to figure out what your top priorities are and maybe they've changed and you adjust them by the hour, by the day, by the week, by the year, but you also want to have in mind what it is you want to accomplish.

MARY CRANSTON: I never had any doubts that the kids came first. When you work this hard as I have with as much pressure as I have, you realize that it's all about prioritization, what comes first. Kids come first. Now these kids turned out to be very squared away without a lot of issues. So I was able to give them my first priority without having it really impinge on the time that I had to do other things as well. I also had a very good domestic set up. I had a live-in housekeeper that we had the whole time the kids were growing up. My twin sister had a live-in housekeeper. We lived very close to each other. And my mother was also willing to be a backup. . . . My husband also was a very involved father. . . . I think being a mother really gave me a lot of motivation to figure out my bullshit.

CATHERINE KIMBALL: After about two months when I had no help and nobody to help me with the children and realized that, making beds and washing dishes and washing clothes and doing those things was nothing that I cared anything at all about, I decided that I would rather go to work and make some money and pay somebody else to do the dishes, and whatever, so in 1970 I think it was they had just appointed a new federal judge in Alexandria, so I went down to apply as a law clerk and he hired me. . . . I felt like I was obviously a terrible mother because I wanted to go to work instead of stay in the house with my children [aged three and one]. I thought something was terribly wrong with me. . . . I didn't really know anyone else, any female professionals at that time, there really was nobody. . . . But I loved working, I enjoyed working.

BETTY ELLERIN: Now, the one thing I will say is working as a law clerk to a judge did give me a certain flexibility. I would go home with work and I'd do charges at night, I would do decisions at night, but if there was a parent-teacher's conference or something like that I would just go during the day. I would never miss one of those. . . . I think I probably would have been very frustrated and short-tempered if I were home all the time, and not participating in the career that I loved. And so that would not have been good for the children. I'm very interested to see how it works for my daughter. Because she also is very involved in her career and is a wonderful mother.

SHIRLEY HUFSTEDLER: My only child was born in 1953 [and I moved my office home]. . . . I found a sitter, but I had to be, as far as I was concerned, at home, so if there was a burst of silence, I would know something was wrong and would find out what happened, or if the decibel level became higher than I thought it ought, I'd check too, but I was at home. . . .

I don't think that's [working harder than male colleagues] any mystery, because any time when a woman is taking care of a family, particularly with young children, and simultaneously working, that woman is working hard, and that's true whether she's working at lower wage income, such as cleaning other people's houses, or whether she's working as a professional, whether a doctor or a lawyer or a professor or whatever. It just takes an awful lot of work.

CARLA HILLS: We had a new baby, a new mortgage and a new law firm, all in the same quarter. But it worked. [We balanced all of that] with vigor. [Laughter] You know, I tried to be a good mom; we always lived within about 20 minutes of my office, less, if possible. . . . When we moved to Washington, D.C., I would not locate our home in the many lovely areas across a bridge because of the commuting delays. Living close by work in Los Angeles, I could get home at lunch when they were very little. And I stayed up late. I'm blessed with good health. I don't think I could have done it except our children also had good health because I did work very, very hard. [Over the years] I had three wonderful housekeepers.

ANTONIA HERNANDEZ: I've always felt that my ability to marry and have children had nothing to do with being a lawyer. I tell people that I think with my brains and I have babies with my tummy. . . . So I met this wonderful fellow who shared my values, who shared my politics, who wanted to do the same thing, who is extremely support-ive, and we just developed this fabulous friendship that mushroomed and developed into a relationship and we married.

CHRISTINE DURHAM: My secret weapon was the man I married; he's a pediatrician by profession, and he loves children. He wanted a lot of children. I really thought I'd be happy with two. He wanted six. So I guess we compromised on four, although we subsequently fostered a nephew who came to us in 1980 at age four. But we were young, we were energetic, and were 50/50 partners in the enterprise. . . . Interestingly, I think [my husband] got more resentment for the role he played in sharing the parenting duties than I did.

ADA SHEN-JAFFE: At the end of April 1983, Ken and I had our son and only child, Noah. . . . When Noah was 6 months old I went back to work full-time, and during the day, left him in the care of a young woman we had known since she was a kid, and who had worked as a nanny to put away money for school. When Noah was a year old, she said, "This kid is like the Energizer Bunny and an electric eel all in one—he needs more stimulation than one person can give him— you've got to get him into daycare." This was in 1984 when childcare options for one-year olds were quite limited.

Happily, he was accepted to the University Temple Daycare near home, where he thrived. . . . To be honest, there were times when it felt like we were just keeping one nostril over the waterline juggling very challenging work lives and a new child, but that would hardly make us any different from the many other families facing the same challenges!

Lucky for us, by the time Noah reached four years of age, it was like a switch got thrown. He had settled down, and from then on, parenting him was like a paid vacation.

Dean Barbara Black, a mother, spoke movingly and at length about how she, her husband, and children participated in caring of another kind, that of an older adult relative.

BARBARA BLACK: In December of 1972 my mother moved in with us. My mother was paraplegic and bedridden; she moved in with us because we insisted that she come. She had lived for 11 years on her own in a wheelchair, in an apartment in Brooklyn. . . . When it did become necessary, she came to us, and she lived with us for a little over ten years, until she died. And for ten years, as Charles used to say, we ran a one-person nursing home. It wasn't difficult because of anything about my mother, who was absolutely wonderful, uncomplaining, funny. She deserved to be taken care of, and we took care of her. But the business of getting help and of keeping help and of changing help. . . . the paperwork, the incredible tax forms, other government forms. The business of not being able to leave her alone in the house for one minute.

So when you talk about balancing that's what I wound up balancing. And the women students used to come and talk to me all the time, and ask "what's it like, juggling home and profession?" And I said, "It's hell on wheels, that's what it's like." Now it wouldn't have been hell on wheels without this extra dimension of caring for an elderly bedridden parent.

* * *

Work-family balance was difficult for these women in the last decades of the twentieth century as they raised families and gave care to elderly parents. In her oral history, Utah Supreme Court chief justice Christine Durham reflected that the issue has only become more difficult for women and their families:

The dominance of the billable hours regime has had a large impact on lifestyle. I believe the profession has been reorganizing itself over the last couple of decades in ways that are very detrimental to the needs of young women, who are in their prime reproductive years, needing time in their lives to devote to family issues. And the problem is that family work still remains women's work and public life offers little or no accommodation of that fact. The United States does not have family-friendly and child-friendly public policies. We do not support families and child raising. We shove all of that into the so-called private sector and that's where women take up the slack.

9

The Case of the Century and Other Tales

Clients make headlines, as do attorneys and judges. Important cases may bring enhanced reputations, financial gain, or a tattered career. Among this group of stellar lawyers and judges, notable cases, whether negotiated to closure, or litigated to a judgment, were remembered both for their substantive importance and for their impact on individual careers. Over long careers, these women were involved in hundreds of notable cases, civil and criminal, that speak to the importance of the rule of law as a central value in American society as well as the full participation of women lawyers in this process of justice.

Who Will Be President?

Florida appellate lawyer Peggy Quince stepped to the other side of the bench in 1994. She served on the Second District Court of Appeal until 1999, when, following a joint appointment by Governor Lawton Chiles and Governor Jeb Bush, she became a member of the Florida Supreme Court. Less than two years later she was in the thick of *Bush v. Gore*, the extraordinary political case of the new century. *Bush v. Gore* was a challenge to the vote-counting procedures in Florida counties, the outcome of which would determine the winner of the year 2000 presidential race. Before the issue went to the United States Supreme Court, Quince and her colleagues on the Florida Supreme Court heard the challenge:

> We were pretty much in this building [the courthouse], you know, 14 and 15 hours a day. A part of it had to do with . . . media types outside that once you came into the building, you wouldn't even go out for lunch. . . . because you didn't want to be accosted by people trying to stick a microphone in your face. . . . [W]e had so much, so many emails, I actually had to change my email address . . . [T]here were some threats. . . . We had to continue on with our oral arguments. . . . [T]he work of the Court didn't

stop just because people wanted to contest the election. So we spent a lot of time on the election cases, but we were also spending a lot of time on the other cases that were before the Court. . . .

I don't think there was less collegiality [in this contentious case]. I think we probably spent more time just discussing it. . . . Because, we'd hope that whatever came out of the Court would be unanimous. And the first one, in fact, the first opinion, full opinion, was, in fact, a unanimous opinion, but then when we got to the second one, it was not a unanimous opinion [by a vote of four to three the court ordered a statewide manual recount of so-called undervotes], but it still required, in order to write the majority opinion, it required understanding what the dissent was taking issue with and vice versa, so it was just more intense and you knew you had to do it in a short period of time. . . . [I]t really came down to your interpretation of the statutory provisions concerning elections and any constitutional provision concerning elections. I think we handled it the way we would have handled any kind of case.

On December 8, 2000, four weeks after the November election, the Florida Supreme Court ordered an immediate recount of undervotes in that state. The following day the U.S. Supreme Court granted a stay application, and scheduled oral argument for December 11. The people of the United States held their breath, waiting to learn who would become president. Only one day later, on the 12th, the high court, in a five to four vote, reversed the Florida Supreme Court's judgment ordering manual recounts, holding that such a recount would be unconstitutional under the Equal Protection Clause. Following the balloting of members of the Electoral College, George W. Bush was elected the forty-third president of the United States.

Addressing Racial Injustice

Every student of constitutional law learns *Hirabayashi v. United States* and *Brown v. Topeka Board of Education*. They are landmark cases, *Hirabayashi* a challenge to the curfew and evacuation orders imposed upon Japanese Americans during World War II and *Brown*, part of a litigation campaign to end de jure racial segregation in American schools. Gordon Hirabayashi refused the order to obey a nighttime curfew and to report for evacuation from his hometown of Seattle. He turned himself in to the FBI, asserting that the government's actions were racially discriminatory. He was convicted by a U.S. federal district court in Seattle of defying the exclusion order and violating curfew. He appealed his conviction to the U.S. Supreme Court and lost.

Forty years later Judge Mary M. Schroeder, newly appointed to the U.S. court of appeals' Ninth Circuit, participated in Hirabayashi's case when he successfully appealed to have it reopened and reconsidered. The presiding judge assigned the opinion to her, an opportunity, she later wrote, "to write what became the opinion of my career."[1] In her oral history Judge Schroeder said,

> Gordon Hirabayashi was a remarkable man. He was a student, graduate student, at the University of Washington when the curfew and then the internment were imposed in 1942 [against Japanese-American citizens]. He refused to obey and decided that he would rather be prosecuted. . . . [T]he case went to the United States Supreme Court. The Supreme Court upheld the curfew and the subsequent internment on the basis of supposed imminent danger to the country by Japanese-Americans. This all turned out to have been based on a report that the Army falsified. And all of the lies were turned up in subsequent research 30 years later when all the original information came to light. The research was done by Peter Irons, an historian. Hirabayashi, by then living in Canada, filed for a writ of *coram nobis* [a request to reopen and reconsider a matter that has been decided, claiming that the decisions was based on a mistake of fact], which is very unusual. The District Court upheld the curfew violation but granted *coram nobis* on the internment violation. So both sides appealed. . . . It was very dramatic because there we were in Seattle, Washington, which is the city where [Hirabayashi] was originally convicted, and the light from the window was shining directly on him during the course of the argument. The Government perceived that it wasn't going particularly well; and when the Government lost it [his conviction was overturned], there was an appeal to the Supreme Court. Their argument was that the case was moot because he was no longer in prison and we rejected that. I think the line that I liked the best in the opinion was that a person convicted on the basis of race is lastingly aggrieved.

At an American Bar Association dinner years later honoring Judge Schroeder, Hirabayashi regaled his table with what happened after the original Supreme Court ruling during World War II. As Judge Schroeder tells the story,

> He explained that the government was supposed to transport him to a prison camp in Arizona to serve his sentence, but the government had no money and no train or truck to get him there. It was the height of the war. For Gordon, however, it was extremely important that he serve his sentence and receive his punishment for standing up for principle. He was a true conscientious objector in the mold of those like Martin Luther King, Jr. and Mahatma Gandhi, only years before the world considered them heroes. What did Gordon Hirabayashi do when the government could not transport him to prison? Always resourceful, he hitchhiked to the Arizona prison camp in the summer. As he described it, the trip was fairly easy until he got to Nevada, where the young man from Seattle began to experience the desert heat. Needless to say, being Gordon Hirabayashi, he kept going. Therefore, nearly fifty years later, it must have been a great day for him when the site of the prison camp on Mt. Lemon, near Tucson, AZ, was dedicated as the Gordon Hirabayashi Rest Area.[2]

At the end of his sentence, Hirabayashi returned to the University of Washington, earned a doctorate, moved to Canada, and taught sociology. He also spoke frequently about the racism experienced by Japanese Americans during World War II. During an appearance at Brown University, he was handed this extraordinary letter, giving a rare insight into the impact of a Trailblazer's work on her family:

Dear Mr. Hirabayashi,
My name is Kate Schroeder. I am the daughter of the Ninth Circuit Court of Appeals Judge Mary M. Schroeder. I wish to take this opportunity to express to you my undying regard for your strength of will. I was nine when your case reached the Circuit Court, but my mother took the time to explain to me and my older sister what a tragic injustice had been done to you and every Japanese-American in the country. Because of your story, I have always been aware of the need to question and examine the actions of our government. And even though it has sought

to provide restitution for its crimes, I, and I believe Mother, feel that no one can ever make up for the wrongs done to you. My family has always admired you for your courage to bring the terrible truths of our nation's racism to the surface. I know that Mother is honored to have had a small part in your search for justice. She has told me many times that this was the most important case she had or will ever have decided. As it has shaped her life, so too, has it shaped my understanding of our history and of the sometimes fragile state of human rights in our country. I give you my highest respect and send you my Mother's most affectionate regards. Sincerely Yours,
Kate Schroeder
Brown University[3]

＊ ＊ ＊

In 1978, nearly a decade before Judge Schroeder and her colleagues ruled in Hirabayashi's *coram nobis* appeal, attorneys had persuaded Linda Brown, lead plaintiff in *Brown v. Board*, to file to reopen *Brown v. Board of Education*. It took a decade for the refiled case to reach the U.S. Court of Appeals for the Tenth Circuit. Judge Stephanie Seymour sat on the panel hearing what many people called "Brown III." It was, she said later, the "most renowned case" that had come across her desk:

I picked up this brief and it was *Linda Brown Smith v. The Board of Education of Topeka, Kansas.* . . . [I]t was the same case as the one the Supreme Court heard [in the 1950s]. Linda Brown was the child over whom school integration in Topeka, Kansas was fought—her mother brought the action on her behalf and she was the plaintiff child in that case. The Supreme Court ordered in the '50s that schools be desegregated in Topeka, Kansas and elsewhere in the country. That child grew up, married, and became Linda Brown Smith. The Supreme Court had remanded the case back to the Tenth Circuit, which had sent it back to Topeka, Kansas, and it had never gotten closed. So Linda Brown Smith reopened the case on behalf of her daughter, claiming that the School Board had never desegregated the schools in Topeka, Kansas, and that was the case.

We decided that [Linda Brown Smith was correct]. . . . The District Court had granted summary judgment for the school district, the Tenth Circuit reversed. There was lots of evidence that nothing much had happened. The City was still segregated and kids went to the same old elementary schools and for economic reasons, the City hadn't really done much by way of integration. . . . We commented in the opinion on how various cities had desegregated, some by busing, some by magnet schools. They ended up settling the case and developing magnet schools in Topeka as a result of that case.

The Tenth Circuit vote was two to one, with Judge Seymour writing for the majority. Settling the case, however, required ten more years of legal and political action. After the Tenth Circuit's ruling, the school district requested that the U.S. Supreme Court take the case on appeal, something the high court declined to do. Instead, the case was returned to the district court for implementation of the Tenth Circuit's mandate. In 1994 a new desegregation plan was approved, along with a bond issue to finance it. New elementary magnet schools were opened and attendance plans redrawn. The standard of racial balance ordered by the court was achieved in 1998, nearly a half a century after *Brown v. Board* was first heard by the U.S. Supreme Court.

New to the Practice of Law

Notable cases also came to several Trailblazers as young lawyers barely out of law school. In May 1970, eleven days after Ohio National Guardsmen killed four students at Kent State University during a demonstration, police shot and killed two black students at Jackson State University, and injured twelve others. The Presidential Commission on Campus Unrest subsequently concluded "that the 28-second fusillade from police officers was an unreasonable, unjustified overreaction."[4] Constance Harvey, a January 1970 graduate of the University of Mississippi Law School, immediately began filing lawsuits, including one representing the families of the victims and the students (*Myrtle Green Burton v. William L. Waller*; Williams was the governor of Mississippi and technically in charge of the Highway Patrol and the National Guard).

Harvey described the state grand jury—Hinds County—that was convened: It brought back no bills, "which meant nobody was indicted." There was also a federal grand jury, presided over by Judge Harold Cox.

Harvey related that when Cox gave the charge to the grand jury, he said "that anybody who would have been a bystander should not have expected not to have been killed or injured." Cox was the same judge, she said, "that referred to black people as chimpanzees and buzzards." Nobody was ever convicted of either student's death, and the state and city were found to be immune from liability for the recovery of damages in the *Burton* decision. Harvey said that the court's decision was "a final bruising and the last that my spirit could endure." She made a conscious choice to leave the practice of civil rights law.

* * *

As a new lawyer at Model Cities in Los Angeles, Antonia Hernandez had the opportunity to litigate what she called "one of the most interesting cases in the country," about the sterilization of Latina women by LA County Hospital:

> If you recall in those days, there was this sterilization of women both in South and North Carolina and the whole issue in the women's movement of freedom of choice. . . . I got to work with the white women's movement. The [pro-]choice movement. I got to work with Nancy Stearns and Rhonda Copelon out of New York. The women that were doing major [women's health] litigation. . . . young and inexperienced, we litigated the case. . . . before Judge Jessie Curtis at the Federal District Court here in LA. And everybody was shocked. It was a three-week trial and everybody was shocked when he ruled against us. . . . We lost in the courts, but we won at the legislative and at the federal levels because the 24-hour waiting period was adopted. You couldn't sterilize women when they were going in there for a c-section. You had to wait 24 hours; so the abuses stopped.

* * *

Yale Law School graduate Nancy Gertner spent twenty-four years as a private practice attorney and seventeen as a federal district court judge before becoming a member of the Harvard Law School faculty. But in 1975, four years out of Yale and, like Harvey and Hernandez, quite inexperienced, she agreed to represent Susan Saxe, an anti–Vietnam War activist charged with murder and bank robbery. Nothing suggested that the case would gloss the new lawyer's reputation. But it did. Against all odds.

Gertner says that the call from Saxe "changed the following 20 years of my practice."[5]

The Saxe case was about five people who had decided that the way to deal with the stalling of the anti-war movement was to, this is 1970, rob banks, to get money to fund more anti-war activities. . . . This group of five— three men, two women were robbing banks up and down the Eastern Seaboard. The men were ex-cons who were part of a re-entry program at Brandeis University. The women were Brandeis students. One was Susan Saxe. . . . 1970 was a turning point in the anti-war movement. . . . It was the time of Kent State, the time of Ohio State. There was very much a sense that we were on the borders of anarchy, a feeling perhaps over-blown in our youthful enthusiasm. Students had been shot on those two occasions. . . . Susan winds up aligned with these four other people. . . . The idea was that one woman would be guarding the getaway car with a "switch car." One of the men would be in front of the bank guarding the bank, watching out if the police arrived. There would be three inside the bank, two men and Susan. The robbery took place. . . . And on the way back to their apartment, they heard over the radio that a police officer was shot. What apparently happened was that the man who was guard-ing the bank in the front saw a police officer enter, go up the sidewalk to the bank. He did not realize that the robbery was over, the other four en route home. . . . He shot the police officer in the back. What had been a serious crime now turned into a capital offense, under the felony murder rule, if you participate in the felony, you are responsible for foreseeable consequences which included this murder. The five of them went under-ground, split up. The men are caught almost immediately. . . . The women disappeared completely and it's one of the ironies that part of the reason they were so successful in disappearing was that the FBI did not know how to deal with women criminals anymore than women anything. So they were literally looking for these women in Las Vegas and strip joints and gambling places. . . . Susan Saxe was apprehended in 1975, five years later. . . . I, of course, said yes when Katie [Roraback] asked me to help. I'd been a lawyer for three years; "what did I know?" . . . [Susan] wanted a woman to represent her. And the irony here was that after I had spent those years fighting because I was the only women, now suddenly it was a strength. . . . I went to my partners, Tom Shapiro and Harvey Silverglate and told them I wanted to take the case. I didn't know how it would be paid for. . . . Harvey and Tom were troubled that this would be a case that would take down the firm. I don't know of any other male partners who would have invested in what was essentially my first high-profile, my first murder case period. I don't know of anyone else who would have had . . . the confidence to say, "you can do it" as they said to me. . . . The case took two years to try. . . . I'd run into men on the street and I asked what should I do about this or that and the answer over and over again was "get out of the case" [or] "You're in over your head."

Gertner found that the newspapers did not know how to cover the case, and paid little attention to her role as Saxe's attorney. In court, however, she was constantly "banging heads" with the judge. And once, when she wore a flouncy dress that was shapeless, the prosecutor told her, "You've no business looking pregnant when you're representing that lesbian."

Gertner wanted to win and to save Saxe's life. In her telling, she set aside just about everything, "boyfriend, friends, fun." The schedule set for the trial enabled her "to learn better how to be a lawyer by the time the trial arrived." She challenged everything—suppression motions, dismissal motions. She brought in jury consultants to help with selection, and ended up with a very young jury, most in their early twenties:

The judge gave us a jury selection procedure that no one in Massachusetts had ever gotten, no doubt on the assumption that we were going to lose anyway. So we had individual voir dire.

[T]he trial began, and the press was covering it not knowing, not having any understanding that we were making some headway. . . . There's the evidence, the physical evidence, the cooperator will testify that Susan was in the bank. [But] there were bank pictures which in fact were very fuzzy. Nobody in the bank could identify the woman. . . . So the physical evidence and even the cooperator did not present a very strong case against Susan. . . . But the prosecutor had two pieces of paper which were devastating. One piece of paper was a letter written by Susan to her rabbi and one to her father after the robbery. And they each began "by the time you get this letter, you'll know what your little girl has been up to." They were essentially confessions. When the trial began, we really had no defense. There were defenses that Susan wouldn't let me do it [men made me do it; I was not the shooter].

Gertner had given the government a list of witnesses before the trial began:

And just in case, although extremely unlikely, we gave them a list of witnesses as if we were going to try the Vietnam War. There had been numbers of anti-war related criminal prosecutions, none as serious as this . . . where the defense essentially had been "we're doing this to protest the Vietnam War and we're asking the jury to nullify." . . . [Historian] Howard Zinn, the Berrigan brothers, all across the country people were flying in to court and the press was covering that. . . . reporting this as if Gertner, the lunatic is going to try the Vietnam War. The prosecutor believed the press.

It became clear that the government planned to end their case without the two confessional letters, hoping to avoid a "prosecution" of the Vietnam War by the defense. When the prosecutor turned to the judge and said, "The prosecution rests," Gertner got up and said, "In that case we rest as well." Hours later she gave the closing argument, predicting correctly what the prosecutor would say and talking about the antiwar effort, though chided for this many times by the judge:

Everybody assumed we were going to lose thunderously. . . . The jury hung at 11 to 1. It was seen as a victory. Everyone understood how close we had come to acquittal. She [Saxe] subsequently pled guilty to manslaughter and got eight years. . . . All of a sudden I had a career and a reputation, no doubt ill-deserved after one case. . . . Only the year before I wasn't mentioned in the [Boston] *Globe* and suddenly I was [a] criminal law superstar. It enabled me to craft a career out of whatever I wanted to do.

Prison Condition Cases

Chicago litigator Joan Hall and federal judge Norma Shapiro each described prison condition cases as among the most important work of their careers. Hall, a partner at Jenner & Block, used the pro bono resources of her firm to bring a class action suit, the *Calvin R.* case, on behalf of all the inmates in protective custody at Stateville, the maximum security prison in Illinois. With an all-women team, in front of a woman judge, Hall argued that the conditions of confinement for protective custody inmates constituted cruel and unusual punishment. She hired experts and obtained a court order enabling the team to go to Stateville with cameras to photograph conditions. The state eventually agreed to a consent decree, Hall reported, "which they subsequently greatly regretted. It required that inmates in protective custody be allowed out of their cells, be able to go to classes, be able to go to the library, be able to get exercise. It [was] a very depressing place. The conditions were very bad."

Long-time Philadelphia lawyer Norma Shapiro, a Republican, moved from private practice to the federal bench in 1978. The following year at a White House reception, Democratic president Jimmy Carter called her "class" of women jurists "his legacy." He wanted women and minorities on the bench; political party was not paramount.

Shapiro was a seasoned federal trial judge when she was assigned a contentious, decades-old case concerning the ancient, overcrowded Holmesburg prison in Philadelphia: *Harris v. Philadelphia.* Holmesburg had been the site of major riots in the 1970s, the subject of a two-year investigation that documented hundreds of cases of the rape of inmates, and the focus of a 1998 exposé, *Acres of Skin: Human Experiments at Holmesburg Prison.*

> *Harris v. the City of Philadelphia* was a class-action, originally on behalf of past, present, and future prisoners at Holmesburg. And you can't have a class action *pro se* [an individual representing her or himself without an attorney], so I appointed David Richman of the Pepper office to represent the class, and what a wonderful job he did. I refused, originally, to entertain the case, because of the role of the state courts that had the case for 25 years and I felt that it was a breach of federal-state relations. They had had something like 365 orders already. And they took me up to the Court of Appeals and got me reversed. It said . . . that the state case was only about injunctive relief and this was about damages. Well, how you give damages to future prisoners was beyond me. But, of course, once it was sent back to me, I fulfilled their mandate. We enlarged the class to include prisoners at all the City's institutions. And, I always thought that one of the reasons the Court of Appeals was so kind to me . . . I think it went up to the Court

of Appeals eight times, and I only got reversed once. I think they felt sorry for me; I think they felt they stuck me with this, and they should be sympathetic. There was terrible overcrowding, and I went out there and inspected a number of times, and then the City realized the conditions there were unconstitutional. It's true, I never made a finding of unconstitutionality, because the City conceded, and they entered into a Consent Decree, which troubled me quite a bit because it involved, ultimately, the release of prisoners. But as I thought about it, and I thought about what else could be done, ultimately, I approved the Consent Decree. One of the problems was that the District Attorney wanted to be a party, and I studied the law and the role of the District Attorney, and I determined that she didn't have a proper interest in having everybody in jail, which was the position that the DA was espousing. The Court of Appeals affirmed me and the Supreme Court refused to take certiorari. Then, the DA went to the State Legislature and got them to pass a bill purporting to give the DA interest. And then I felt that that was an unconstitutional separation of powers issue, and I refused to let her intervene again, and the Court of Appeals again affirmed. That created a terrible problem, because she wasn't a party, and she couldn't appeal approval of the Consent Decree, and it also got her goat. And, as I look back on it, I'm sorry that I didn't let her intervene permissibly, because she would have been subject to my jurisdiction and I could have enforced orders against her. So that one never knows, you don't get the chance to do something over, but she was very uncooperative in matters where cooperation was essential. What I came to see was that the problem of over-crowding could not be corrected by the prisons; they had to accept the people the judges sent them. It had something to do with, first, the amount of crime and the amount of facilities. Second, it had to do with the poverty of the people who were arrested; they couldn't raise bail in what were bail offenses. Then there was a problem about just general disorganization and communication. We were just beginning the use of computers, and people would be in jail for a week, a month, sometimes several months, when there was no order keeping them there. So, there were a tremendous amount of problems that could only be corrected by cooperation between the court system, the District Attorney, the Sheriff of the jails, and so on. We made marvelous progress in many respects. What happened, unfortunately, after I approved the Consent Decree which provided, ultimately, that if you couldn't get the population down, you must release the people on the lowest bail and the least violent crimes. Once we started to release people, we got very, very bad press. For a couple of months I was on the [Philadelphia] *Daily News* front page as public enemy number one, ahead of the robbers, the murderers, the rapists [whose crimes were described by the newspaper each day as they were released under the decree].

Shapiro made clear that the politics and the publicity that followed the Consent Decree situation were very painful:

It was hard to be called an activist judge when I knew I had refused to take this case to begin with. And none of these people who criticized me came up with any thoughtful solutions to the problem. I was, I wouldn't say begging, but I was very receptive to any ideas about what we could do better. We hired some consultants from Temple; the prison did, under my orders. It turned out that one of the provisions in the, I hope I get this right, in the first Consent Decree, was to build a 400 bed prison downtown near the Criminal Justice Center, because, in the state courts, if someone didn't show, and lots of times witnesses or the police wouldn't show, they wouldn't postpone the case for a day, they would postpone it for four months. That delay was part of the problem. When I first got involved, at least three quarters of the people in the jails were pretrial detainees; they hadn't been convicted of anything. And they would stay in jail until they were there longer than their sentences if they were convicted, and then they would be released for time served. Then the DA would arrange to have them come for trial and they'd be released. The whole system, it seemed to me, was crazy. Well, we did a number of things. First, we arranged for the first house arrest program that had electronic bracelets. We got 250 of them. I had fine money because the City didn't meet some of their [sic] goals, and the Court of Appeals held that it was appropriate to fine them. So I had this money that could be spent, and we spent money for electronic bracelets so some people could be released from house arrest. We arranged, ultimately, for . . . good time credit and that is a very desirable thing as far as penology is concerned because it encourages good behavior. So we worked out that system. As I recall, the District Attorney agreed to that system, so that reduced sentences. My orders, when we finally began to implement releases, were for people nearest to the end of their sentence with the least violent crimes.

The adverse media publicity and interoffice conflict created tremendous tension and raised concerns about Judge Shapiro's safety. The district attorney was so angry that she had her staff draft legislation to stop Shapiro. During the hearings, the DA accused Shapiro of killing a policeman's son. (The man was shot and killed by someone who had been in prison, but Shapiro had not signed a release order for the assailant.) After passage of the Litigation Reform Act, the district attorney visited various citizen groups, lecturing about how awful Shapiro's decisions were, how they were imperiling public safety:

And I did get a number of death threats and very scurrilous letters. But, you have to ignore them. I had some advice from the Marshals about how to deal with it, which I followed, and, fortunately, nothing ever happened.

[There were] other solutions to overcrowding, one of which, of course, was to build more capacity. We had this proposal for a building in Center City, and, as with all City projects, there was a provision for the hiring of women and minorities. And the people building it did not comply, and it was also getting over-budget. So the Mayor stopped the construction, leaving a huge hole in Center City. You may remember this, "Shapiro Hole." And he came up for re-election, and it was very embarrassing to have this hole there, so he was anxious to get out from my contempt order. What I did was freeze all the construction funds; I just issued an injunction. They couldn't touch it. And I remember at the time, they were trying to build the new stadium, and I let it be known that they weren't going to build a new stadium if they didn't do something about the prisons. So we got involved in some very unusual negotiations. Also a bond issue was coming due, and they would have been in default on that. So, I think it was General Motors that helped. They had a financing corporation. So they got together, and they all worked out something that I would lift my order, and the funds they would provide, maybe $292 million, to build a prison facility out with the other prison facilities and a courthouse where the "Shapiro Hole" was. And, of course, there was a desperate need for a new criminal courthouse. And I agreed, provided that the new bond issue had a clause that nothing over $100,000 could be expended without my approval, which was very unusual, but the bond attorney didn't see any reason why not, and the result was that PICC, the Philadelphia Industrial Corrections Center, was finished. The Criminal Justice Center was built; the Curran-Fromhold Prison was built in memory of Warden Curran and Assistant Warden Fromhold who were murdered in the last prisoner uprising, then about 25 years before. And they were all built on time and under budget, and, of course, the excess money was returned to the City. So that turned out to be very advantageous.

Pleased with improvements in health care services and other matters, and conscious of the limits of her powers as the result of the Prison Litigation Reform Act, Shapiro entered into a new Consent Decree in 2000 that ended her oversight while also requiring the city to complete certain improvements. Holmesburg, described by Shapiro as "one of the dankest, most dismal places you have ever seen," had already been closed (used only for overflow).

While the case was under her jurisdiction, Shapiro was repeatedly criticized as an activist judge. In summing up the many aspects of the case, she commented,

> There was no other way. As a matter of fact, at one point, they wanted to join, as defendants, the entire Philadelphia court system. . . . There are some things that if you had a great leader, you can pull everything together and accomplish something, but the hardest thing to do is to get independent institutions to work together. The federal courts are ill-suited for that job. . . . But, I think, the criticism of activist judges is wrong; it just makes no sense. And I think the activist judges are those judges that do things that people don't like. It's another way of saying we don't like your attitude, or the way in which you enforce the law. I know very few judges who say, "don't care what the law is, I'm going to do this anyway." You do what you think you're required to do, and I did what I thought the Third Circuit was requiring me to do.

> I want to just tell you about something amusing. When I left this case, there were 7,000 inmates. Now the newspapers report about 9,000, and I understand the *Daily News*, sometime ago, had some editorial that what they needed was Judge Shapiro back again. That gave me some pleasure.

Tax Policy and the State of California

California tax attorney Joanne Garvey had been active in the ABA as a founding member of the Women's Caucus, head of the Standing Committee on Legal Aid and Indigent Defendants, and member of the Board of Governors. After one of her partners suggested that she run for the presidency of the association, Garvey said that she began to put together a small coterie of supporters, knowing that she would have to run against Trailblazer Roberta Ramo. And then, as she started to campaign in earnest, Garvey was surprised by a positive turn in a fifteen-year-old case. Needing to give all her attention to this work, including arguing for her client at the U.S. Supreme Court, she dropped out of the race, throwing her support to Ramo. Garvey never became head of the ABA, but she won headlines, and praise from the legal community.

In its final iteration, before the U.S. Supreme Court, Garvey's case was known as *Barclays Bank PLC v. Franchise Tax Board*. Some people referred to it as the California Unitary Tax case. Garvey spoke of it as "this never-ending tax case which had been winding its way through the California courts, testing the constitutionality of California's tax system." It was a devilish piece of work: interminable, complex, and very political. Unsettled questions of multinational corporations' tax liability were at stake.

The syllabus reporting the Supreme Court decision laid out the legal question of the *Barclays* appeal:

> During the years at issue in these consolidated cases, California used a "worldwide combined reporting" method to determine the corporate franchise tax owed by unitary multinational corporate group members doing business in California. California's method first looked to the worldwide income of the unitary business, and then taxed a percentage of that income equal to the average of the proportions of worldwide payroll, property, and sales located within California. In contrast, the Federal Government employ[ed] a "separate accounting" method, which treats each corporate entity discretely for the purpose of determining income tax liability. In *Container Corp. of America v. Franchise Tax Bd.* this Court upheld the California scheme as applied to domestic-based multinationals, but did not address the constitutionality of the scheme as applied to

domestic corporations with foreign parents or to foreign corporations with foreign parents or foreign subsidiaries. Both petitioner Barclays Bank PLC (Barclays)—a foreign multinational—and petitioner Colgate-Palmolive Co. (Colgate)—a domestic multinational—have operations in California. In separate cases, two members of the Barclays group and Colgate were denied refunds by the California authorities.[6]

When Garvey accepted representation in 1977, she attempted administrative resolution. She also approached members of the California legislature, "because the simpler answer would be to get legislation," but had no success. And so she talked to her client, Barclays, suggesting that they had a shot with litigation that would put pressure on the legislature, which eventually did happen: "So in 1987, we had started the litigation and everybody was shocked and surprised that we had won in the trial court, and had California's taxing laws declared unconstitutional. So we are at the Court of Appeal, and ordinarily, you spend a couple years at the Court of Appeal on the appellate process. We spent something like seven years [five actually] at the Court of Appeal. . . . [E]ventually we won 3-zip. But, in the meantime, we had been delayed, so eventually we got to the California Supreme Court."

The California high court reversed and remanded the case back for consideration of another issue. The case bounced back and forth. The California Supreme Court overturned the court of appeal seven to zero. Finally, Garvey filed to have the U.S. Supreme Court hear the case and, to the "shock and surprise" of everyone but Garvey, it did.

Garvey argued *Barclays* in March 1994.[7] It was a moving moment for court watchers of a certain age: Justices Sandra Day O'Connor and Ruth Bader Ginsburg listening to Garvey—three women of a similar age who each, early in their career, had experienced professional discrimination, facing one another in the great chamber of the highest court in the land, pursuing their daily work.

Garvey lost *Barclays Bank* seven to two, in part, she felt, because the U.S. Solicitor General's Office, which had been with her as an amicus from the trial court on, altered its position after Bill Clinton was elected president. The Supreme Court held that the Constitution "does not impede application of California's tax to Barclays (and Colgate)."

In evaluating the outcome Garvey said, "We got two votes . . . a strange pair, Sandra O'Connor and Clarence Thomas. . . . When Thomas started, his first job was with the Department of Revenue in the State of Missouri, and he knew this law. And Sandra Day O'Connor had been a state legislator and so she knew it. So the two people who were the most knowledgeable [were the two we got]. We lost the case, but we won the war because we got the legislation."

Sex Discrimination

Women lawyers in government service, NGO lawyers, and women in private practice have played an important part in addressing issues of sex discrimination. Many Trailblazers reported having experienced sex discrimination, and that such experience gave them insight into the problem and a commitment to fair hearing.

Betty Murphy did not have to seek out clients with claims of sex discrimination. In the 1960s, *Time* magazine published a special issue on women. Among the articles was one about Murphy, describing her as a young woman lawyer "successfully moving up." In her oral history Murphy relates the impact of the article:

As a result, I received letters and telephone calls from women—literally— from all over the United States, all of whom had work related problems, which they said were based on the fact they were women. Fortunately, I knew a lot of lawyers in a lot of places in the United States and elsewhere. So I asked my lawyer friends who happened to be all men to give one hour of free advice to a woman in his state who had asked for my help, and they did.

There was one woman who was very persistent. She was an American married to a retired American citizen and she was employed as a Foreign Service Staff employee at our Embassy in Venezuela. I'll call her "Lucy."

Lucy claimed that once she was married, she never received another promotion, and in fact was demoted from being the Secretary to the Ambassador to becoming the Secretary to the Vice Consul. I took her case against the U.S. Department of State and it was expanded to include women in the same position as she, in all levels at State.

This case was so easy to win, we never had to go to trial. Lucy's personnel file contained comments like: "Lucy wants the best of both worlds. She wants to be a mother and have a career." There were never any negative comments about her work. Only about her marital status. . . . When Lucy had her first child, her personnel file reflected this. It said "Lucy thinks she can be married, have a child and still have a career." So I negotiated our victory.

Lucy received a promotion of ten steps plus married couples' benefits. The settlement also included inviting the women who had had to retire after marrying men active in the Foreign Service to return to their positions if they wanted to. And most of them did, and did well. Dorothy Sampas, for example, later became ambassador to Mauritania in President Clinton's administration.

Murphy also handled a number of cases involving women who were or had been flight attendants, then called stewardesses:

[They were] really the front runners of the women's movement. They were the most discriminated against group of women I ever ran across. They were required to maintain a certain weight and no more. They had to wear girdles, and their supervisor—a woman, of course, had the authority to inspect their underwear to make sure they were wearing a girdle and a bra. I'm not joking. No stewardess could be married, divorced, or have a child, and remain a stewardess. . . . Pilots could weigh 300 pounds and no one checked their underwear or weighed them. They could have three or four wives, all sorts of children and mistresses, and nothing was said about that either. . . . These cases were not hard to win once there was a law which prohibited discrimination in employment based on sex, which is what Title VII of the [1964] Civil Rights Act did.

In the last decades of the twentieth century, women in academia also faced multiple forms of discrimination. They were paid less than men and could go only so far as professors or administrators. But Murphy found women in academia harder to deal with because many did not want to pay lawyers anything, "not even when we obtained terrific promotions, tenure and extra benefits for them. The ones I met thought all legal assistance should be completely free because, after all, they were women. I never understood their logic." Murphy went on to accept more public-sector discrimination cases and joined the Individual Rights Section of the ABA: "It was a natural for women lawyers in private practice to take these cases and we did little by little, we changed the face of America to get more women and more minorities the opportunities previously denied to them. Those were fun days."

* * *

In New York Trailblazer Judith Vladeck was known as one of the few attorneys in the 1970s and 1980s who represented female plaintiffs in employment cases. She never represented employers. Vladeck graduated from Columbia Law School in 1947, when, as she was fond of saying, "the placement office didn't send women on job interviews." She first made headlines with a case a class of women plaintiffs pursued against Chase Manhattan Bank in the mid-1970s:

> Sometime in the late 70s–early 80s, the Department of Labor did a major study on what was the most effective device for ending discrimination. And they looked at the work of the various government agencies that were empowered to deal with these issues and looked at voluntary programs that had been adopted by various corporations and what was the conclusion? That class actions were the most effective device for ending discrimination in the workplace. I believe it still is. . . . Most every case I take is an element of my own personality. . . . [M]y version or view of my kind of work is it's really a "them against us" and they're daring me and I get mad enough. . . . I think Chase became the model. I'm very pleased looking back on it, the process was I think an education for the [unclear] that became part of efforts of responsible companies.

As Vladeck took on more employment discrimination cases, she worked on how best to proceed with class actions, how to use statistics and regression analysis, and when and how to use a hostile witness. In fighting powerful private businesses and public universities, she employed detailed analyses of salary histories, sometimes involving data on thousands of employees. Unlike Murphy, she took academic cases. Her most notable case was *Melani v. The Board of Higher Education of the City of New York*. In this class action suit, women employees of the City

University of New York, in a Title VII action, alleged that the university "as a general practice pays less to female members of the instructional staff than it pays to similarly qualified male members, raising a claim of disparate treatment."

The City University of New York, known as CUNY, is the largest urban university in the United States. It began with a single institution, City College, which dates to 1847. By the time of the lawsuit, in the early 1980s, a coordinated higher education community had been formed from the integration of a number of public senior, junior, and professional schools. Thousands of women constituted the affected class. Any finding of discrimination with a monetary settlement would be costly and, more critically, a landmark decision at a time when more and more Title VII and Title IX cases were finding their way into federal courts.

Vladeck spent days arguing the complex salary data of the case in a lower Manhattan federal court. She built her case for the women of the instructional staff around various forms of statistical analyses, and her approach paid off. In March 1983 federal district court Judge Lee Gagliardi found for Vladeck's clients, stating that the university had discriminated against women for fifteen years. The ensuing settlement gave City University's female instructional staff a small one-time across-the-board cash payment as well as the right to file individual appeals, some of which resolved particularly egregious discrimination by adjusting that individual's salary by thousands of dollars per year. A *New York Times* reporter later asked Vladeck whether she thought the multimillion-dollar settlement was equitable. Her answer became the paper's quotation of the day. "If we were to calculate the real back pay in this case, they'd have to take Brooklyn College and City College and auction them off to pay the damages."[8]

* * *

Over the years, the issue of single-sex education has divided feminists, often in highly contentious debate. Trailblazer Anne Marie Whittemore, Yale Law class of 1970, became part of the debate when she was selected to be on the McGuire, Woods & Battle team defending the Virginia Military Institute's (VMI) male-only admissions policy. She was the only senior woman on the team formed by the firm.

Virginia Military Institute's legal battle began in 1990 when a female high school student filed a suit saying that her constitutional right to equal protection under the law was violated when she was not admitted to VMI, a public institution of higher education that received funds from the state of Virginia.

Whittemore later said she was chosen as a member of the legal team "because it was known that I felt very strongly about the value of single-sex education." She went on to say that "for me, it was an opportunity as a lawyer to advance arguments that I personally felt strongly about and that I felt were very significant to education in the country." Whittemore had attended an all-girls high school and then Vassar when the college only accepted women. She believed that men and women learn differently and benefited from single-sex educational institutions.

After Yale, Whittemore had clerked for Judge Albert Bryan on the Fourth Circuit Court of Appeals in Alexandria (Virginia). At the end of her clerkship, Bryan connected Whittemore with members of Virginia's McGuire, Woods & Battle firm. In 1971 the firm hired her as its first woman associate and, six years later, elected her its first woman partner.

Whittemore began working on the VMI case two decades after beginning her career at McGuire, Woods. In those years Whittemore had gained extensive experience participating in big, complex, team-based litigation. In addition, she served on several boards, including the Federal Reserve Bank of Richmond. Later, she would become president of the Richmond Bar Association.

In her oral history, Whittemore explained her client's position:

VMI felt that as an educational experience the fact that it was all male was critical to that experience because the admission of women, it felt, would require changes in what they called "the adversative method," which was essentially barracks life; that was one component of the position. The other component was the educational value of single-sex education—both for men and for women. The sense that within the diversity of the system of public higher education in Virginia there was a role and a value to have an offering, in at least one institution of a single-sex program for men. It was based upon an educational philosophy in both respects as opposed to a social issue of gender discrimination.

Whittemore said further,

> We knew we would likely go to the Supreme Court, and we were very
> conscious of focusing on the Supreme Court opinion in *Hogan v. Missis-*
> *sippi University for Women* in which the Supreme Court found that the
> record in that case did not support maintaining a female-only nursing
> program at Mississippi University; so throughout the litigation, we were
> influenced by that decision in making sure that our record plugged all
> the holes, so to speak, that the Supreme Court found deficient about the
> *Hogan* decision. We also were consulting on and off with constitutional
> lawyers to make sure that we were focused the right way to make the best
> record we could.

In 1991 VMI won in federal district court. U.S. Justice Department
lawyers had argued that VMI's failure to admit women constituted
sex discrimination. Robert Patterson, representing VMI and the VMI
Foundation, argued that the Justice Department was attacking the sovereignty of the state of Virginia—that "the Constitution doesn't require
what they ask for here."[9] He asked if the court would permit the VMI
system of education, indeed, single-sex education—to them a way of
life—to survive.

When the Justice Department appealed its loss in *United States v. Vir-*
ginia to the Fourth Circuit Court of Appeals, established women's public
interest law organizations came together to write, and file, an amicus
brief that underscored the central issue as one of constitutional gender
equality. The names on the brief included those of Marcia Greenberger
of the National Women's Law Center and Isabelle Katz Pinzler of the
ACLU's Women's Rights Project. They were two of several lawyers at
public interest organizations who maintained a significant involvement,
helping to bring about a successful outcome.

A brief submitted by the Virginia Women Attorneys Association took
another direction, emphasizing statutory issues: single-sex diversity
was not an important state interest, and under existing state statutes it
should not be part of Virginia's educational policy. When Justice Department lawyer Judith Silver opened her argument before the justices of the
appeals court on April 8, 1992, she claimed that the VMI policy violated
the Equal Protection Clause of the Fourteenth Amendment, and could

be upheld only if, under the standard established in *Hogan*, the policy was supported by an exceedingly persuasive justification. She further argued that VMI's mission was to "educate citizen soldiers," a mission that "women can take part in."[10]

Robert Patterson again appeared for VMI but did not do well in his presentation of the Fourteenth Amendment issue despite an attempt by team member Griffin Bell to discuss with the court the implications of the ruling in *Hogan* for the VMI case. In October, the Fourth Circuit justices, often described as conservative, held that Virginia was in violation of the equal protection clause and now had three options: admit women to the college; turn VMI into a private college; or create parallel institutions of programs for women. According to legal historian Philippa Strum, the Fourth Circuit ruling "did not mean the government had won . . . for the court clearly indicated that it thought VMI should remain male."[11] The appeals court remanded the case to the district court, directing the state "to select a course it chooses . . . that conforms with the Equal Protection Clause."[12]

VMI appealed, moving for a stay of the appeals court's first decision, but the appeals court prevailed and a second trial began on February 9, 1994. This time Anne Whittemore replaced Patterson in court. In her argument she focused upon the state's compliance with the court of appeals' suggestion that Virginia create a different, parallel program for women who wanted a citizen-soldier education. The plan submitted to the trial court, Whittemore said, would be an education that paralleled that of the VMI male student but would not be identical because, Virginia continued to argue, women learned differently from men. Whittemore called witnesses to explain how men and women learn differently as the result of socially, not biologically, constructed needs.

Whittemore succeeded. Trial court judge Jackson Kiser ruled that the state's plan to establish a separate program for women with educational goals similar to VMI's was the constitutionally acceptable remedy proposed by the appeals court. The United States appealed and, again, the case was heard by the Fourth Circuit with Whittemore arguing for VMI. Once more she contended that the parallel program met the demands of the equal protection clause, and she promised good-faith funding and judicial oversight of its progress. The decision—with a contentious dissent—handed down in January 1995 accepted Whittemore's argument: VMI could maintain its single-sex status as long as the parallel education program for women was maintained. The Justice Department again appealed and the Supreme Court granted certiorari. On January 17, 1996, the high court heard oral argument in *United States v. Virginia.*

Anne Marie Whittemore sat at counsel table with Theodore B. Olson, who later argued in *Bush v. Gore* and became George W. Bush's solicitor general, and Virginia attorney general James S. Gilmore III. It was her first appearance at the Supreme Court. Robert Patterson had wanted Whittemore to argue. He believed that she had done an outstanding job at the court of appeals. The VMI Foundation and the VMI Alumni Association, however, made it clear that they expected someone who had experience arguing appeals at the Supreme Court. Olson was hired but Whittemore sat with him and was a keen observer of the justices and Olson's words:[13]

> I would say it was remarkable even for the United States Supreme Court. The courtroom was absolutely packed. There were a huge number of VMI supporters there. . . . You could just sense in the room a great deal of enthusiasm . . . and there was a strong group of women there who were opposed to the VMI position. . . . I recall vividly sitting at counsel table; and counsel table is very close to the bench where the Justices are seated; and Justice Ginsburg was directly above me, which turned out to be rather fortuitous or ironic, depending upon how you want to view it. Ted Olson's argument focused principally on the State policy of diversity; and he chose not to really argue the uniqueness of the VMI methodology, which I know I personally felt that that deserved to be laid out before the Court, as well as the State policy of diversity in higher education. I know that afterwards many of the VMI folks asked me, "Why didn't he talk about VMI? Why did he only talk about the State policy?" The fact of the matter is though that at the end of the argument, he did say a few things about VMI and the adversative method. I will never forget that Justice Breyer just snapped right back at him and said "The adversative method? So what?" At that point, my heart sank because I knew that the Court just did not accept the inherent value of the VMI methodology, and that meant we were relegated to the State policy of diversity; and it was apparent to me from the questions that had been asked of Ted Olson that we did not have a receptive court on that argument.

Whittemore was correct. The arguments made by Olson on behalf of VMI's all-male admissions policy did not find a positive reception. The justices voted seven to one against VMI (Clarence Thomas had recused himself from the case because his son was a cadet at VMI), with Antonin Scalia the lone justice to vote in favor of the school. Justice Ginsburg wrote the majority opinion; Chief Justice William Rehnquist wrote a concurring opinion. Like the *Barclays Bank* case, *U.S. v. Virginia* demonstrated the extraordinary change that had occurred by the mid-1990s with respect to the status of women lawyers. Once again, a woman, Whittemore, sat at the counsel table looking across at the members of the Supreme Court bench that included Sandra Day O'Connor and, since August 1993, Ruth Bader Ginsburg.

Whittemore recalled her feelings when she first heard Ginsburg's opinion:

The opinion came down when I was on vacation at Block Island up in Rhode Island. My secretary called me; and she was all excited, "The opinion's come down! The opinion's come down!" And I said, "Well who wrote it?" And she said "Justice Ginsburg." At that point, I knew that we had lost. In reading the opinion. . . . she discussed at great length all of the history of equal protection with respect to gender. It was apparent to me having studied about Justice Ginsburg that she was rewriting in the opinion the analysis that she had written in briefs to the Supreme Court for years; and so, I felt that for Justice Ginsburg, this was a vindication of the position for which she had been a very staunch advocate throughout her career before she became a Justice.

Commenting upon Ginsburg's assertion that there was no reason to believe that VMI's unique adversative method would need to be changed to accommodate women, Whittemore said,

It really resulted or reflected what I may have referred to earlier as the "one woman argument"; that if one woman can handle the adversative method and wants it, she should not be denied admission even though the admission of even a single woman inherently changes the fact that it is no longer a single-sex institution; and she may want the adversative method, but sound educators may conclude that it is not in her interest. In fact, VMI's adversary method has changed with the admission of women. . . . They have also now adopted dual standards in physical education. Even though Justice Ginsburg says if one woman wants it, she should be able to have it; well, she cannot have it at VMI now because the VMI educators have concluded in their judgment that you do have to have different physical standards for men and women just like we saw at West Point and The Naval Academy, just like we put into evidence in the VMI litigation.

Ruth Bader Ginsburg wrote the opinion two and a half decades after cofounding the Women's Rights Project at the American Civil Liberties Union, and having argued numerous landmark gender-equity cases before becoming a judge. She crafted a careful opinion mindful of the difficulties of using a strict scrutiny test in which a law must further a compelling governmental interest. Wishing to have as many justices as possible signing onto her opinion, Ginsburg was cautious in the standard of scrutiny she employed: "Parties who seek to defend gender based government action must demonstrate an 'exceedingly persuasive justification' for that action. . . . Without equating gender classifications, for all purposes, to classifications based on race or national origin, the Court, in post-*Reed* decisions, has carefully inspected official action that closes a door or denies opportunity to women (or to men). . . . The burden of justification is demanding and it rests entirely on the State."[14]

In this instance, Ginsburg concluded, the state of Virginia and VMI had not persuasively argued the case for diversity or the impossibility of providing the adversarial method, unmodified, to women; nor had the state proffered an acceptable remedy to the Fourteenth Amendment violation by creating a parallel program, which, she wrote, "affords women no opportunity to experience the rigorous military training for which VMI is famed. . . . Virginia has closed this facility to its daughters and, instead, has devised for them a 'parallel program,' with a faculty less impressively credentialed and less well paid, more limited course offerings, fewer opportunities for military training and for scientific specialization."[15]

Members of the women's rights community did not hold back their praise for the landmark decision. They lauded the ruling as a historic victory for women's "shot at educational opportunity" because it outlawed the use of gender-based stereotypes.[16] Newspapers from Texas to New York to Virginia supported the outcome, with the *Chattanooga Times* declaring the decision "a victory for equality not 'political correctness.'"[17] But in her oral argument Anne Marie Whittemore argued that the changes instituted at VMI following the decision have altered the adversative method, causing VMI to lose a valuable aspect of its educational program.

Conclusion

In their oral histories Trailblazers testified to their involvement in important, headline-grabbing, justice-seeking cases. It is exciting to describe a small number of cases and, at the same time, to urge readers to access the original oral histories to gain an even fuller appreciation of all of the cases that happened on their watch: the establishment of employment rights for pregnant teachers and male and female airline attendants, tobacco company settlements, defense of Guantanamo inmates, the Exxon Valdez and BP lawsuits, the expansion of athletic competition opportunities for girls and women, the representation of indigent criminals as well as the defense of gangsters, right-to-choose trials and appeals, the Dalkon Shield and breast implants litigation, superfund environmental cases, the Meritor Savings Bank hostile environment case, the Google Street View case, the General Motors switch litigation, Iran Contra, and, of course, Ann Hopkins's appeal of the Price Waterhouse decision not to elect her a partner, in part, the company said, because she needed to walk and talk less aggressively.

Women in court—on the bench and arguing cases—are now a commonplace sight. This reality dulls our minds to the many decades of the twentieth century when society did not seek out or, in most cases, tolerate women judges and litigators. But these oral histories bear witness to the change that has occurred, and the fact that woman lawyers have participated, on both sides of the bench, in many of the most important cases of the past several decades.

Epilogue

In 1954 the sports columnist Red Smith announced the presence of the first woman sportswriter credentialed to sit in the press box at the Yale Bowl. In the *New York Herald Tribune* Smith reported that Anne Morrissy "is a slick little chick whose name probably will be linked in history with those of other crusading cupcakes such as Lady Godiva, Susan B. Anthony, Lydia Pinkham and Mrs. Amelia Bloomer."[1] Following the sarcasm, Smith doubled down on the real issue: "The first sports writing doll to thrust her shapely foot through the door of an Ivy League press coop, she has breached the last bastion of masculinity left standing this side of the shower room."[2]

Smith, of course, was wrong. In the mid-1950s, and later still, many bastions of masculinity remained in the world of work. But Smith was correct in understanding the male privilege that permitted, even encouraged him to write so openly, in a major American newspaper, of his contempt for Anne Morrissy's career ambitions.

It is part of the legacy of the Trailblazers and their activist allies that blatant efforts to dismiss or block women's workplace ambitions are no longer easily tolerated. Crusading "cupcakes" and everyday folk now have civil and criminal law with which to joust. In the twenty-first century, legal and social weapons exist to use against acts of workplace discrimination. Women do not always use them. Only the naive would say that there are no repercussions for those who come forward. Still, surveys of state and federal court cases, as well as cases filed with agencies like the Equal Employment Opportunity Commission (charged with investigating complaints of discriminatory workplace practices), do indicate substantial use of such institutions.[3]

So what has happened with respect to women in law, and what do Trailblazers and other observers argue remains to be done to create fair and equal career opportunities for women lawyers?

Law schools have responded to legal and social pressure to end gender discrimination. In the 1950s and 1960s, women accounted for only 3 percent of enrolled law students. That figure started to change in the 1970s, and by 2016 women held just over 50 percent of the seats at accredited law schools.[4] They are taught by a far larger number of women professors at institutions where the percent of women deans is approaching one-third. Curriculum and clinics focus on issues of gender. Nearly one-half of law review leadership positions go to women students.[5]

Women law graduates do reasonably well obtaining law associate positions, gaining tenure-line tracks at law schools, and finding government employment. Nevertheless, according to studies by the American Bar Association, the National Association of Women Lawyers, the National Association for Law Placement (NALP), and other groups, sometime after women are hired, explicit and implicit gender, and racial, bias may occur, affecting promotion, retention, and job satisfaction. To quote law school professor Deborah L. Rhode, "One irony of this nation's continuing struggle for diversity and gender equity in employment is that the profession leading the struggle has failed to set an example in its own workplaces."[6]

Rhode continues to argue that part of the problem "lies in lack of consensus on what exactly the problem is. . . . [and] who is responsible for addressing [it]," as well as determining what is effective.[7]

After graduation, two-thirds of law students join a private law firm or a general counsel's office of a large corporation. Initially, opportunities for women appear to be good. In 2016 women comprised 45 percent of associates in private practices.[8] Ten or more years later, however, those women face a decline in opportunities. At that point only 27 percent of women have made partner, and a mere 19 percent are equity partners or a managing partner at one of the two hundred largest law firms.[9] At Fortune 500 firms, women held only 25 percent of general counsel positions.[10] These statistics tell us more when broken down. Analyses show that the opportunity to make partner varies according to city for all women and, in particular, for minority women: "Among the largest of these cities (those with more than 900 partners represented), Los Angeles and San Francisco show the highest representation of women, minorities, and minority women among both partners and associates."[11] Cities such as Boston, Portland, Oregon, and St. Louis were at or above average on most measures with respect to women but lagged on minority representation.[12]

A report by NALP documents the failure of law firms to keep and promote minority women. Several years ago when women accounted for just under one-third of lawyers at law firms across the country, the percent of minority women was only slightly over 6 percent. This report further stated that "minority women continue to be the most dramatically underrepresented group at the partnership level, a pattern that holds across all firm sizes and most jurisdictions. Minority women make up just over 2% of the partners in the nation's major law firms."[13]

Data on compensation logically reflect these patterns. In 2015, according to the Bureau of Labor Statistics, compensation for women lawyers as a percentage of male lawyers' salaries was 89.7. Between 2005 and 2015, this figure was fluid, rising and falling as much as fifteen points. Broken down, these figures reveal other significant differences. Reports from thirty of the two hundred largest law firms, for example, indicate that "the typical female equity partner earns 80% of the compensation earned by the typical male partner."[14]

* * *

Reading various surveys reporting on male and female lawyers, as well as general studies of working women, reveals a number of reasons why substantial progress is still needed if women are to have equal opportunities to succeed in the field of law. In their book *What Works for Women at Work*, Joan C. Williams and Rachel Dempsey argue that equality will not occur until organizations change. They believe that the gender revolution has stalled (other observers describe "diversity fatigue"). Williams and Dempsey chalk the lack of equality up to implicit bias that leads "men [to] get promoted based on fewer accomplishments than women would need." They also argue that "women are more likely than men to be penalized if they make a mistake. . . . and when women have children, they need to start proving themselves all over again."[15]

Williams and Dempsey suggest that for organizations to change in ways that will retain and promote women, leaders need to implement several policies. Changing time norms is high on their list: "[W]hat's needed . . . are careers in which *men as well as women* can, without stigma, take a family leave or a career break or reduce their hours *with-*

out falling off the career track."[16] They also believe that organizations "with structures that imbed accountability" lead to the greatest increases in both race and gender diversity over time.[17] And, last, Williams and Dempsey make a case for the creation of salary systems where women are told that their supervisors expect them to negotiate their pay, eliminating prejudice against those women who do and are considered too assertive.

Writing about her research on private practitioners and general counsel, Deborah Rhode also makes a case for the impact of what she calls "unconscious" bias. She contends that "lawyers who are truly committed to a just and inclusive workplace need a better understanding of what gets in the way."[18] This includes, she maintains, "deeper appreciation of how racial, ethnic, and gender stereotypes affect not just evaluations of performance but performance itself, and the relative value attached to specific performance measures." She cites surveys that indicate a very large number of female lawyers believe that "they are held to higher standards than their male colleagues," that they do not enjoy the presumption of competence enjoyed by white men. Women lawyers who are mothers also tell interviewers that even when they work full-time, colleagues assume they are less available or less committed. Many women report reluctance to use maternity leave for fear of being passed over for good assignments, or being subject to poor performance reviews.

Women lawyers also identify insufficient mentoring as a problem. They seek more social "work" situations such as meals or sports in which they might be included. Mentoring has many aspects, not the least important being a role in who gets credit for business brought in (origination credit), and long-term control of books of business.

In recent years surveys have just begun to explore the impact on women's opportunities of mergers, mega firms, and the increasing number of global firms. Speaking of the increasing pressure of law firms to behave like corporations, women, and some men, urge diminished pressure to bill. Decades ago Trailblazers were expected to have about fifteen hundred chargeable hours a year. Today the figure ranges from eighteen hundred to more than two thousand. Women also ask for more opportunity to shape the future of their workplaces, and encouragement to use child and elder care leave.[19]

A 2017 article by Meghan Tribe, "Study Shows Big Law Women Pulled to Certain Practice Areas," points out that despite increasing gender diversity in large law firms, women continue to "lag significantly behind male counterparts in certain key Big Law practice areas."[20] The greatest proportion of women was found in education, family law, health care, immigration, and labor and employment. In contrast, areas such as banking, corporate, and litigation had the lowest number of female lawyers. Tribe quotes one recruiter as saying that certain practices are more attractive to women because they have more control over the hours that they work. The status and compensation of different practice areas certainly require more study on the part of researchers as well as law firms.

* * *

Stories from Trailblazing Women Lawyers chronicles the stories of one hundred extraordinary women lawyers. In their oral histories these women narrate their progress, and pain, as they sought to enter a profession that was, in Red Smith's words, a bastion of male power.

The entry of women into a profession inevitably provokes a particular question: Did the women join the men and adopt male career values, or did they bring new values and methods to their workplace, with an eye to changing the profession? In their oral histories some women report that they slid into the world of law and changed it only by their presence, which, in Smith's terms, would represent a considerable imprint. Most of the Trailblazers, however, had an even larger impact, bringing gender and racial diversity to the profession through their personal presence and by effecting institutional changes.

First, of course, their demands for equal opportunity and consideration altered the number of women law school graduates in the United States, and made the job interview process fairer. These women successfully challenged the gender hiring bias at American law schools and also transformed legal education institutions by challenging the absence of attention to women and law in the curriculum. A feminist-influenced jurisprudence of gender flowed from the pens of a number of these women, including Ruth Bader Ginsburg, Wendy Williams, Nancy Gertner, Barbara Babcock, Lynn Hecht Schafran, and many others, ultimately changing the way state and federal institutions approached gender questions. New public interest law organizations, such as the Women's Legal

Defense Fund and the National Women's Law Center, represented institutional change by their very existence, augmenting gender justice on the ground level in private and public sectors.

In their oral histories, Trailblazers also speak about efforts to change institutional workplace practices. Mentoring always received comments. Taking second chair was recognized as the obligation of the newcomer. Male clubs and restaurants that barred women drew caustic comments and were targeted as discriminatory adjuncts to the workplace. These Trailblazers entered a profession with no child care policies. Quite early, several women successfully lobbied the first maternity leave policies at their law firms. Other Trailblazers described efforts to bring part-time and flex-time practices to universities and law firms.

While women today still reach fewer of the middle- and high-level federal government positions than men, the problem was far worse in the 1970s. President Jimmy Carter's late 1970s initiative to add women and minorities to the federal judiciary has significantly increased the number of women judges. Thirty-three percent of federal district court positions are currently filled by women, with the percent slightly higher—36 percent—for the U.S. Court of Appeals.[21] The Carter initiative succeeded for several reasons. None was more important than the commitment on the part of women lawyers to bring one another along into leadership positions. Women also realized that the American Bar Association criteria used in rating judicial candidates was a problem. Through the work of the ABA's Standing Committee on the Federal Judiciary, new experience criteria were adopted, aiding Carter's efforts to diversify the federal bench. Trailblazers such as Brooksley Born and Roberta Ramos (the first woman ABA president, followed now by six others) recognized the importance of bringing about institutional change through change at the ABA itself.

* * *

The oral histories presented in *Stories from Trailblazing Women Lawyers* have intrinsic value as the life stories of women lawyers at a critical time in the history of the legal profession. They describe the values that governed the profession in the first decades after World War II, and the lengths that many men would go to in order to keep the field of law a male preserve. The oral histories are sometimes painful, sometimes funny, and always inspirational. They illuminate what women did, what they would temporarily tolerate in order to become lawyers, and how brilliantly they succeeded.

The Trailblazers batted down contemporary prejudice against middle-class women acquiring higher education degrees and holding jobs. They condemned the dearth of women lawyers employed by the public and the private sectors. They created public interest law groups to improve public policy and judicial decisions as they affected women and their families. And they identified how family-work balance constituted one of the most pressing issues of our time.

Now largely retired, these women see that the profession of law is a better place because of the diversity they helped to bring about. They also realize, however, that some issues they identified have yet to be resolved in ways that serve women. And, equally critically, these lawyers appreciate that the world they were changing was not itself a static place. For example, to the degree that they contended with the globalization of law firms, they did so at the end of their careers. They look, then, to new generations of female and male lawyers to bring about the still-elusive goal of equal opportunity in the profession of law.

NOTES

INTRODUCTION

1 October 9, 1869, entry, Allan Nevins and Milton Halsey Thomas, eds., *The Diary of George Templeton Strong: Post-War Years, 1865–1875* (New York: Macmillan, 1952), 4:256.

2 "The Surprise," *Lockport Daily Journal*, February 17, 1879, 2. Lockwood, Lura Ormes, her daughter, or their friend Mary Walker may have written the article.

3 All quotations in this paragraph are drawn from Catharine Waugh, "Women as Law Clerks." Mary Earhart Dillon Collection, 1869–1945, Schlesinger Library, Radcliff Inst., Series VI. Undated.

4 Robinson to Equity Club members, April 9, 1887, in Virginia G. Drachman, *Women Lawyers and the Origins of Professional Identity in America: The Letters of the Equity Club, 1887 to 1890* (Ann Arbor: University of Michigan Press, 1993), 199.

5 Lavinia Goodell, "Women as Lawyers," *Chicago Legal News*, April 26, 1879, 260–61.

6 Catharine G. Waugh to Equity Club members, April 26, 1889, in Drachman, *Women Lawyers*, 177.

7 Ibid., 175.

8 "Women Lawyers at the Isabella Club House," *Chicago Legal News*, August 26, 1893, 451.

9 Lura McNall Ormes, "Our Washington Letter," *Lockport Daily Journal*, November 21, 1873, 2.

10 Barbara Babcock, *Woman Lawyer: The Trials of Clara Foltz* (Stanford, CA: Stanford University Press, 2011), 152–57, 184–88.

11 Grace Hathaway, *Fate Rides a Tortoise: A Biography of Ellen Spencer Mussey* (Chicago: John C. Winston, 1937), 107–8.

12 Felice Batlan, "Legal Aid, Women Lay Lawyers, and the Rewriting of History, 1863–1930," in Tracy A. Thomas and Tracey Jean Boisseau, eds., *Feminist Legal History* (New York: NYU Press, 2011).

13 Felice Batlan, "Notes from the Margins: Florence Kelley and the Making of Sociological Jurisprudence," in Daniel W. Hamilton, ed., *Transformations in American Legal History* (Cambridge, MA: Harvard Law School, 2011), vol. 2; and Kathryn Kish Sklar, *Florence Kelley and the Nation's Work* (New Haven, CT: Yale University Press, 1995).

14 "Woman Will Help in War against Trusts; Mrs. Quackenbos, Attorney General's Assistant, a Lawyer and Member of Old New York Family," *New York Times*,

September 15, 1907; "Woman Lawyer Who Solved Murder of Ruth Cruger, Once Employed Here," *Washington Post*, June 18, 1917, 4.

15 Mary L. Clark, "Women as Supreme Court Advocates, 1879–1979," *Journal of Supreme Court History* 30 (2005): 47, 52.

16 ABA, Women Trailblazers in the Law. Oral History of Shirley Hufstedler, 147.

17 "Ignore Sex in Jobs Women Are Told," *New York Times*, September 30, 1929, n.p.

18 Naomi Blumberg, "Mabel Walker Willebrandt," *Encyclopedia Britannia*, www. britannica.com. Visited October 11, 2017.

19 Jacqueline A. McLeod, *Daughter of the Empire State: The Life of Judge Jane Bolin* (Urbana: University of Illinois Press, 2011).

20 Ibid., 38.

21 Pauli Murray, *Song in a Weary Throat: An American Pilgrimage* (New York: Harper & Row, 1987), 363.

22 251 F. Supp. 401 (1966). Murray and Kenyon's portion of the brief argued that the Fourteenth Amendment forbids state action that arbitrarily discriminates on the basis of sex.

23 Constance Baker Motley, *Equal Justice under Law: An Autobiography* (New York: Farrar, Straus, and Giroux, 1998), 58.

24 Ibid., 193–202.

25 "Biographical Note," Constance Baker Motley Papers, Five College Archives and Manuscript Collections. www.asteria.fivecolleges.edu.

26 Motley, *Equal Justice*, 213–14. LBJ intended to nominate her to the United States Court of Appeals for the Second Circuit. Edward Lumbard, chief judge of the Second Circuit, adamantly opposed Motley's appointment, as did many Wall Street lawyers, apparently because she was a woman. The president withdrew her name. Ibid., 218–19. Mississippi senator James Eastland held up her nomination to the district court for months.

27 Letter of Bella S. Abzug to Constance Baker Motley, February 6, 1964. Constance Baker Motley Papers, Sophia Smith Collection, Smith College, Box 8, folio 6.

28 Dorothy S. Shawhan and Martha H. Swain, *Lucy Somerville Howorth: New Deal Lawyer, Politician, and Feminist from the South* (Baton Rouge: Louisiana State University Press, 2006).

29 Olga Herrmann Lapin lived from 1894 to 1978. All quotations in this paragraph draw upon materials from Mart Lapin, *The Lady Lawyer of the Opposite Persuasion* (unpublished manuscript, 2014), 34–35, 57, and 61.

30 Anne Firor Scott, Foreword, in Shawhan, xii.

31 Ibid., xii.

32 "List of Federal Judges Appointed by Harry Truman," *Wikipedia*, www.wikipedia. org. Visited August 10, 2017.

33 *Roe v. Wade*, 314 F. Supp. 1217 (1970); *Roe v. Wade*, 410 US 113, 93.

34 Judge Larry A. Jordan, "Four Questions about the First Woman to Clerk at the United States Supreme Court," *Washington State Bar News*, November 2011, 27–29.

35 When 150,000 women joined the army during World War II, Margaret Sanger wrote in the New York *Herald-Tribune* that the Women's Army Auxiliary Corps "appears to be the final realization of woman's dream of complete equality with men." The famous family planning activist was "dismayed" that the government didn't provide contraceptives for the WAACS. Jill Lepore, "The Last Amazon," *New Yorker*, September 22, 2014, 70–71.

36 "Sex Balance by Edict," *New York Times*, August 15, 1971, section 4, 14; Karen Blumenthal, "The Truth about Title IX," *Daily Beast*, June 22, 2012.

37 Steve Wolf, "Title IX: 37 Words That Changed Everything," ESPN W., April 29, 2012.

CHAPTER 1. CATALOGUING CHILDHOOD INFLUENCES

1 Adam Bryant, "Making Room for Differences: An Interview with Lois Braverman," *New York Times*, Sunday Business Section, February 8, 2015, 2.

2 Boris Kachka, "Who Is the Author of Toni Morrison?" *New York Magazine*, May 7, 2012, 40.

3 One-third of the women interviewed divorced once or more. Only one woman indicated that she had a woman partner.

CHAPTER 2. THE LURE OF LAW

1 District of Columbia Historical Society Oral History Project. Interview with Joan Bernstein, 29–30.

2 Elizabeth Warren, *A Fighting Chance* (New York: Henry Holt, 2014). E-book, 269.

CHAPTER 3. LAW SCHOOL

1 Academy of Achievement Interview with Justice Ruth Bader Ginsburg, August 17, 2010. Formerly posted, now available in the Academy's archives.

2 Mary J. Mullarkey, "Two Harvard Women: 1965 to Today," *Harvard Women's Law Journal* 27 (2004): 367, 371.

3 Academy of Achievement Interview with Justice Ruth Bader Ginsburg, August 17, 2010.

4 Judith Richards Hope, *Pinstripes and Pearls* (New York: Scribners, 2003), 98–99.

5 Hope, *Pinstripes*, 97.

6 Mullarkey, "Two Harvard Women," 370.

7 Ibid., 370.

8 Ibid., 370.

9 All quotations in this paragraph cite to ibid., 371.

10 O'Neil is one of the few Trailblazers who acknowledged having read Judith Richards Hope's *Pinstripes and Pearls*, a book about the women of Harvard Law's class of 1964. O'Neil found Hope's book to be "an apology for what to me was sadistic behavior on the part of much of the faculty at Harvard Law School. They were sadistic towards men, and the men were sadistic to each other—cutthroat compe-

tition, demeaning each other." ABA, Women Trailblazers in the Law. Oral History of Katherine O'Neil, 101.

11 Ibid., 98–99.

12 ABA, Women Trailblazers in the Law. Oral History of Wendy Williams, 27.

13 Herma Hill Kay, "First Women." *Ms. JD. Blog* (February 20, 2007), www.ms-jd. org. Visited April 24, 2015.

14 Ibid.

15 *Frontiero v. Richardson*, 411 U.S. 677 (1973).

CHAPTER 4. WORK PROFILES

1 Robert O. Boorstin, "Hufstedler Meets Washington," *Harvard Crimson*, April 2, 1980, www.thecrimson.com. Visited April 24, 2017.

2 ABA, Women Trailblazers in the Law. Oral History of Shirley Adelson, Section III, 13.

3 David Garrow, *Liberty and Sexuality* (New York: Macmillan, 1994), 260.

4 Betty Roberts (with Gail Wells), *With Grit and by Grace: Breaking Trails in Politics and Law, A Memoir* (Corvallis: Oregon State University Press, 2008), 209.

5 The profile of Betty Binns Flectcher draws upon her ABA, Women Trailblazers in the Law oral history and the oral history that she gave to the Ninth Judicial Circuit Historical Society in 2003.

6 Nina Shapiro, "Judge Betty's Revenge," *Seattle Weekly News*, www.seattleweekly. com. Viewed May 14, 2017.

ENTR'ACTE

1 "Should a Woman Lawyer Wear Her Hat in Court?" Reprinted in the *Washington Law Reporter*, April 1, 1876, 47.

2 "L.A. Judge Makes Woman Lawyer Doff Hat in Court," *Los Angeles Herald Express*, April 7, 1947, 1, 8.

3 "Bella Abzug, 1920–1998: Activist for Women's Rights Was Known for Her Large Hats and Strong Opinions." *Stories About People*, www.manythings.org. Visited October 11, 2017.

4 Judith Richards Hope, *Pinstripes and Pearls* (New York: Scribners, 2003), 35.

5 Benjamin Mueller, "Immigration Lawyers, a Surprise Speaker Who Asks Them to Change Lives," *New York Times*, September 5, 2014, A22.

6 Nancy Gertner, *In Defense of Women* (Boston: Beacon, 2011), 53.

7 Ibid., 124.

CHAPTER 5. THE NEXT GENERATION

1 David J. Danelski, "Lucile Lomen: The First Woman to Clerk at the Supreme Court," *Journal of Supreme Court History* 23 (1999): 43–49.

2 In 1966, Justice Hugo Black selected Harvard Law School graduate Margaret J. Corcoran as his clerk, the second woman to serve in this capacity. Justice Fortas selected a woman clerk in 1968. Title IX was enacted in 1972. Perhaps because

of the impact of Title IX, during the later 1970s, female U.S. Supreme Court law clerks increased in number. Two dozen women served in this decade, all but three between the years of 1974 and 1979. "List of Law Clerks of the Supreme Court of the United States," *Wikipedia*, www.wikipedia.org. Visited August 10, 2017.

3 Cynthia L. Cooper, "Women Supreme Court Clerks Striving for Commonplace," *Perspectives* (Summer 2008), www.americanbar.org.

4 Sheryl Sandberg, *Lean In: Women, Work, and the Will to Lead* (New York: Knopf, 2013).

CHAPTER 6. BREAKING NEW GROUND

1 Barbara Babcock, "Falling into Feminism: A Personal History," *Stanford Journal of Civil Rights & Liberties* (June 2015): 110–11.

2 Before the publication of these casebooks, Leo Kanowitz's 1969 monograph, *Women and the Law,* was the sole book on the subject. Historian Linda K. Kerber has chronicled who taught the early women and law courses, who developed material for these courses, and what feminist law reviews were founded in her article "Writing Our Own Rare Books," *Yale Journal of Law and Feminism* 14 (2002): 429.

3 *Women's Legal History* (WLH) website, wlh.law.stanford.edu. Visited August 10, 2017.

4 Babcock, "Falling," 110.

5 Judith Resnik, "Visible on 'Women's Issues,'" *Iowa L. Rev.* 77 (1991–1992): 41.

6 Ibid.

7 Interview with the Honorable Dorothy Nelson, 2005, *YouTube*, www.youtube. com. Accessed August 15, 2016.

8 Ibid.

9 In 1981 the WRP separated from CLSP and became the independent National Women's Law Center.

10 Ruth Bader Ginsburg Interview, Academy of Achievement, August 17, 2010. Available at Academy archives.

11 For Lardent's account of the issues behind the founding of the six projects, see ABA, Women Trailblazers in the Law. Oral History of Esther Lardent, 61–62.

12 In the year 2000, three U.S. legal departments had formal, organized pro bono programs. In 2014, those programs number in the hundreds. Pro Bono Institute, "Letter from Esther: The Future of In-House Pro Bono," *Pro Bono Wire*, November 2014, 1.

CHAPTER 7. THE NEW FACE OF GOVERNMENT

1 ABA, Women Trailblazers in the Law, Oral History of Ruth Burg, 123.

2 "Clinton Expected to Name Woman Attorney General," *New York Times*, December 9, 1992.

CHAPTER 8. "JUDGE COOKIE TO YOU"

1 Barbara Babcock, *Fish Raincoats: A Woman Lawyer's Life* (New Orleans: Quid Pro Books, 2016), 141 (e-book ed.).

2 Ibid., 141 (e-book ed.).

3 Ibid., 160 (e-book ed.).

4 Ibid. (e-book ed.).

5 Sally J. Kenney, *Gender & Justice: Why Women in the Judiciary Really Matter* (New York: Routledge, 2013), 71.

6 Ibid., 75.

7 The committee eliminated the fifteen-year trial experience requirement and specifically provided that, in assessing professional experience, the committee would take into consideration that women and people of color had come to the Bar in significant numbers only in recent years and therefore could not be expected to have the length and depth of professional experience traditionally required by the committee. Personal communication from Brooksley Born to Jill Norgren, June 20, 2016.

8 Ibid.

9 Josh Barbanel, "7 Are Found Well Qualified for Judgeship by Bar Group," *New York Times*, August 3, 1983. Zita Weinshienk, confirmed as a U.S. district court judge in 1979, described a less combative relationship with a potential competitor: "Another female Denver district judge was also mentioned [for federal judge] and was being pushed as well. But she and I talked to each other and decided that if either one of us made the short list that we would help the other one." ABA, Women Trailblazers in the Law. Oral History of Zita Weinshienk, Section III, 3.

10 Academy of Achievement. 2010 Interview with Ruth Bader Ginsburg. Available in the Academy archives.

11 Ibid.

ENTR'ACTE

1 Brittany Wong, "The Truth about the Divorce Rate Is Surprisingly Optimistic," *Huffington Post*, December 2, 2014. www.huffingtonpost.com.

CHAPTER 9. THE CASE OF THE CENTURY AND OTHER TALES

1 Judge Mary M. Schroeder, "What Gordon Hirabayashi Taught Me about Courage," *Seattle Journal for Social Justice* 11 (1), article 6, 65. Available at www.digitalcommons.law.seattle.edu.

2 Ibid., 69–70.

3 Ibid., 71.

4 U.S. President's Commission on Campus Unrest, *Campus Unrest* (Washington, DC: GPO, 1970), 450.

5 Taped interview with Nancy Gertner, April 23, 2014, www.youtube.com. Visited October 10, 2017.

6 Cornell Law School, Legal Information Institute, "Syllabus." www.law.cornell.edu. Visited October 9, 2017.

7 To hear Garvey's argument, go to *Oyez*, www.oyez.org.

8 Susan Antilla, "Profile: Workplace Discrimination? Don't Try It around Her," *New York Times*, Business Day, February 13, 1994, www.nytimes.com.

9 Philippa Strum, *Women in the Barracks: The VMI Case and Equal Rights* (Lawrence: University Press of Kansas, 2002), 142. Strum's study is the most complete and exacting analysis of the case.

10 Ibid., 193, quoting from the transcript of the appeals court oral transcript.

11 Ibid., 194.

12 Ibid., 196.

13 Ibid., 264.

14 *U.S. v. Virginia*, 518 U.S. 515, 531 (1996).

15 *U.S. v. Virginia*, 518 U.S. 515, 548, 557.

16 Strum, 295.

17 Ibid., 296.

EPILOGUE

1 Sam Roberts, "Anne Morrisssy Merick, Barrier Breaker, Dies at 83," *New York Times,* May 10, 2017, B15.

2 Ibid., B15.

3 Elizabeth Olson, "Suit Presses Issue of Lower Pay for Female Law Partners," *New York Times*, May 8, 2017, B3. In this article Olson reports on one of the most recent compensation lawsuits brought by female partners.

4 Elizabeth Olson, "Women Make Up Majority of U.S. Law Students for First Time," *New York Times,* December 16, 2016, B4. For a list of American Bar Association reports on professional diversity, see www.americanbar.org.

5 American Bar Association, *A Current Glance at Women in the Law* (Chicago: ABA, 2017). All statistics in this paragraph are drawn from this report.

6 Deborah L. Rhode, "Chapter 4: Women in Law," in *Women and Leadership* (New York: Oxford University Press, 2017), location 1678.

7 Ibid., 1678.

8 American Bar Association, *A Current Glance*, 2. Women comprised 48.7 percent of summer associates.

9 Ibid., 2; Jacqueline Bell, "The 2017 *Law360* Glass Ceiling Report," *Law360,* July 23, 2017, www.law360.com.

10 American Bar Association, *A Current Glance*, 3.

11 National Association for Law Placement, "Representation of Women among Associates Continues to Fall, Even as Minority Associates Make Gains" (Washington, DC: December 13, 2012), 2–3.

12 Ibid., 3.

13 Ibid., 1–2.

14 ABA, *A Current Glance*, 6. See also the 2016 compensation study conducted by the firm of Major, Lindsey, and Africa.

15 Joan C. Williams and Rachel Dempsey, *What Works for Women at Work* (New York: NYU Press, 2014), 299.

16 Ibid., 301.

17 Ibid.

18 Rhode, "Women in Law," 1739–63. All quotations in this paragraph cite to this location.

19 Gita Z. Wilder, *Are Minority Women Lawyers Leaving Their Jobs?* (Washington, DC: NALP, 2008), 21.

20 Meghan Tribe, "Study Shows Big Law Women Pulled to Certain Practice Areas," *Law.Com,* April 18, 2017, www.law.com.

21 *A Current Glance,* 5. These figures are for judges on active status.

CASE REFERENCES

Arizona v. California, 373 U.S. 546 (1963).

Barclays Bank PLC v. Franchise Tax Board, 512 U.S. 298 (1994).

Brown v. Topeka Board of Education, 347 U.S. 483 (1954); 349 U.S. 294 (1955).

Bush v. Gore, 531 U.S. 98 (2000).

Container Corp. of America v. Franchise Tax Bd., 463 U.S. 159 (1983).

Eastern Railroads Presidents Conference v. Noerr, 365 U.S. 127 (1961).

General Electric v. Gilbert, 429 U.S. 125 (1976).

Griswold v. Connecticut, 381 U.S. 479 (1965).

Harris v. City of Philadelphia, No. CIV. A. 82–1847, 1994 WL 408231 at *1 (E.D. Pa. Jun. 28, 1994).

Hirabayashi v. United States, 320 U.S. 81 (1943).

Hirabayashi v. United States, 828 F.2d 591 (1987).

Hoyt v. Florida, 368 U.S. 57 (1961).

In Re Browning, 568 So.2d 4(Fla. 1990).

Johnson v. Transportation Agency, 770 F.2d 752 (1984).

Johnson v. Transportation Agency, 480 U.S. 616 (1987).

Keyes v. School District, 413 U.S. 189 (1973).

King v. Smith, 393 U.S. 309 (1968).

Melani v. Bd. of Higher Education of the City University of New York, 561 F. Supp. 769 (1983).

Mississippi University for Women v. Hogan, 458 U.S. 718 (1982).

Morrow v. Crisler, 491 F.2d 1053 (1974).

Myrtle Green Burton v. William L. Waller, 502 F.2d 1261 [5th Circuit, 1974].

Oliver Brown et al. v. Board of Education of Topeka, 892 F.2d 851 (1989).

Plyler v. Doe, 457 U.S. 202 (1982).

Poe v. Ullman, 367 U.S. 497 (1961).

Reed v. Reed, 404 U.S. 71 (1971).

Roe v. Wade, 314 F.Supp. 1217 (1970).

Roe v. Wade, 410 U.S. 113 (1973).

Sail'er Inn, Inc. v. Kirby, 5 Cal 3d 1, 485 P.2d 529 (1971).

Taylor v. Sterrett, 344 F. Supp. 411 (1972).

U.S. v. Virginia, 518 U.S. 515 (1996).

White v. Crook, 251 F. Supp. 401 (1966).

SELECT BIBLIOGRAPHY

Abramson, Jill, and Barbara Franklin. *Where They Are Now: The Story of the Women of Harvard Law 1974*. New York: Doubleday, 1986.

Allen, Florence E. *To Do Justly*. Cleveland, OH: Case Western Reserve Press, 1965.

American Bar Association. *A Current Glance at Women in the Law*. Chicago: ABA, January 2017.

Babcock, Barbara. *Fish Raincoats: A Woman Lawyer's Life*. New Orleans: Quid Pro Books, 2016.

———. *Woman Lawyer: The Trials of Clara Foltz*. Stanford, CA: Stanford University Press, 2011.

Biskupic, Joan. *Breaking In: The Rise of Sonia Sotomayor and the Politics of Justice*. New York: Farrar, Straus & Giroux, 2014.

———. *Sandra Day O'Connor*. New York: Harper, 2005.

Bowling, Kristy, and Lynn Hecht Schafran, eds. "Women of the Courts Symposium." *University of Toledo Law Review* 36 (Summer 2005).

Carmon, Irin, and Shana Knizhnik, *Notorious RBG: The Life and Times of Ruth Bader Ginsburg*. New York: HarperCollins, 2015.

Clark, Mary L. "The First Women Members of the Supreme Court Bar, 1879–1900." *San Diego Law Review* 36 (1999): 87.

———. "Women as Supreme Court Advocates, 1879–1979." *Journal of Supreme Court History* 30 (2005).

Drachman, Virginia G. *Sisters in Law: Women Lawyers in Modern American History*. Cambridge, MA: Harvard University Press, 1998.

———. *Women Lawyers and the Origins of Professional Identity in America: The Letters of the Equity Club, 1887 to 1890*. Ann Arbor: University of Michigan Press, 1993.

Epstein, Cynthia Fuchs. *Women in Law*. New York: Basic Books, 1981; 1993.

Freeman, Frankie Muse. *A Song of Faith and Hope: The Life of Frankie Muse Freeman*. St. Louis: Missouri History Museum Press, 2003.

Fricke, Amber, and Angela Onwuachi-Willig. "Do Female 'Firsts' Still Matter? Why They Do for Female Judges of Color." *Michigan State Law Review* (2012).

Gertner, Nancy. *In Defense of Women: Memoirs of an Unrepentant Advocate*. Boston: Beacon, 2011.

Hope, Judith Richards. *Pinstripes: The Women of the Harvard Class of '64*. New York: Scribner, 2003.

Kay, Herma Hill. "The Future of Women Law Professors." *Iowa Law Review* 77 (1991): 5.

Kaye, Judith S., and Anne C. Reddy. "The Progress of Women Lawyers at Big Firms." *Fordham Law Review* 76 (2008): 1941–74.

Kennedy, Flo. *Color Me Flo*. Englewood Cliffs, NJ: Prentice Hall, 1976.

Kenney, Sally J. *Gender and Justice: Why Women in the Judiciary Really Matter*. New York: Routledge, 2012.

Kerber, Linda K. "Writing Our Own Rare Books." *Yale Journal of Law & Feminism* 14 (2002): 429.

Lockwood, Karen M. *The Road to Independence: 101 Women's Journeys to Starting Their Own Law Firms*. Chicago: American Bar Association, 2011.

Mack, Kenneth M. *Representing the Race: The Creation of the Civil Rights Lawyer*. Cambridge, MA: Harvard University Press, 2012.

McLeod, Jacqueline A. *Daughter of the Empire State: The Life of Judge Jane Bolin*. Urbana: University of Illinois Press, 2011.

Morello, Karen. *Invisible Bar*. New York: Random House, 1986; Boston: Beacon, 1988.

Mossman, Mary Jane. *First Women Lawyers*. Portland, OR: Hart Publishing, 2006.

Motley, Constance Baker. *Equal Justice under Law: An Autobiography*. New York: Farrar, Straus & Giroux, 1998.

Norgren, Jill. *Belva Lockwood*. New York: NYU Press, 2007.

———. *Rebels at the Bar*. New York: NYU Press, 2013.

O'Connor, Sandra Day. *Out of Order: Stories from the History of the Supreme Court*. New York: Random House, 2013.

Rhode, Deborah L. "Chapter 4: Women in Law," in *Women and Leadership*. New York: Oxford University Press, 2016.

———. *Lawyers as Leaders*. New York: Oxford University Press, 2013.

Roberts, Betty. *With Grit and by Grace: Breaking Trails in Politics and Law*. Corvallis: Oregon State University Press, 2008.

Rosenberg, Rosalind. *Jane Crow: The Life of Pauli Murray*. New York: Oxford University Press, 2017.

Schneider, Elizabeth M., and Stephanie M. Wildman, eds. *Women and the Law Stories*. New York: Thomas Reuters/Foundation Press, 2011.

Shawhan, Dorothy S., and Martha H. Swain. *Lucy Somerville Howorth: New Deal Lawyer, Politician, and Feminist from the South*. Baton Rouge: Louisiana State University Press, 2006.

Sotomayor, Sonia. *My Beloved World*. New York: Knopf, 2013.

Strebeigh, Fred. *Equal: Women Reshape American Law*. New York: Norton, 2009.

Thomas, Gillian. *Because of Sex: One Law, Ten Cases, and Fifty Years That Changed American Women's Lives at Work*. New York: St. Martin's Press, 2016.

Trestman, Marlene. *Fair Labor Lawyer: The Remarkable Life of New Deal Attorney and Supreme Court Advocate Bessie Margolin*. Baton Rouge: Louisiana State University Press, 2016.

Wilder, Gita Z. *Are Minority Women Lawyers Leaving Their Jobs?* Dallas: NALP Foundation, 2008.

Williams, Joan C., and Rachel Dempsey. *What Works for Women at Work*. New York: NYU Press, 2014.

INDEX

Abrams, Ruth: choice of college, 33; Harvard Law School experience, 51–53; state judge, 204; told by judge to wear hat and white gloves, 100

Abzug, Bella, 11–12; and hats, 100; member of Congress, 163

Adams, Annette Abbott, 7

Allen, Judge Florence: appointed to the U.S. Court of Appeals (Sixth Circuit), 14–15

Alschuler, Martha F., 16

American Bar Association (ABA), 8, 173, 185; and Commission on Women in the Profession, x, xiii; interest in pro bono programs, 1551–56; Joanne Garvey considers running for presidency of, 237; new judicial selection criteria, 187, 264n7; Section on Individual Rights and Responsibilities (SIRR), 154, 156; Senior Lawyers Division, x, xiii; Standing Committee on the Federal Judiciary, 187, 256; Women Trailblazers in the Law Project, xiii

American Civil Liberties Union (ACLU), 10–11; Women's Rights Project, 68–69, 141, 148, 244, 248

American Lawyer (magazine): and definition of pro bono, 158

American University Washington College of Law, 39

Areen, Judith: Georgetown Law School dean, 144; opinion about all-girls schools, 27

Argrett, Loretta: early career as a scientist, 32, 40; enters Harvard Law School, 40–41; experience at Howard University, and in D.C., 32

Arnold & Porter: encourages pro bono work, 157

Atkinson, Judge Edith, 12, 14

Babcock, Barbara: co-author of a women and law casebook, 64, 141–142; comments on law school dressing habits, 100; comments on next generation of women and their influence, 142; committee to identify women for government positions, 185; creates women's legal history course, 143; first woman hired on a tenure line at Stanford Law School, 143, 145; on having children, 216–217; heads up the Public Defender Service, 141; serves as assistant attorney general for the DOJ Civil Division, 143, 186; teaches at Georgetown, 64; teaches women and law courses, 61, 64, 141–142; writes biography of lawyer Clara Foltz, 143

Bair, Sheila: appointed to the Federal Deposit Insurance Corporation, 178; derivatives policy, 179; graduate of University of Kansas Law School, 178; heads FDIC, 179–181; member of the Commodity Futures Trading Commission, 1781–79; runs for Congress, 178; works at Department of Health, Education, and Welfare, 178; works at New York Stock Exchange, 178; works for Senator Robert Dole, 178

ABOUT THE AUTHOR

Jill Norgren is Professor Emerita of Political Science and Legal Studies, John Jay College of Criminal Justice, and the Graduate Center, The City University of New York. She writes on law and legal history, currently the history of women lawyers in the nineteenth and twentieth centuries. She is the co-author (with Serena Nanda) of *American Cultural Pluralism and Law* and (with Petra T. Shuttuck) *Partial Justice*, and the author of *The Cherokee Cases: Two Landmark Federal Decisions in the Fight for Sovereignty*. In 2007 she wrote *Belva Lockwood: The Woman Who Would Be President*, as well as a young adult biography about Lockwood, titled *Belva Lockwood: Equal Rights Pioneer*. Her next book on women lawyers was *Rebels at the Bar: The Fascinating, Forgotten Stories of America's First Women Lawyers* (2013). She has received fellowships and awards from the Rockefeller Foundation, the Woodrow Wilson International Center for Scholars, the American Society for Legal History, the United States Supreme Court Historical Society, and the American Library Association. With colleagues, she has created www.herhatwasinthering.org, the first website featuring biographical entries of U.S. women who ran for political office before ratification of the woman suffrage amendment in 1920.